AF594467

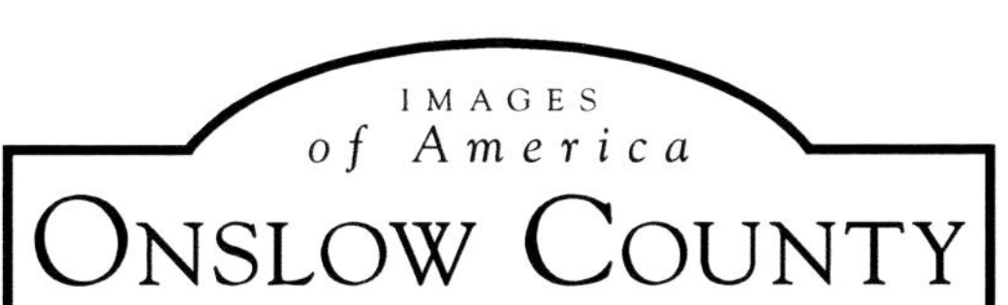
IMAGES
of America
ONSLOW COUNTY

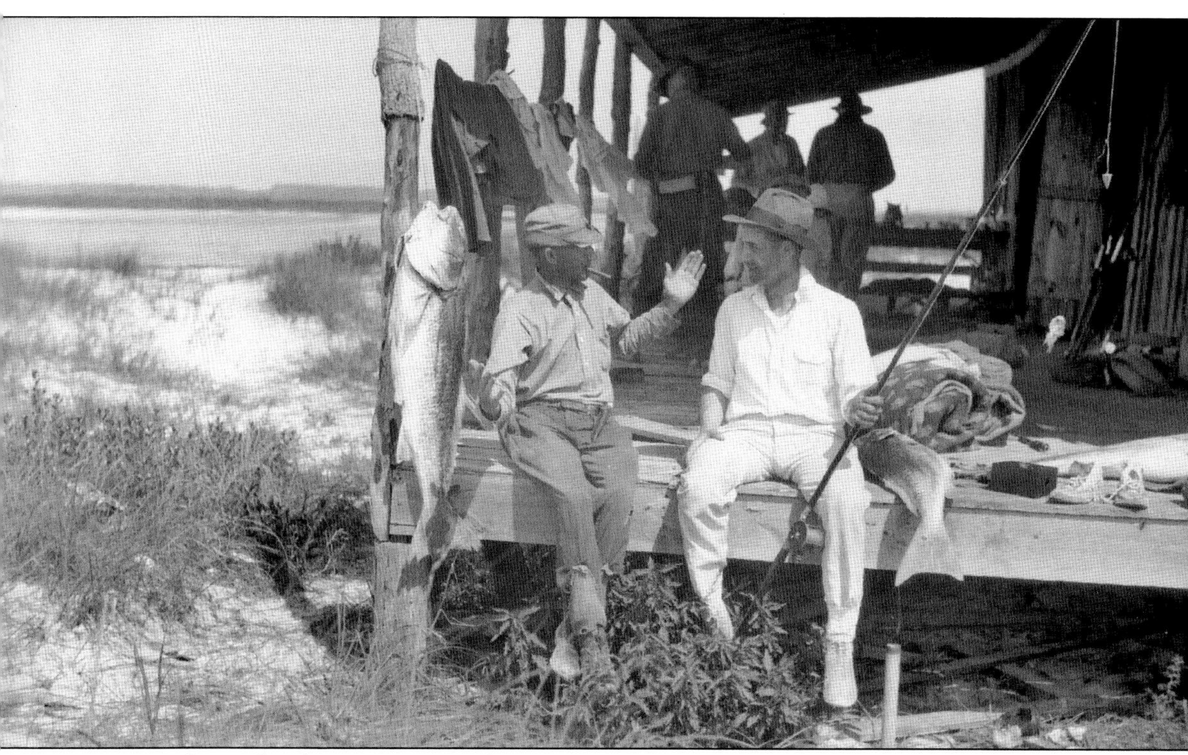

An enduring local pastime in Onslow County is fishing. This picture was taken in the 1920s at one of the beach shacks used by sporting anglers. It appears that a "big fish" story was being told, but in fact, Onslow was known for its record-setting fish. (Courtesy of State Archives of North Carolina.)

ON THE COVER: Taken in about 1938 at the community of Fulcher's Landing on the New River by Charles Anderson Farrell, this nostalgic image captures the innocence of the pre–World War II era and recalls the easygoing way of life on the river before the coming of the US Marine base. (Courtesy of State Archives of North Carolina.)

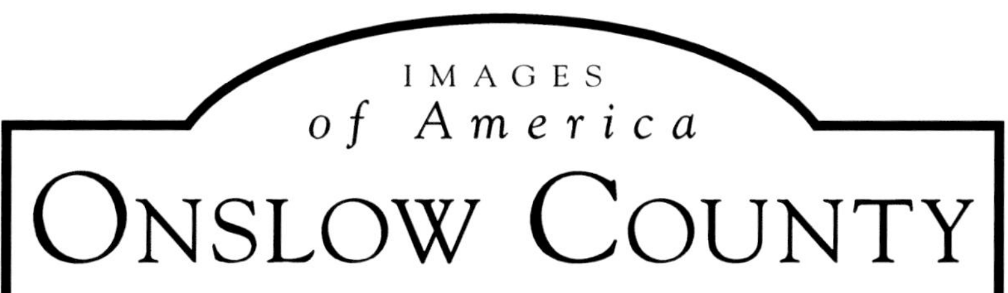

Onslow County

Patricia M. Hughey

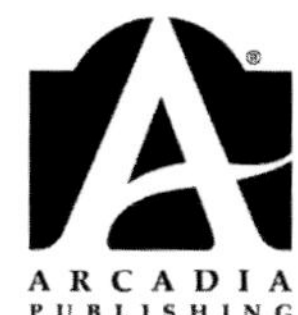

ISBN 978-1-4671-1736-4

Published by Arcadia Publishing
Charleston, South Carolina

Printed in the United States of America

Library of Congress Control Number: 2016947831

For all general information, please contact Arcadia Publishing:
Telephone 843-853-2070
Fax 843-853-0044
E-mail sales@arcadiapublishing.com
For customer service and orders:
Toll-Free 1-888-313-2665

Visit us on the Internet at www.arcadiapublishing.com

To my family

Contents

ACKNOWLEDGMENTS

A number of individuals assisted me in the creation of this book. My special thanks go to Onslow County Museum director Lisa Whitman-Grice, my friend and former boss, for all her encouragement and help in this endeavor and for allowing the use of the museum's large photograph collection. Thanks also go to collections manager Chance Hellmann, who greatly assisted me with scans. Also graciously providing me with historical images were Kara Newcomer of Marine Corps Special Collections, archivist Kim Andersen of the Audio Visual Materials Unit at the State Archives of North Carolina in Raleigh, and her assistant, Mathew Waehner. Additionally, Dennis E. Jones and Robert Royster contributed important images.

I appreciate the moral support given to me by many friends and family members, including my children and my fiancé. Lastly, the spiritual support of the Almighty was, as always, invaluable.

Introduction

Onslow County has the distinction of being one of the oldest coastal counties in North Carolina. Settlement is known to have begun as early as 1713, after the end of the Tuscarora War opened new avenues and opportunities for land speculation and homesteading. The landscape of the area—with its thick, vast longleaf pine forests, numerous waterways, and proximity to the ocean—proved to be an enticement to both farmers and potential businessmen, eager to profit from the resources of this new land.

By 1730, there were at least 200 families living in the area that would become Onslow, enough to cause difficulties for inhabitants needing to do court business in Carteret Precinct. The governor was petitioned for the formation of a new precinct (county) in 1731 to be named in honor of the Honorable Arthur Onslow, Speaker of the House of Commons of Great Britain. After several legal delays, Onslow Precinct (County) was officially formed in 1734.

The new county had no courthouse and court was held in a number of private homes along the New River until 1744. A beautiful spot along the south side of the New River was chosen for the establishment of a town called Johnston, named after Onslow resident Samuel Johnston's brother Gabriel Johnston, the governor of North Carolina. The town streets and lots were mapped out for purchase, and a courthouse was planned and built. Unfortunately, in September 1752, the coast was ravaged by a tremendous hurricane that left Johnston devastated. County leaders deemed Johnston's location to be "inconvenient," determining that the seat of government should be situated further up the New River, and chose the area of Wantland's Ferry (present-day Jacksonville). Ferry owner James Wantland sold an acre of land on the river to the county for the establishment of a new courthouse.

Onslow grew slowly but steadily, with an estimated population of 4,900 by 1774. Drawn to the area by its bountiful natural resources, many were engaged in farming and in the naval stores industry, which used slave labor and vast stands of longleaf pine to be profitable. Fishing also played a role; many families were dependent upon the bounty of the sea and the waterways for their livelihood and subsistence. Between 1783 and 1812, at least 16 maritime vessels were built in the Swansboro area.

Settled by a people who were often resistant to authority, Onslow County rallied as a patriot force during the American Revolution, raising a militia company to fight for freedom from Britain. By 1777, nearly 700 men were enrolled in the militia force. After the end of the Revolution and the establishment of the new nation, life continued apace in Onslow. With some slight changes, the framework of county governance remained similar, with county commissioners and justices of the peace enforcing laws and meting out justice. As houses, taverns, and ordinaries sprang up around the courthouse at Wantland's Ferry, the town was soon referred to as Onslow Courthouse, a name that remained in place until 1842, after the initially proposed name Cedarville was rejected in favor of Jacksonville, chosen to honor Pres. Andrew Jackson.

The Civil War brought hardship and destruction, but a new way of life emerged with the emancipation of the slave population and with improvements in infrastructure that only came gradually to the South and agonizingly slowly to Onslow. The sleepy town of Jacksonville attracted few investors, and commerce was restricted by the absence of a railroad. Numerous attempts to bring the railroad to Onslow for over 20 years after the conclusion of the war had all ended in failure. In 1889, an enterprising businessman from New York saw the untapped potential and formed a partnership to bring the railroad to Jacksonville. Thomas A. McIntyre fell in love with Onslow County and soon built not only a railroad, but also a large mansion on the New River. The railroad was finally connected to Jacksonville in 1891. McIntyre's estate, which included both the mansion house named Onslow Hall, completed about 1892, and his innovative model farm called Glenoe, became well-known showplaces.

In spite of the economic boost of the railroad, Onslow remained predominantly rural. Tobacco and cotton were the major crops. At the turn of the 20th century, the lumber industry prospered for a time, with mills at Swansboro and Jacksonville providing lumber for the nationwide building boom. In time, the once vast resource of longleaf pine would be reduced to a much smaller remnant of its originally widespread acreage.

In 1940, the threat of war loomed large over the entire country. The War Department (now the Department of Defense) searched for a new area to establish a Marine Corps training base and soon discovered Onslow; with its low population, natural resources, and pristine coastline, it was the ideal location for what would become the world's largest amphibious training base.

The establishment of Camp Lejeune would change the face of Onslow County forever. The government initially acquired 111,000 acres for the new installation. Hundreds of families who had lived in Onslow for generations were displaced from their land and homes. In a short time, the population of Jacksonville would burgeon from 873 to thousands. The temporary Army base at Camp Davis in Holly Ridge would have a similar effect, but the land was leased rather than purchased. At its peak, approximately 22,000 military personnel were stationed there.

New faces from across the country found a home in Onslow County, bringing fresh ideas, innovations, and customs, yet blending with the traditional values and lifestyles of the once slow-paced farming and fishing communities. One only has to look at population figures to comprehend the magnitude of growth in Onslow. Post–World War II Onslow had a population of 42,047 in 1950; it has grown steadily, recording 177,772 inhabitants by 2010, making it the 11th largest county among the 100 counties of North Carolina.

One

Rural Life

The rich soil, winding waterways, and abundant wildlife of the land that became Onslow attracted settlers from the early 1700s. Early residents arriving after the end of the Tuscarora War in 1713 established small farms and plantations. There was a great diversity of crops in the early years as farmers experimented with raising rice, indigo, and flax. Indian corn was a staple crop and livestock such as cattle, chickens, and pigs were successfully raised. Families were self-sufficient, producing most of their own food, building their own houses, and making their own clothing.

Encouraged by the British government, the harvesting of tar, pitch, and turpentine made what was called "turpentine farming" a lucrative venture for many landowners with stands of longleaf pine. This enterprise required extensive acreage and used slave labor. By 1830, about 40 percent of the population was enslaved, though most were owned by a very small number of white residents.

After the ending of the Civil War in 1865, the area began its recovery. Cotton reigned as the most valuable crop, followed by corn. Other commonly grown crops included peanuts, sweet potatoes, apples, and peaches. By the end of the 19th century, tobacco production would quickly ascend as the predominant crop, holding that distinction for much of the 20th century.

Because of its proximity to the ocean, many of Onslow's farmers were also fishermen. It was common for a farmer to raise crops, harvest resin from pine trees, and bring in a catch of fish or shellfish. The isolation of Onslow preserved many of its natural resources; fish were said to be so plentiful that they were simply scooped into boats during certain times of the year.

As in the rest of the United States, the number of farms and farmers has been steadily decreasing in Onslow County. The presence of Camp Lejeune removed a number of farms during its establishment; the accompanying urban growth and corporate farm acquisition are also factors in the decline. More than 2,000 farms existed in Onslow County in 1940; in 1974, only 874 were counted, declining to 401 by 2007.

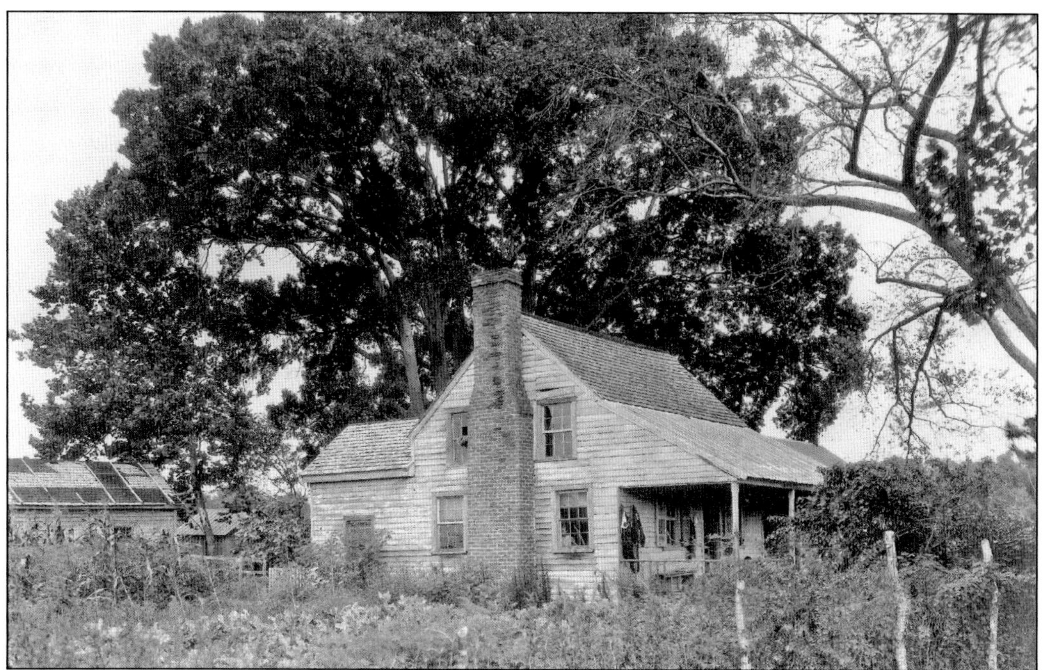

The coastal cottage was a common form of home architecture all along eastern North Carolina. Believed to have been brought here by early West Indies traders in the 18th century, the style endured into the early 20th century. The 1939 image of the Pearson house, seen here, shows a typical farm home in the coastal cottage style. The home was torn down with the coming of Camp Lejeune. (Courtesy of Onslow County Museum.)

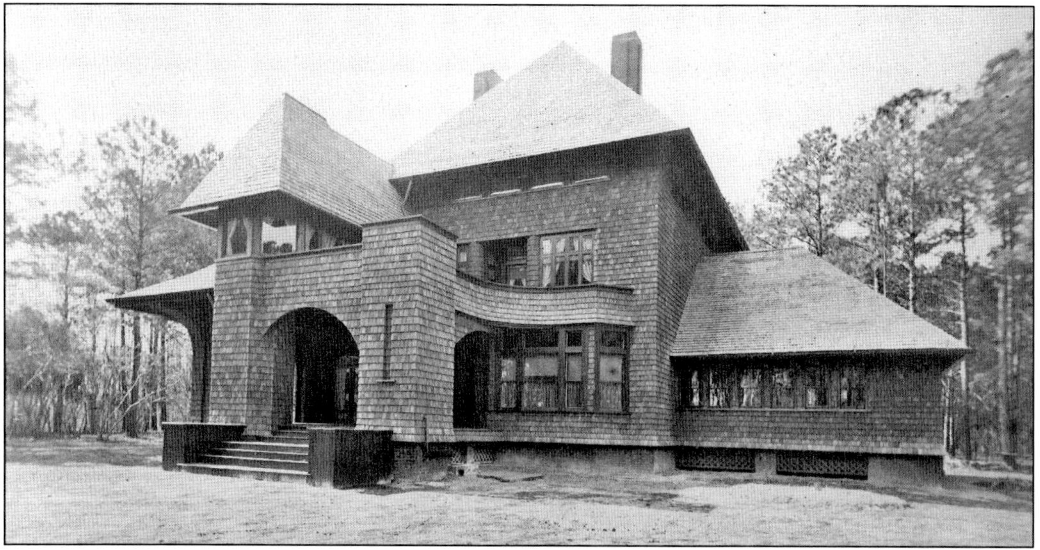

Onslow Hall was a large 27-room mansion unlike any that had been seen before in Onslow County. The house was built in 1892 by New York financier and railroad investor Thomas A. McIntyre on a 2,600-acre tract of land at Town Point on the New River; another part of the estate was Glenoe, a model farm where McIntyre raised extensive crops and livestock. McIntyre was the key investor in the long-awaited completion of the railroad tracks into Jacksonville in 1891. (Courtesy of Onslow County Museum.)

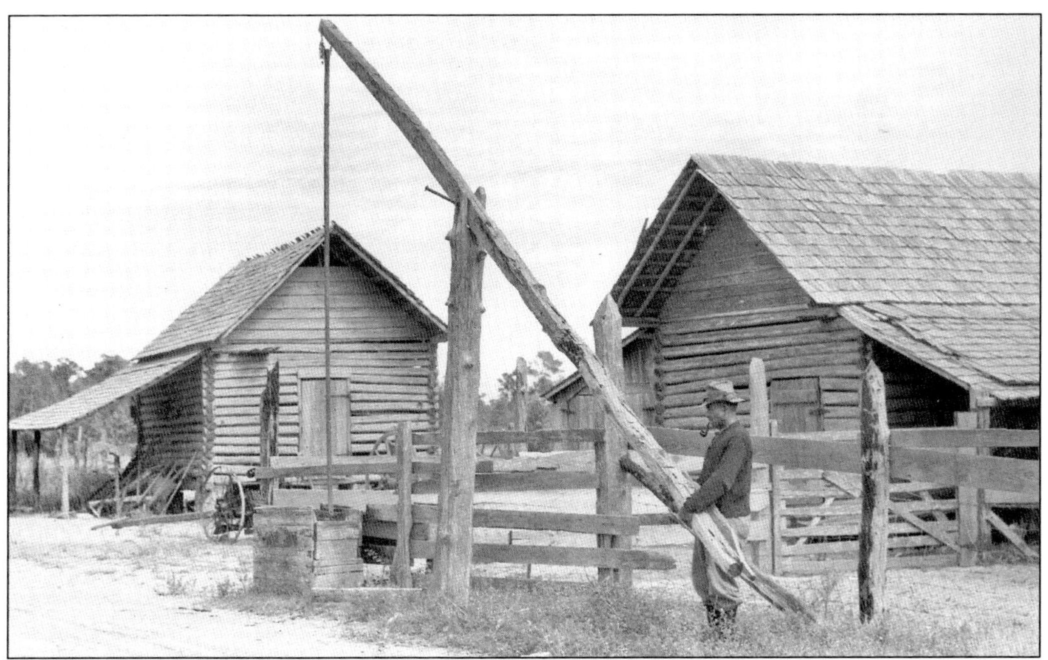

In this image, a local farmer operates a well sweep at a farm near Richlands in 1939. A well sweep was a simple but ingenious wooden device that functioned as a fulcrum to bring water up from a well. (Courtesy of Onslow County Museum.)

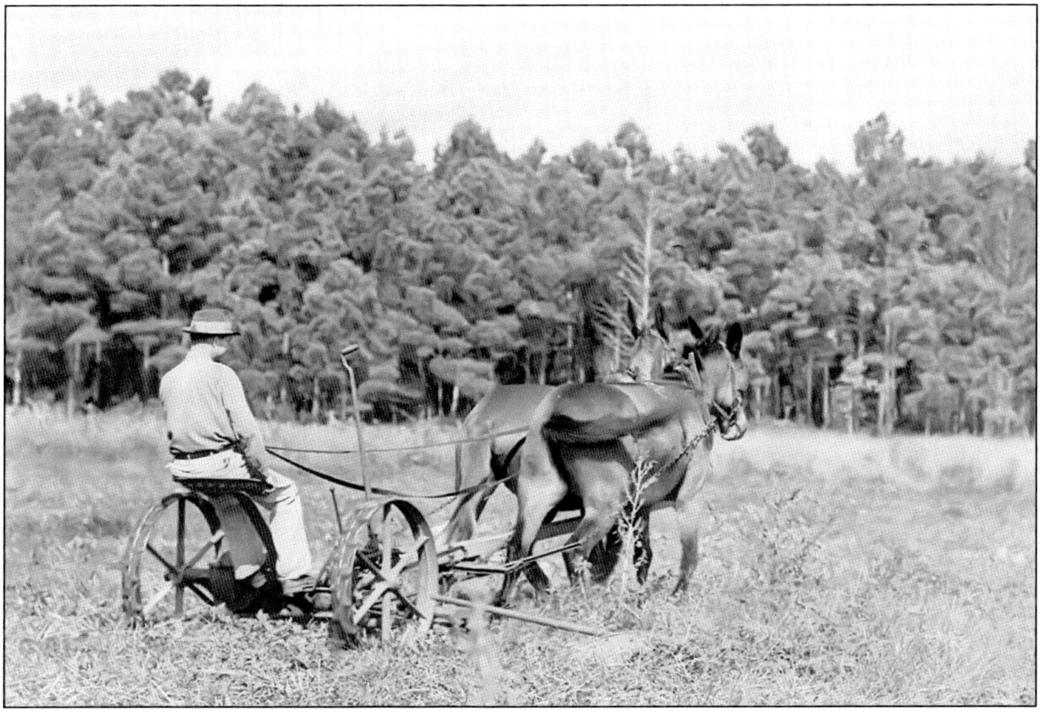

Farmer Telfair Best plows a field with a mule in about 1939, near Richlands. Common crops at this time were corn and tobacco. (Courtesy of Onslow County Museum.)

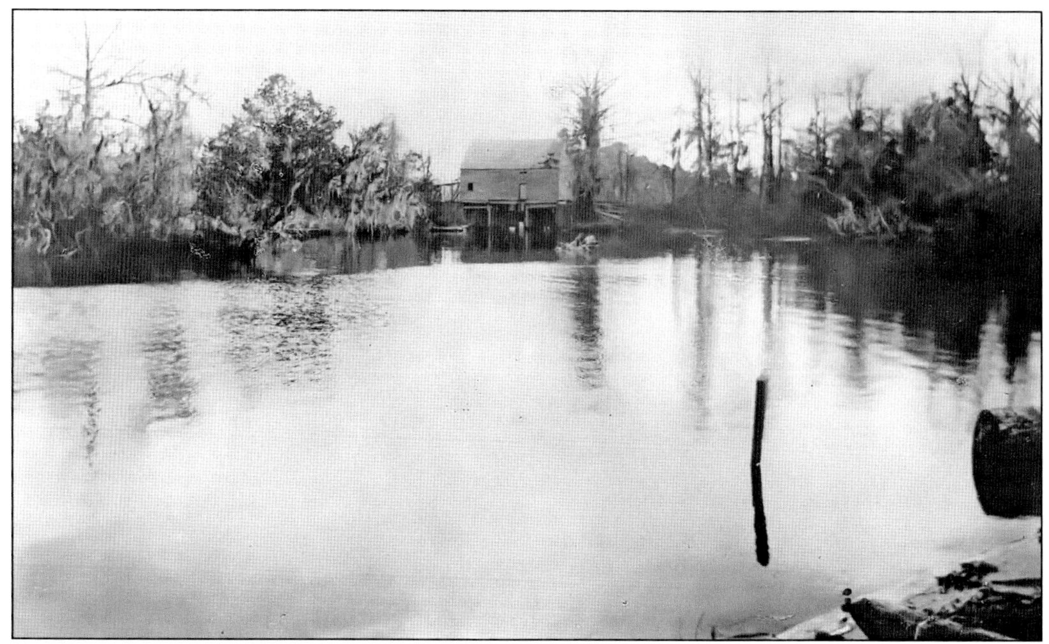

A number of mills were located throughout the county from earliest settlement. This tranquil view of Henderson's Millpond on Queen's Creek near Hubert was taken in the late 1930s. This facility served as a gristmill and lumber mill. (Courtesy of Onslow County Museum.)

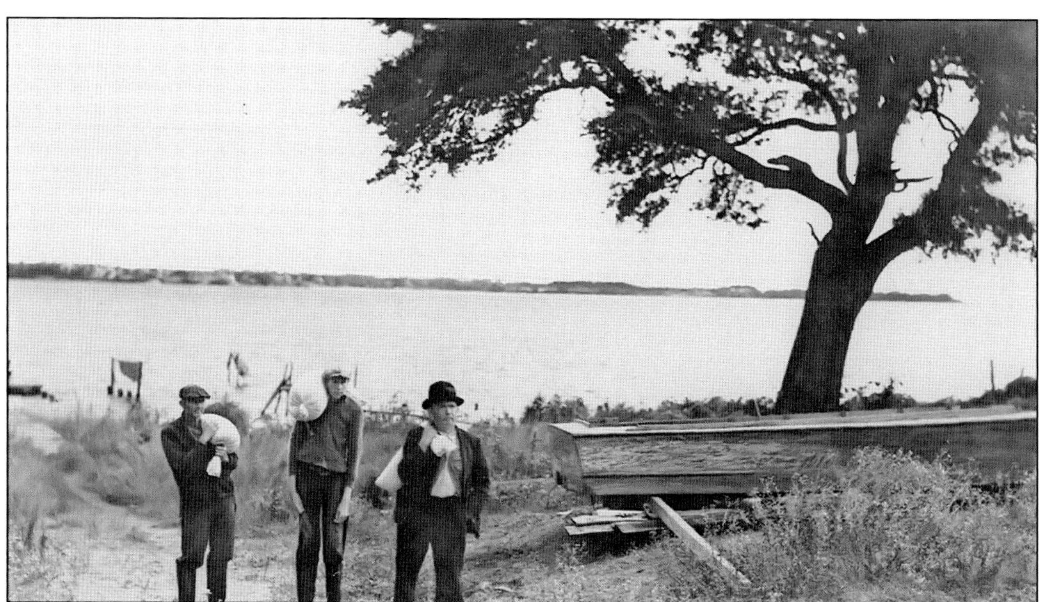

A small corn mill was located at Marines; in the late 1930s, people from across the river at Fulcher's Landing, like these three men, came to have their sacks of corn ground into meal. (Courtesy of Onslow County Museum.)

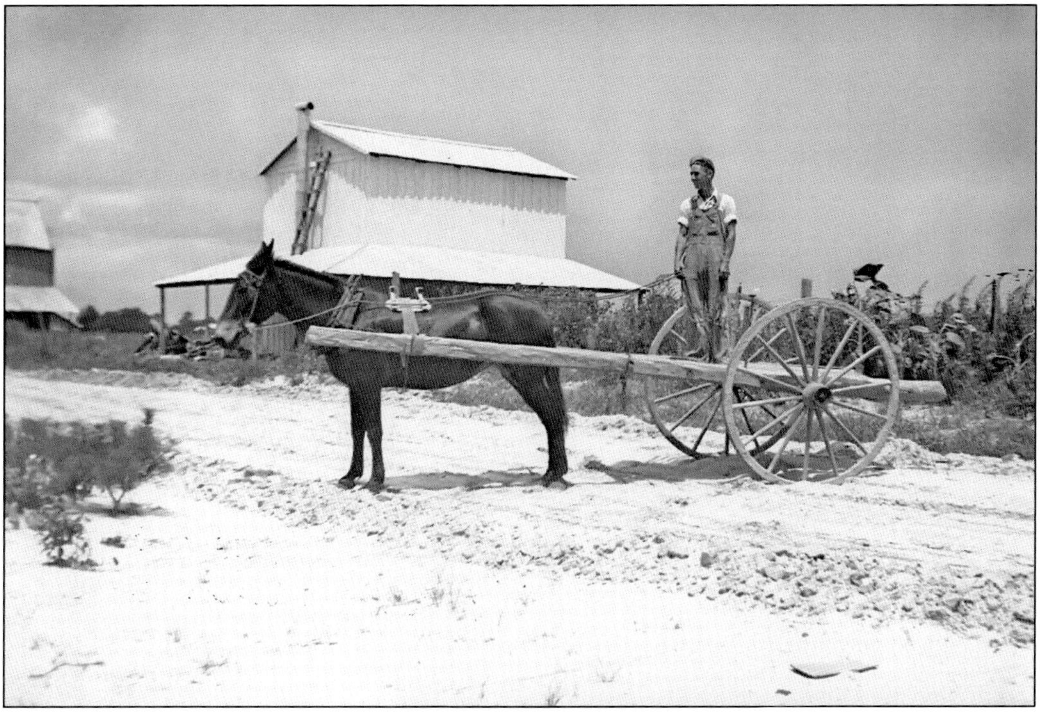

This Onslow farmer stands on his wagon, obviously proud of it and his mule. Note the tobacco barns behind him. In the late 1930s, the economy, including farming, was beginning to recover from the Great Depression. (Courtesy of Onslow County Museum.)

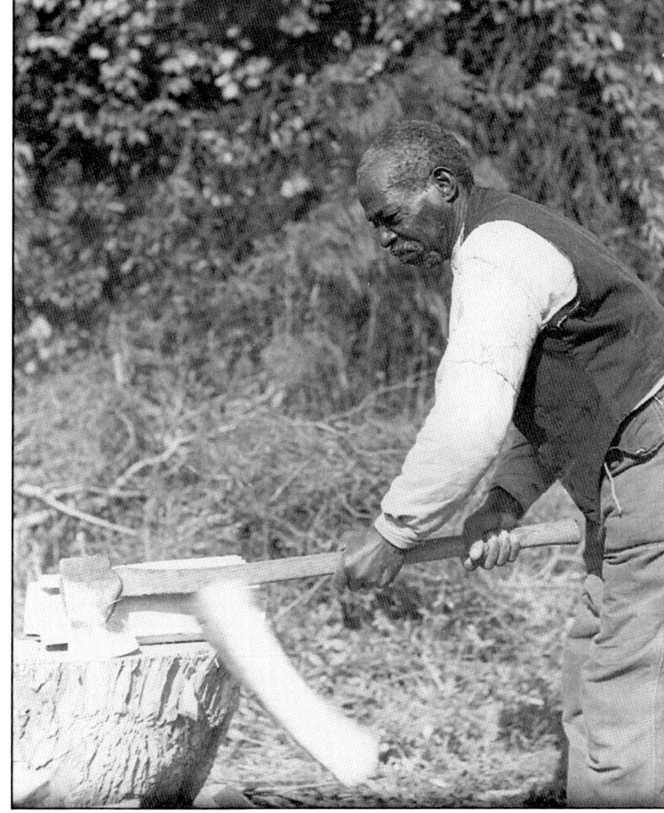

James "Jim" Bell splits wood, possibly for shingles, about 1939. At this time, about half the farmers in Onslow were tenant farmers, although Bell owned his farm near Swansboro. (Courtesy of Onslow County Museum.)

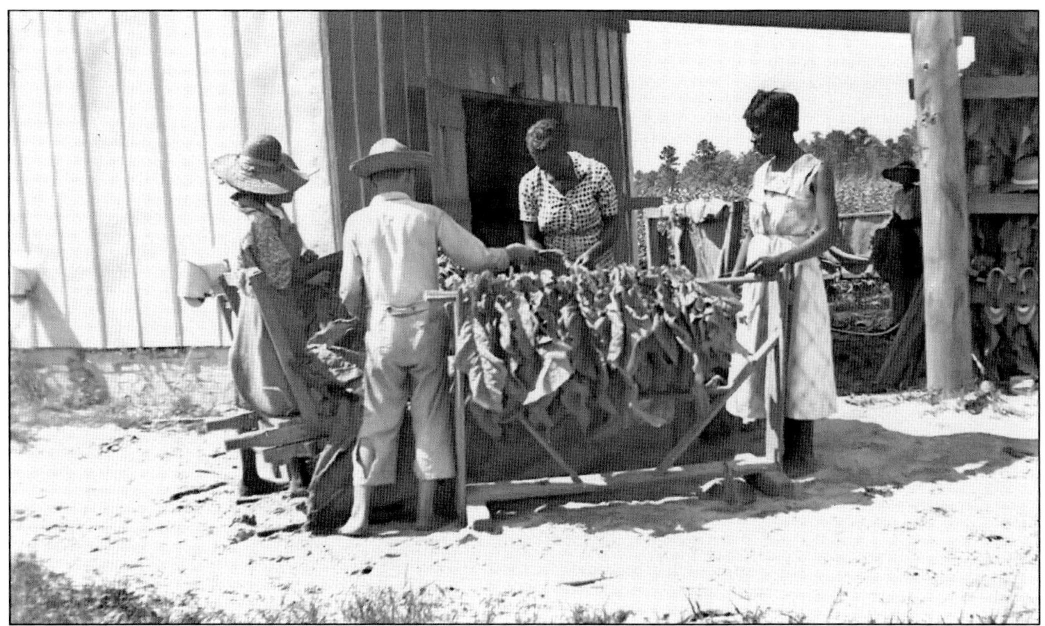

Harvesting tobacco usually started in late July and continued through the end of summer. Here, members of the Will Montford family and an unidentified young boy are looping tobacco to be hung in the curing barn. (Courtesy of Onslow County Museum.)

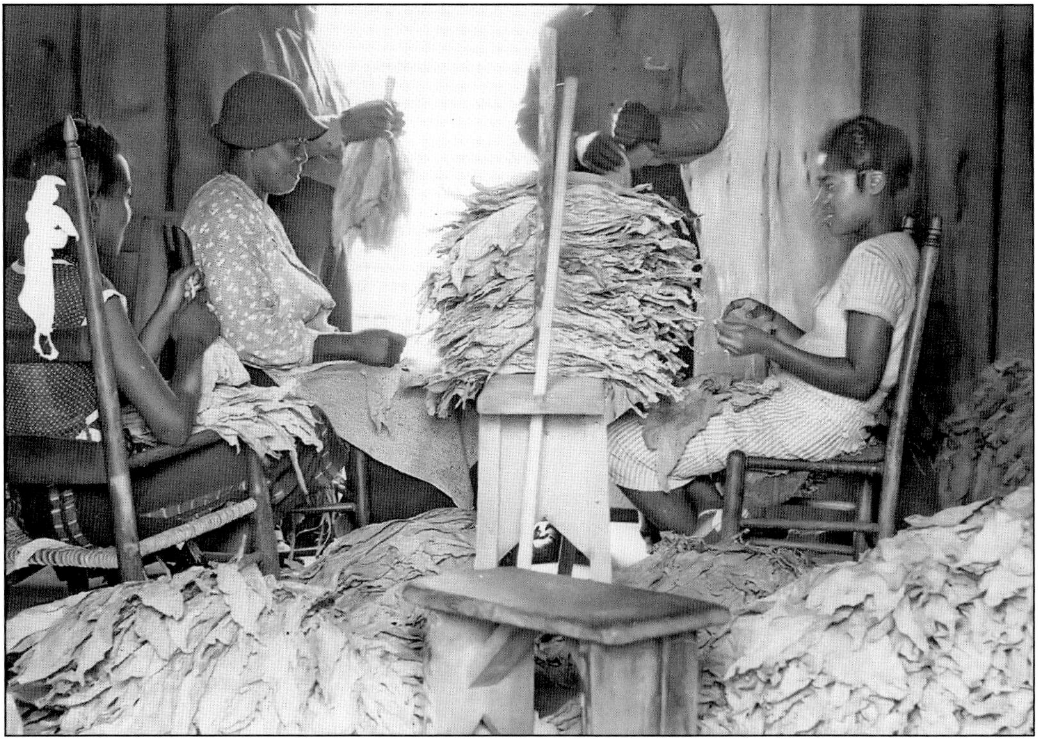

After the curing process was complete, the leaves were taken down and graded according to color and quality, as seen in this late-1930s image of the Will Montford family at work. (Courtesy of Onslow County Museum.)

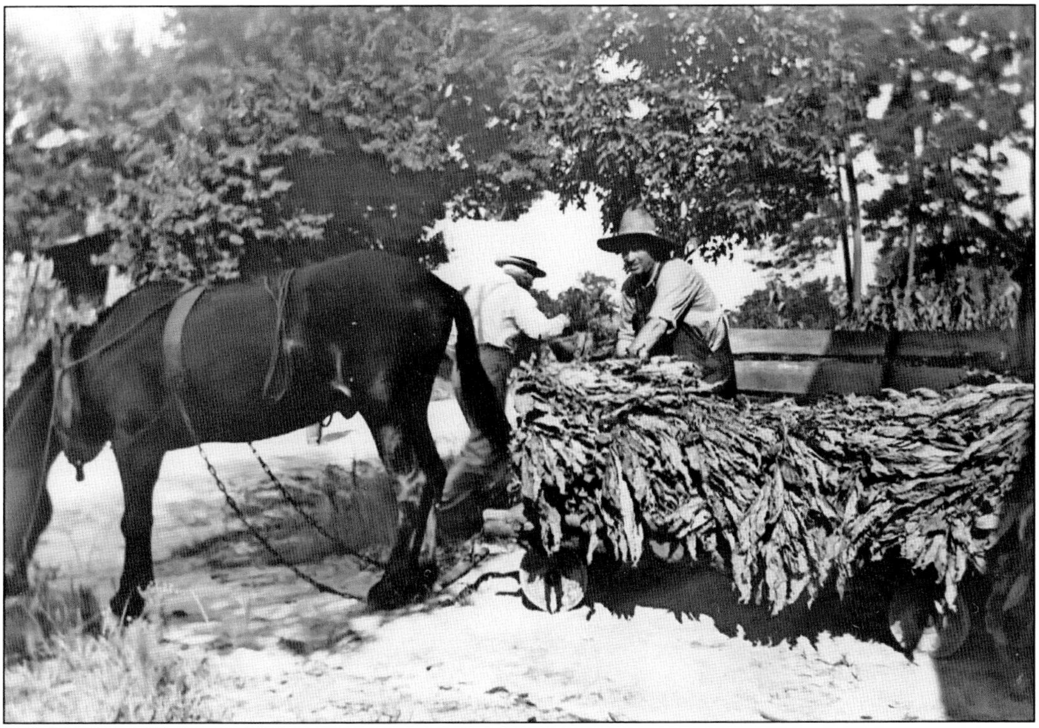

The family stacks and loads bright leaf tobacco leaves to be taken to the market in Kinston. Tobacco was the primary cash crop for decades in Onslow County. (Courtesy of Onslow County Museum.)

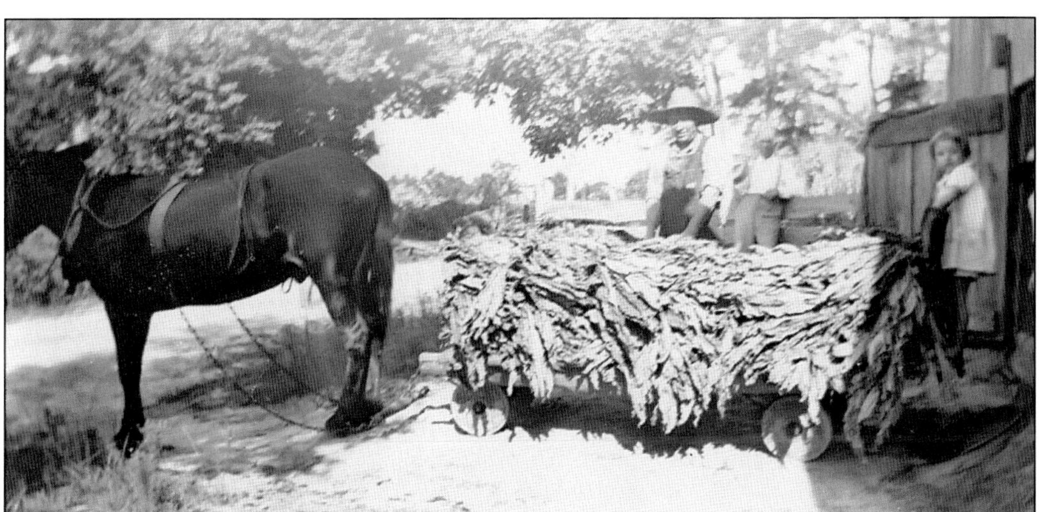

Loading tobacco for market often involved the entire family, as seen in this 1939 image. Often, children were assigned the task of watching the fire in the tobacco barn and ensuring that it did not go out. (Courtesy of Onslow County Museum.)

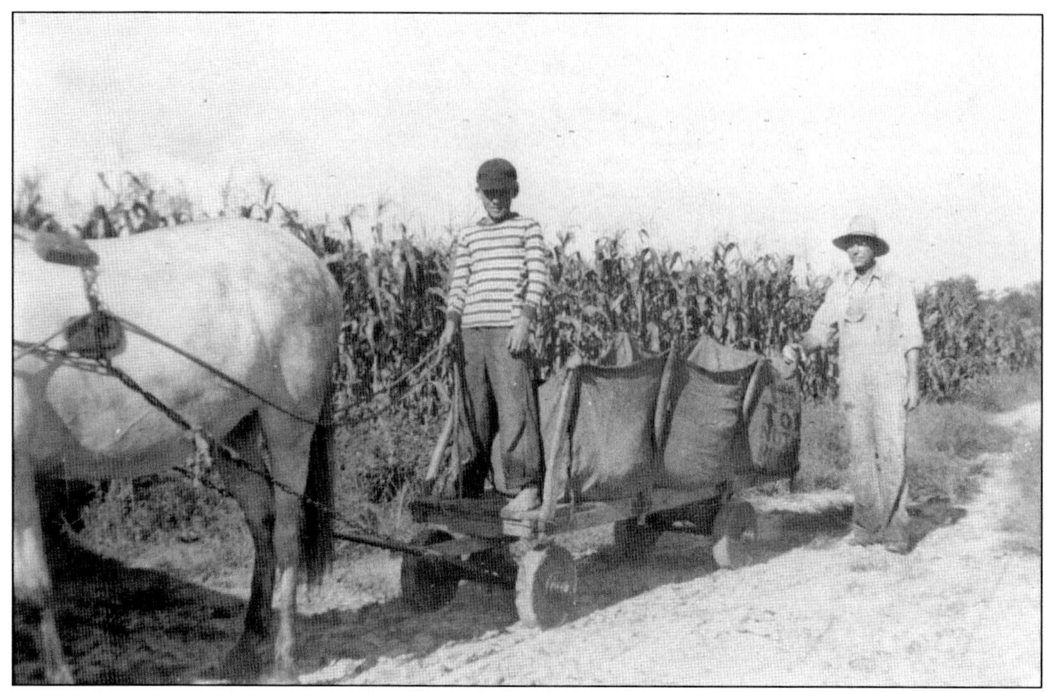
Dennis E. Jones (young boy on tobacco sled) and his grandfather Charlie Huffman are pictured on their farm near Richlands, about 1956. (Courtesy of Dennis E. Jones.)

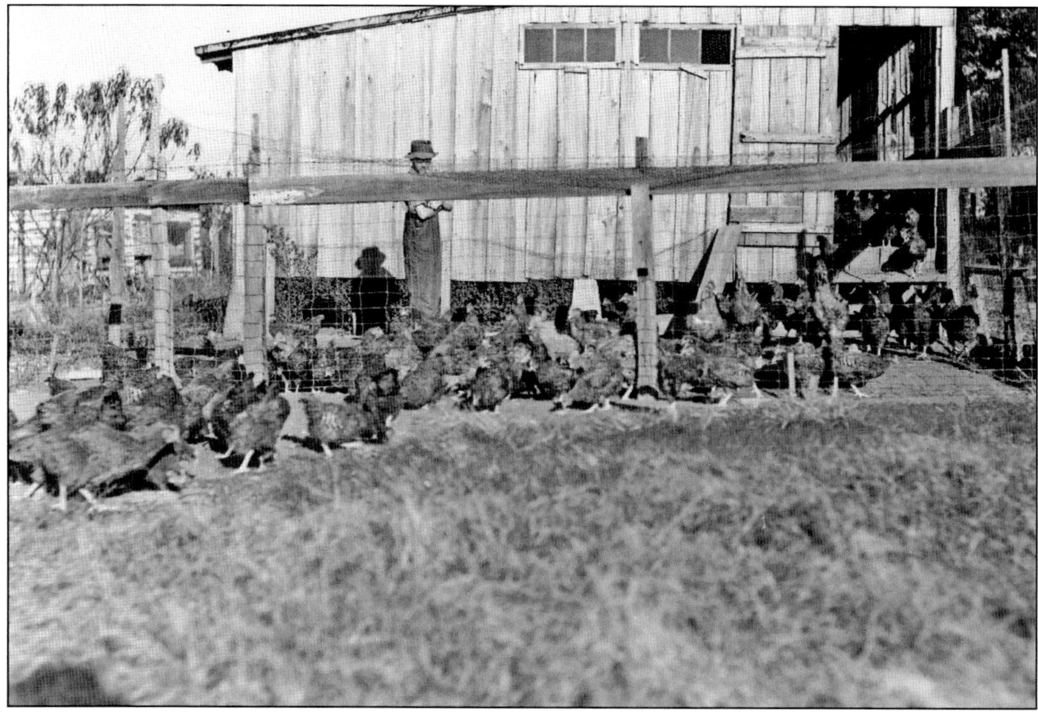
Most farm families raised chickens for eating and for their eggs. This flock with its large coop behind them was photographed in the late 1930s, probably at the James Taylor farm near Richlands. (Courtesy of State Archives of North Carolina.)

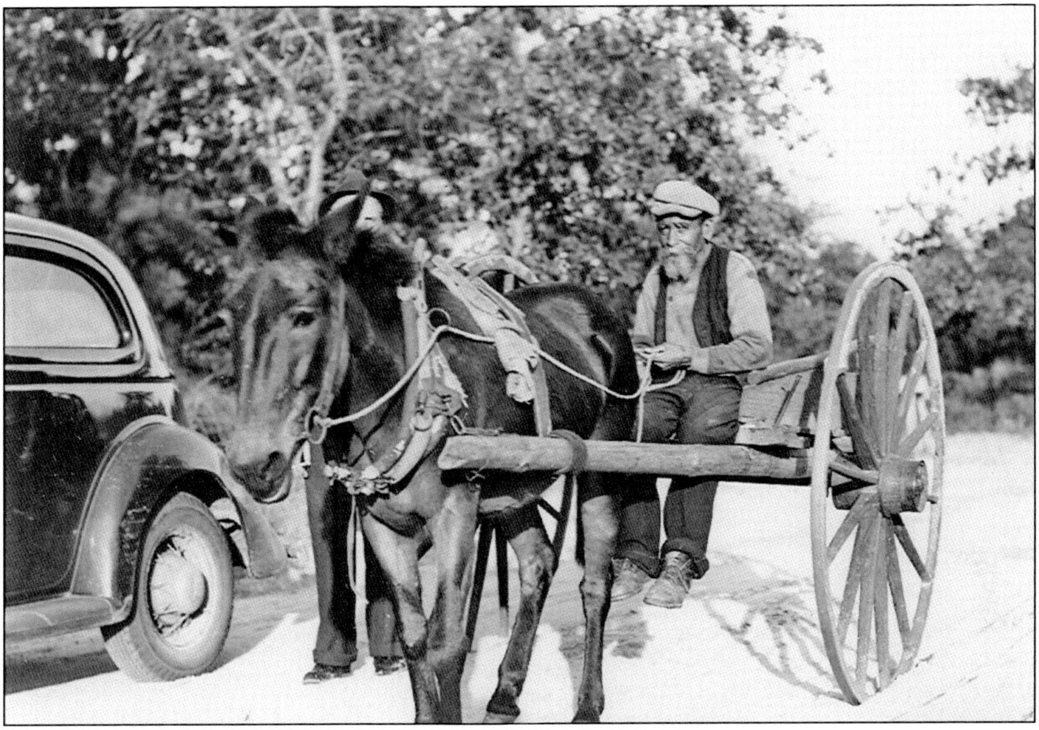

In 1930s Onslow County, it was not unusual to see modes of transportation reflecting the old and the new. Here, a farmer driving a traditional pole cart passes by a parked automobile. (Courtesy of Onslow County Museum.)

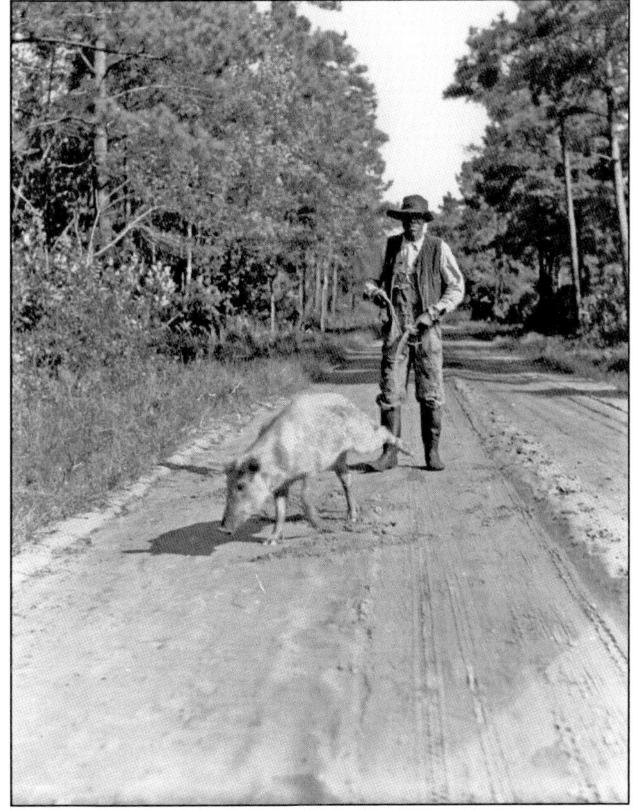

Jim Henderson transports a hog. Hogs were an important part of rural life in the 19th century and into the 20th century. Often called "pine-rooters," hogs were sometimes turned loose into wooded areas to forage for food. Longleaf pine seedlings were consumed by the hogs because of the high starch content of the roots. (Courtesy of State Archives of North Carolina.)

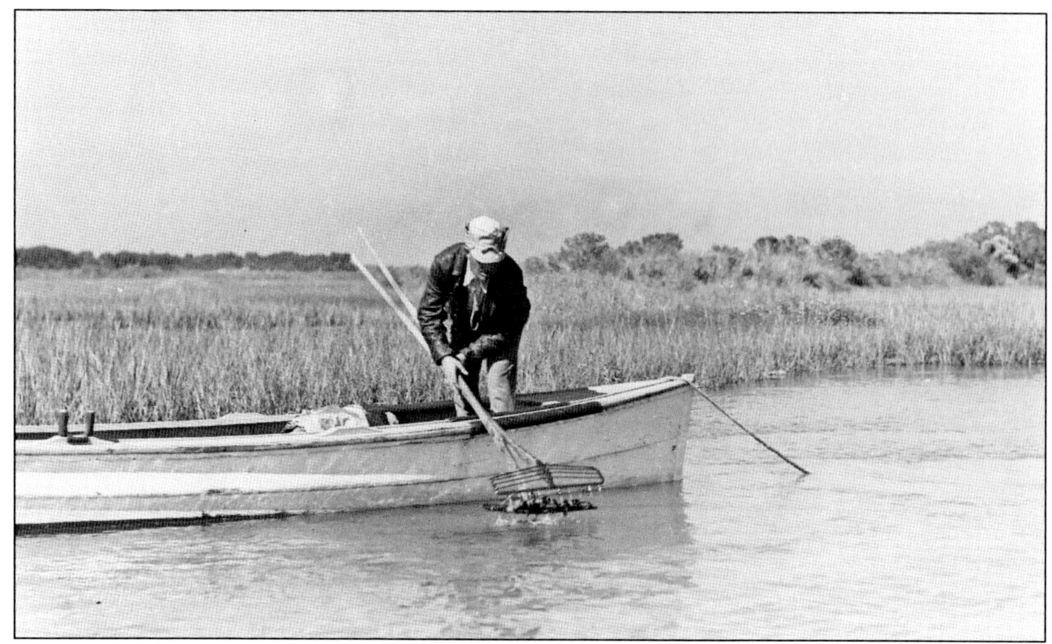

Bill Hanes, a former accountant, made his home in Onslow in the 1930s. He enjoyed clamming in the New River. Clamming became more prevalent when the oyster population declined due to habitat-altering storms. (Courtesy of Onslow County Museum.)

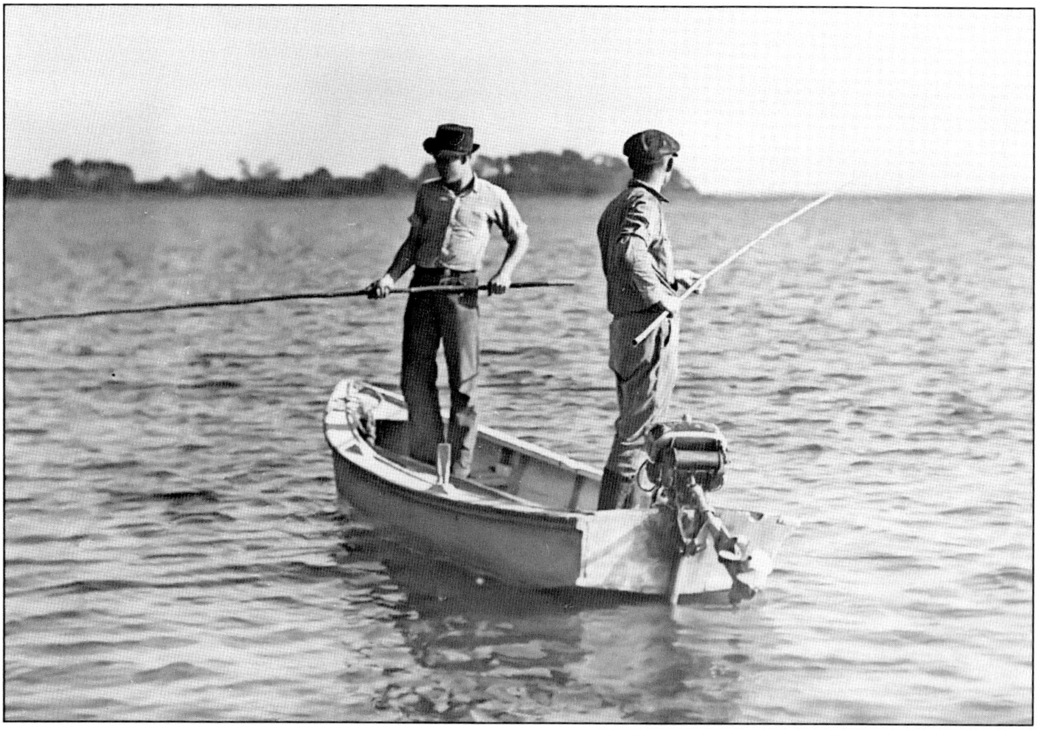

Fishing buddies Wiley Taylor (left) and Ollie Marine are seen here fishing in the New River. Their respective families were some of the earlier settlers of Onslow County. (Courtesy of Onslow County Museum.)

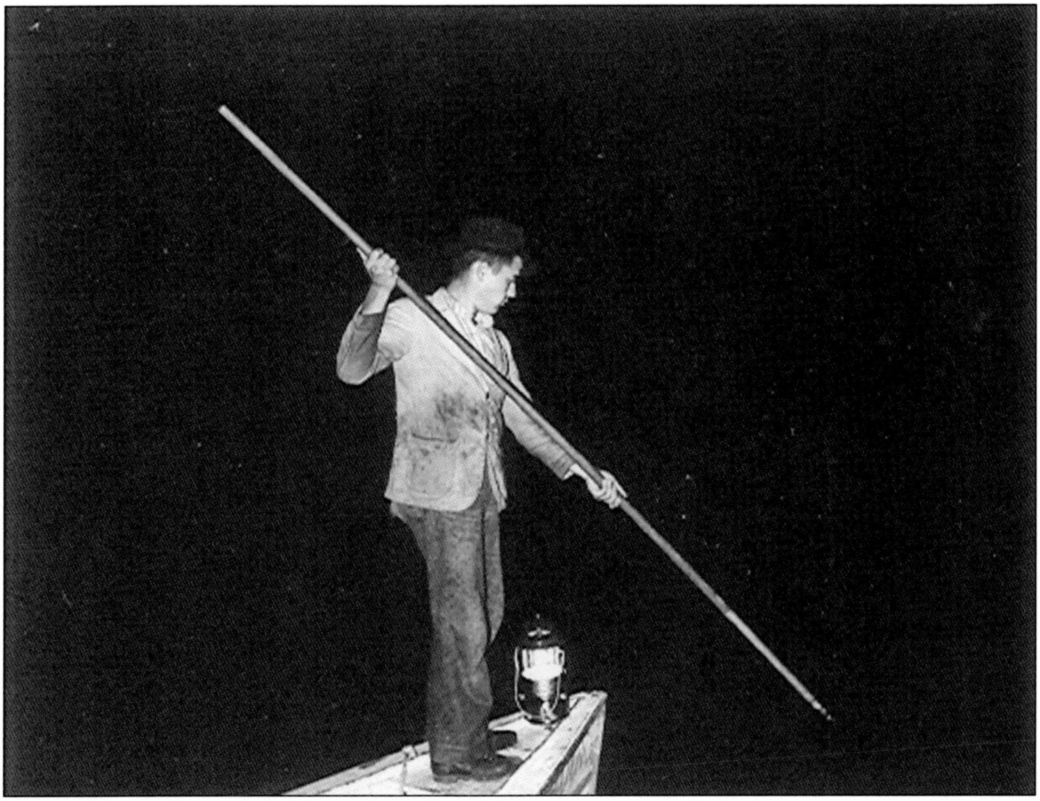

Here, Wiley Taylor gigs fish or frogs at night. Night gigging using a three-pronged metal spearhead on a wooden pole was a traditional and popular pastime. (Courtesy of Onslow County Museum.)

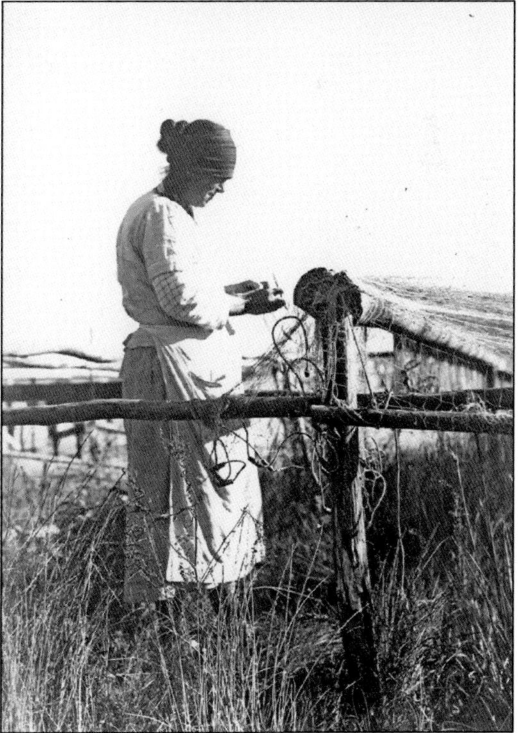

Women were also active in the fishing trade; fishing families took good care of their nets, washing them, and arranging them on net spreads to dry. Net fishing for spot and mullet was a common enterprise of most Onslow residents before World War II. In this image, Annie Millis Norton Wiggins is shown mending a fishing net drying on a net spread in Sneads Ferry about 1939. (Courtesy of Onslow County Museum.)

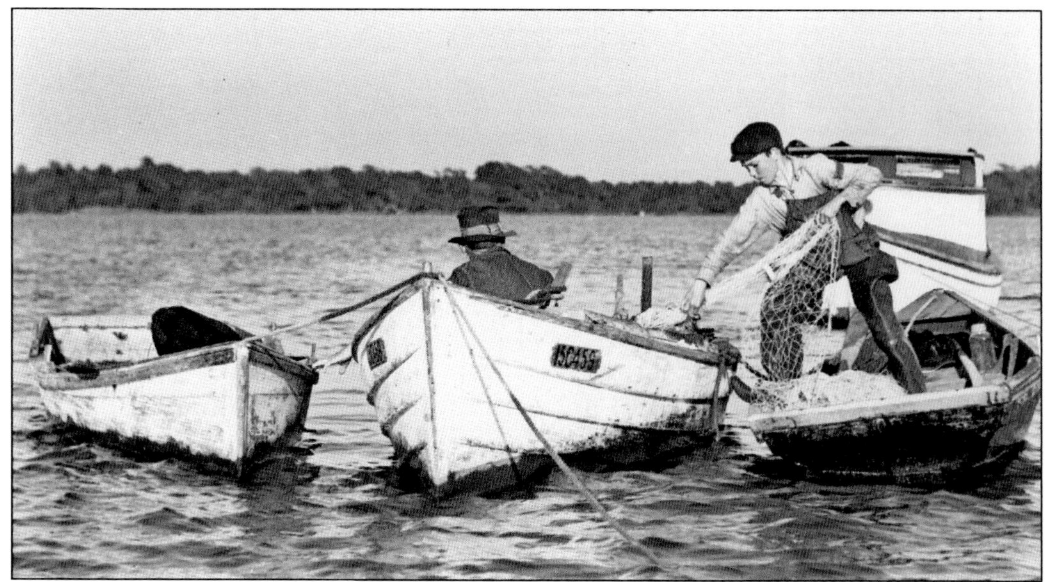

Fishing with nets required the use of at least two boats. Here, a boy helps his grandfather bring in a catch on the New River. Children were raised with the expectation that they would help the family and learn the traditional lifeways. (Courtesy of State Archives of North Carolina.)

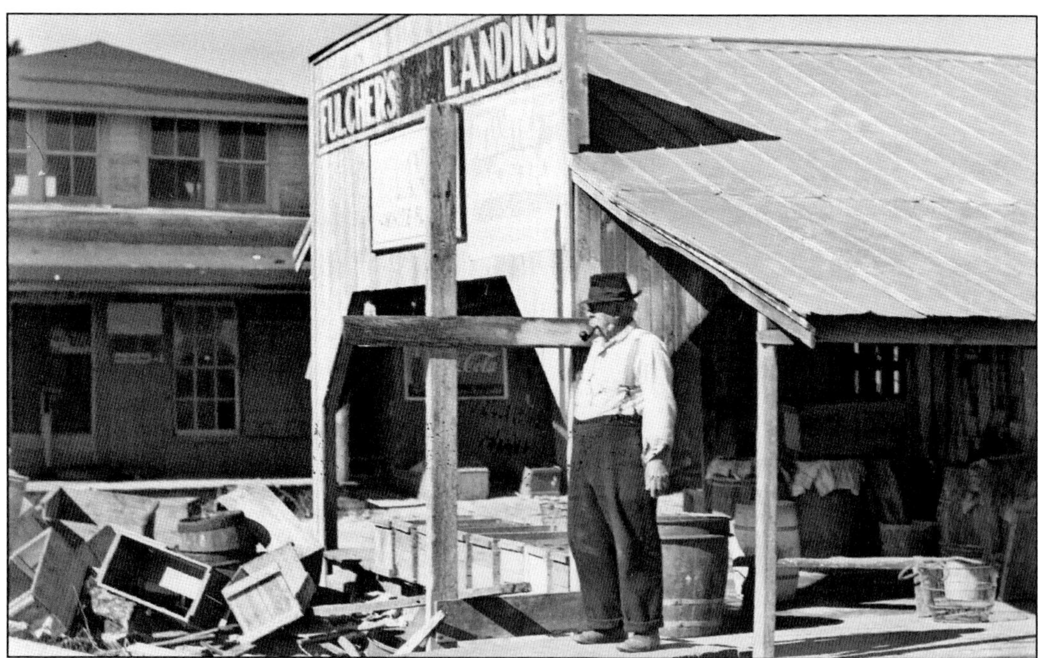

James "Jim" Fulcher was a farmer, fisherman, and storekeeper in the old community of Fulcher's Landing near Sneads Ferry. Born in Carteret County in 1869, he lived most of his life in Onslow County and died in 1940 as big changes in the county were beginning. (Courtesy of Onslow County Museum.)

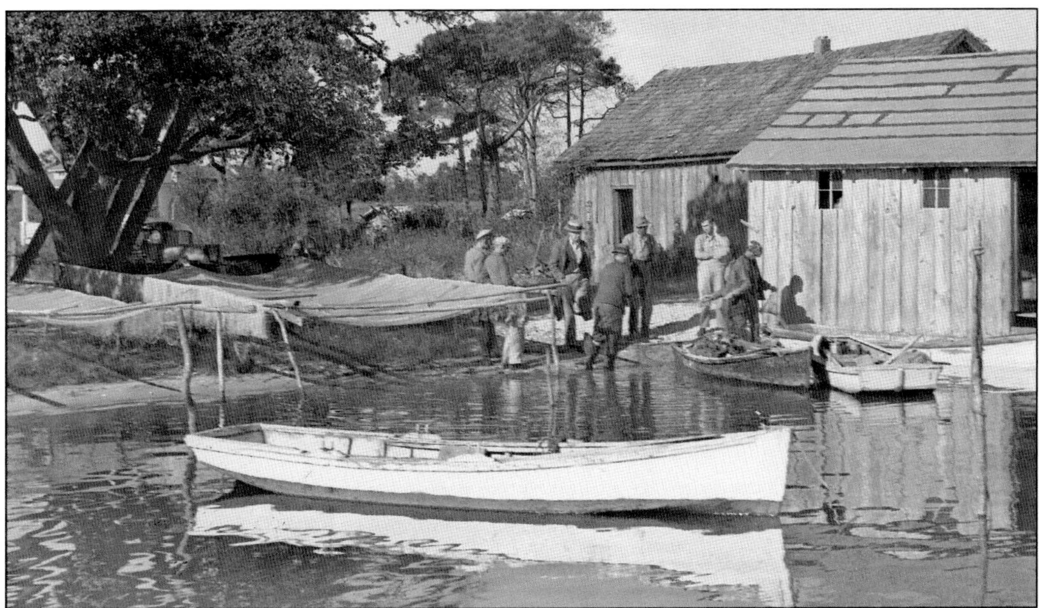

Fishermen unload a catch at Fulcher's Landing in the late 1930s. (Courtesy of Onslow County Museum.)

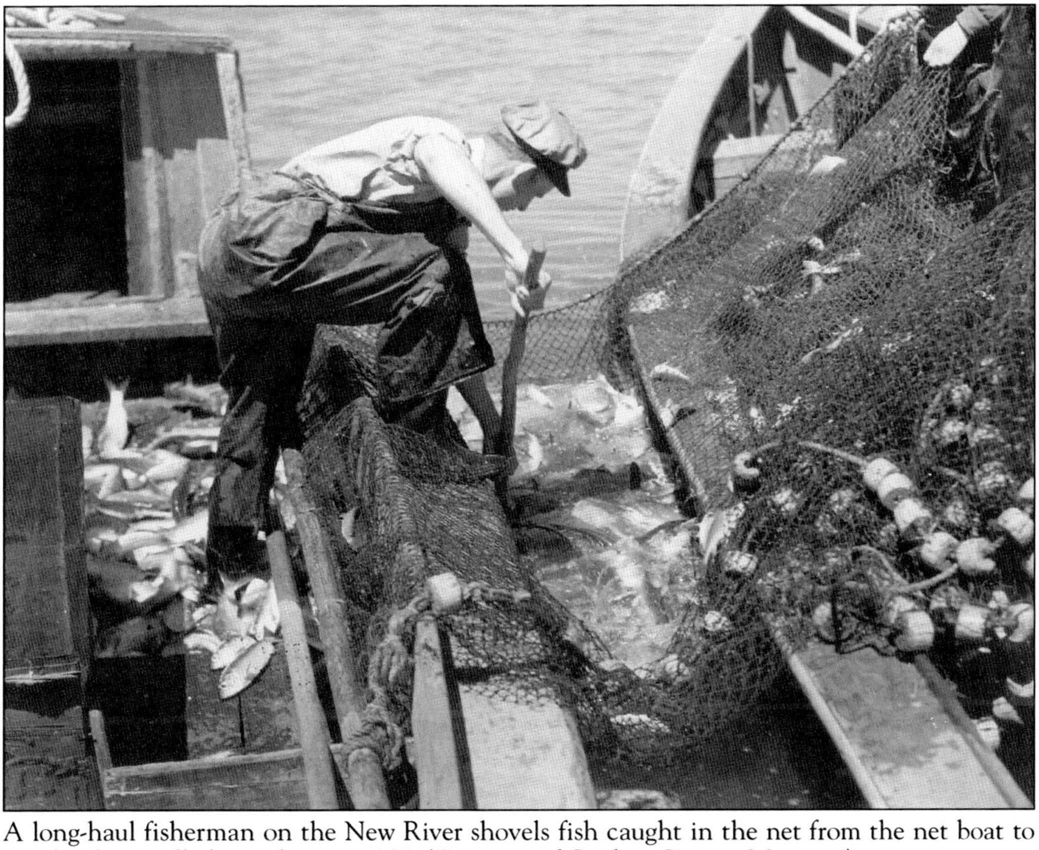

A long-haul fisherman on the New River shovels fish caught in the net from the net boat to another boat called a runboat in 1939. (Courtesy of Onslow County Museum.)

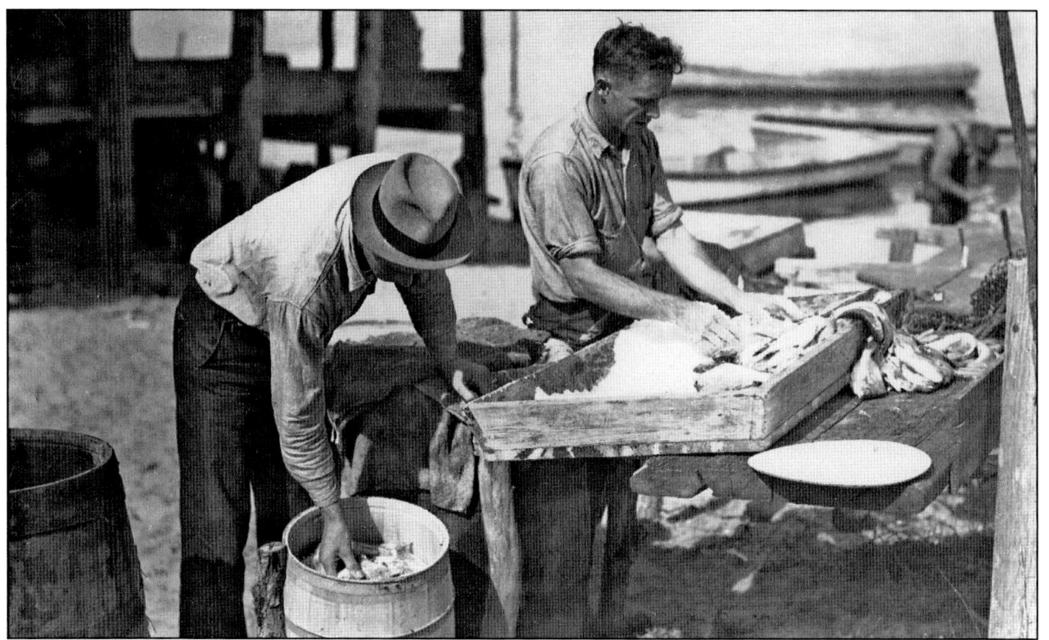

In this photograph, men work at a salting spot for packing at Swansboro in about 1939. This ancient method of preservation provided long-term storage. (Courtesy of Onslow County Museum.)

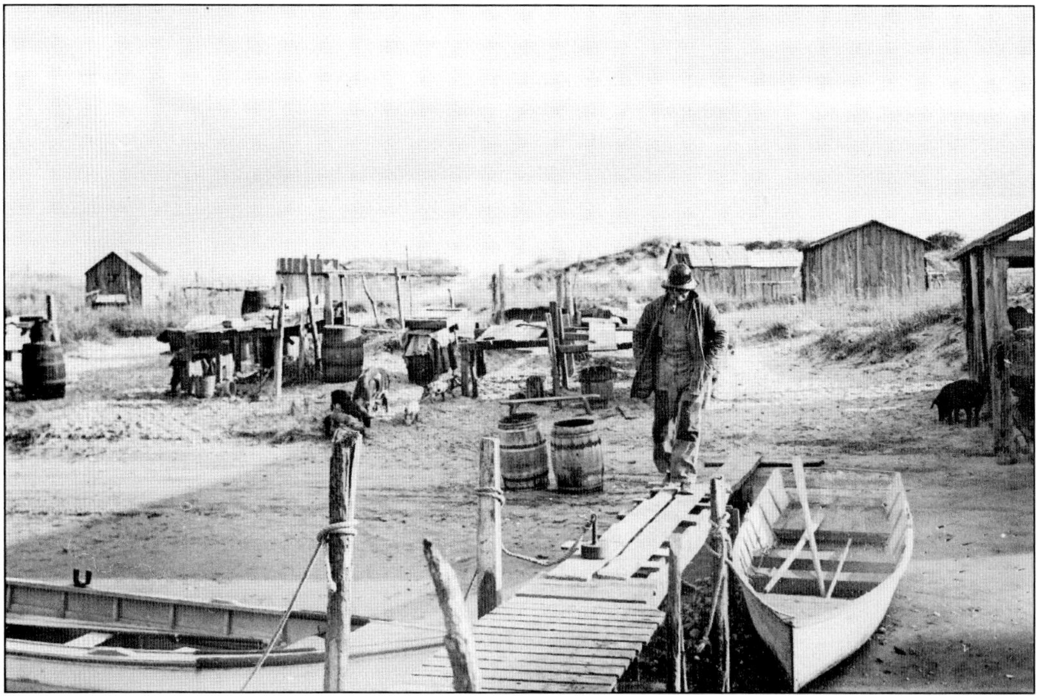

A number of fish camps dotted the shores of Onslow County. One of the larger ones was on Gillikin Island at Brown's Inlet. This temporary community was occupied by mullet fishermen for several months a year. (Courtesy of State Archives of North Carolina.)

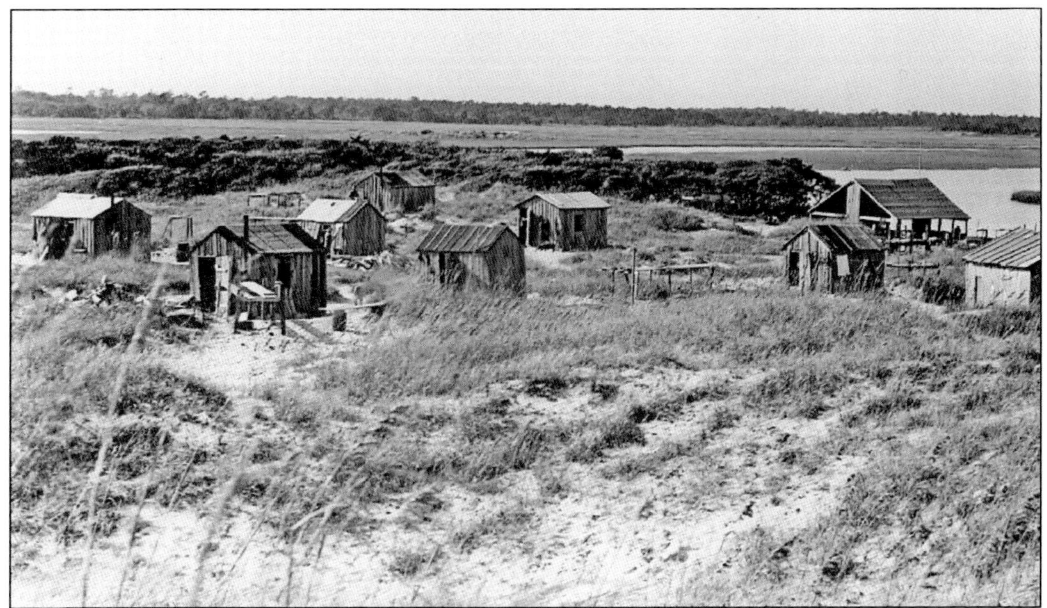

The fishermen built their fishing shacks at Gillikin Island out of scrap lumber and cardboard. Life was primitive here, but the shacks had bunks and small stoves for warmth during the cold, mullet-fishing season in 1939. (Courtesy of State Archives of North Carolina.)

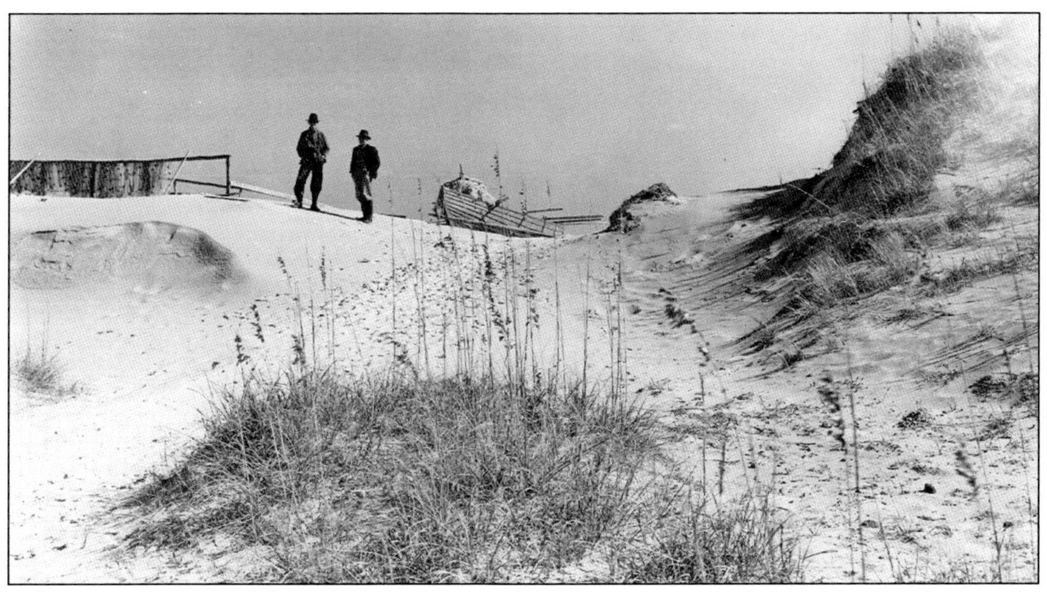

Fishermen wait on sand dunes at Brown's Inlet. Nets are drying on the left in this 1939 photograph. (Courtesy of Onslow County Museum.)

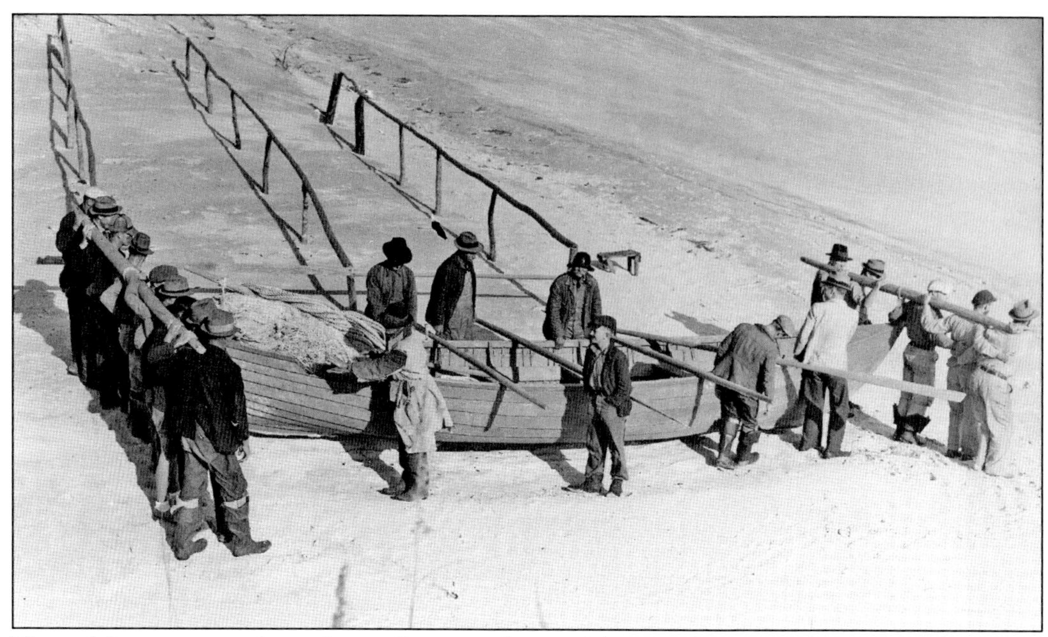

These fishermen are taking the surfboat out for net fishing at Brown's Inlet in 1939. (Courtesy of Onslow County Museum.)

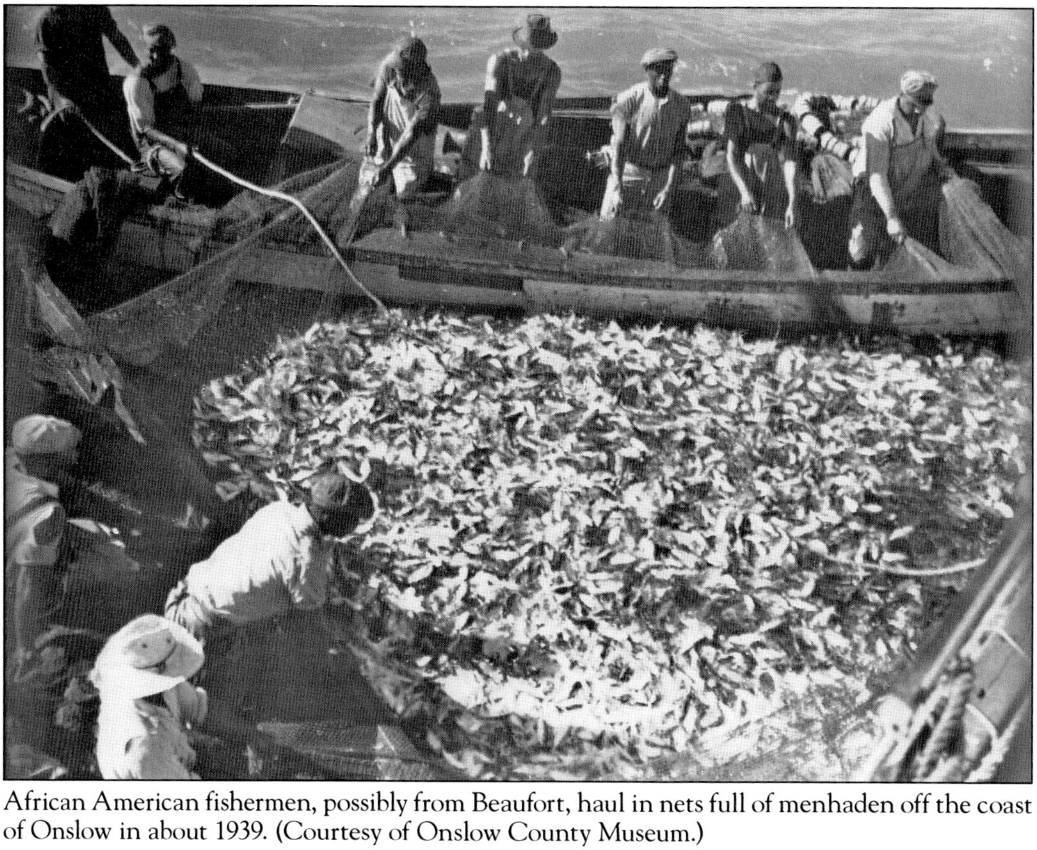

African American fishermen, possibly from Beaufort, haul in nets full of menhaden off the coast of Onslow in about 1939. (Courtesy of Onslow County Museum.)

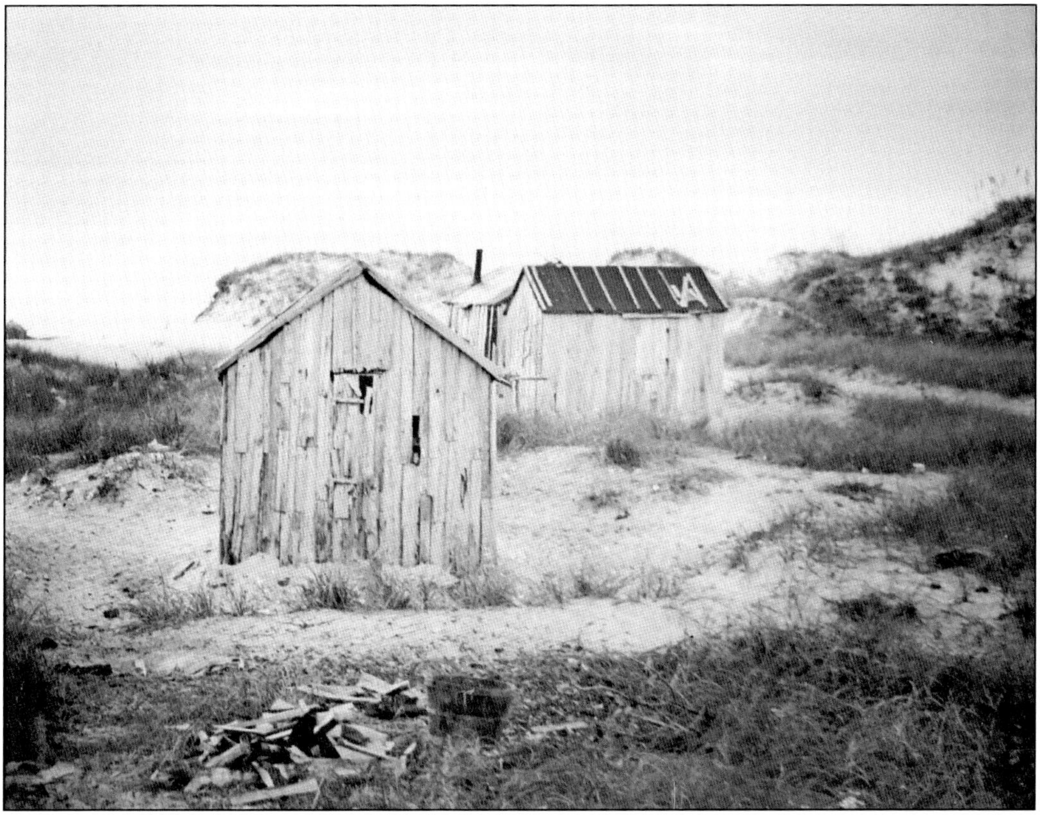

Fishing shacks at Gillikin Island are pictured here in 1938 or 1939. (Courtesy of State Archives of North Carolina.)

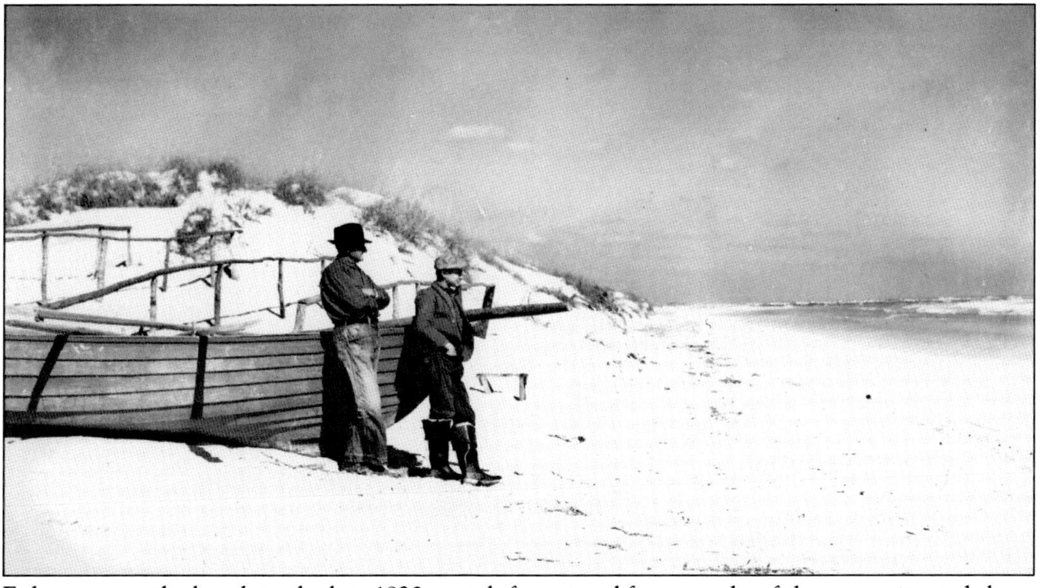

Fishermen on the beach in the late 1930s watch for a signal from another fisherman, situated about half a mile away, that the fish are coming in. (Courtesy of State Archives of North Carolina.)

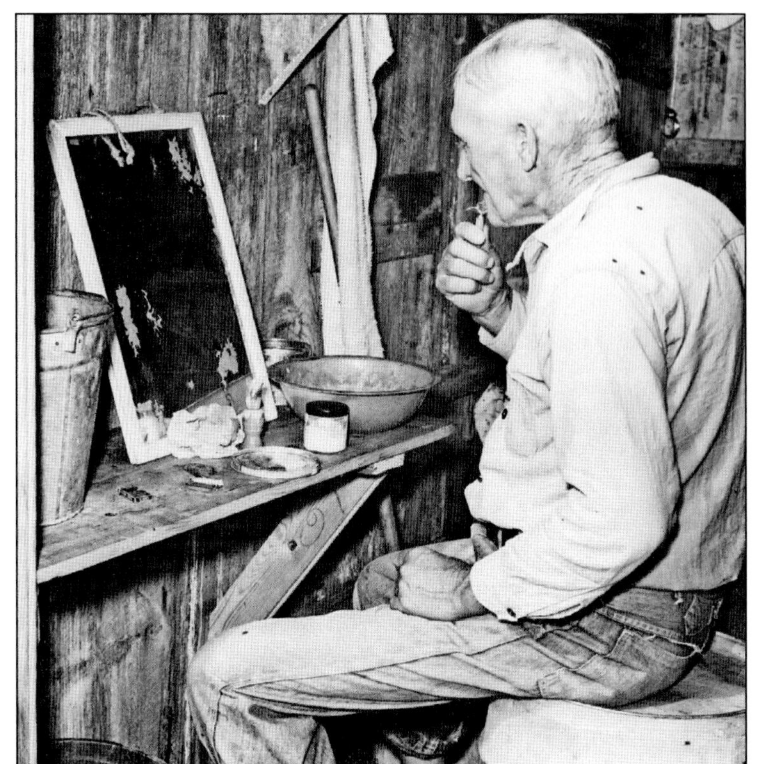

Bryant Gillikin shaves in a small fishing shack at Gillikin Island in about 1939. The fishermen usually arrived in the camp for the first mullet run in mid-September and stayed until the beginning of December. (Courtesy of State Archives of North Carolina.)

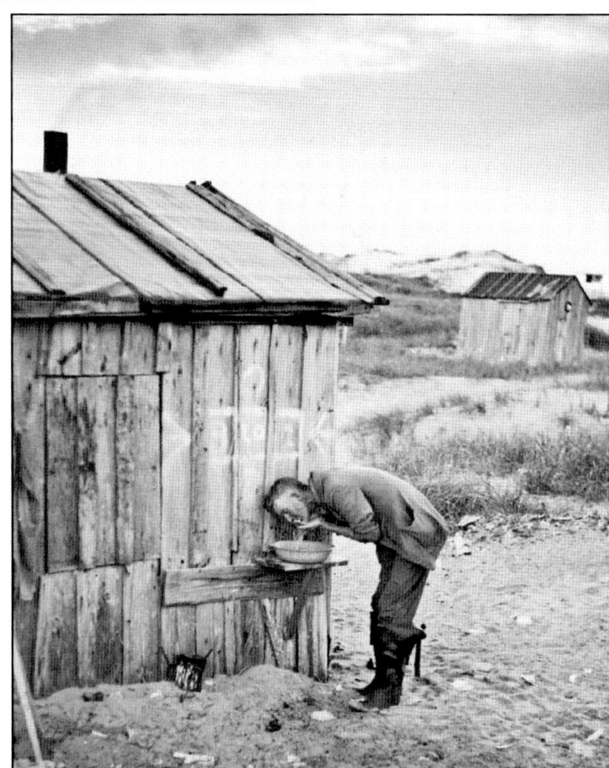

A fisherman washes up outside of fishing shack after a long day on the water in 1939. (Courtesy of State Archives of North Carolina.)

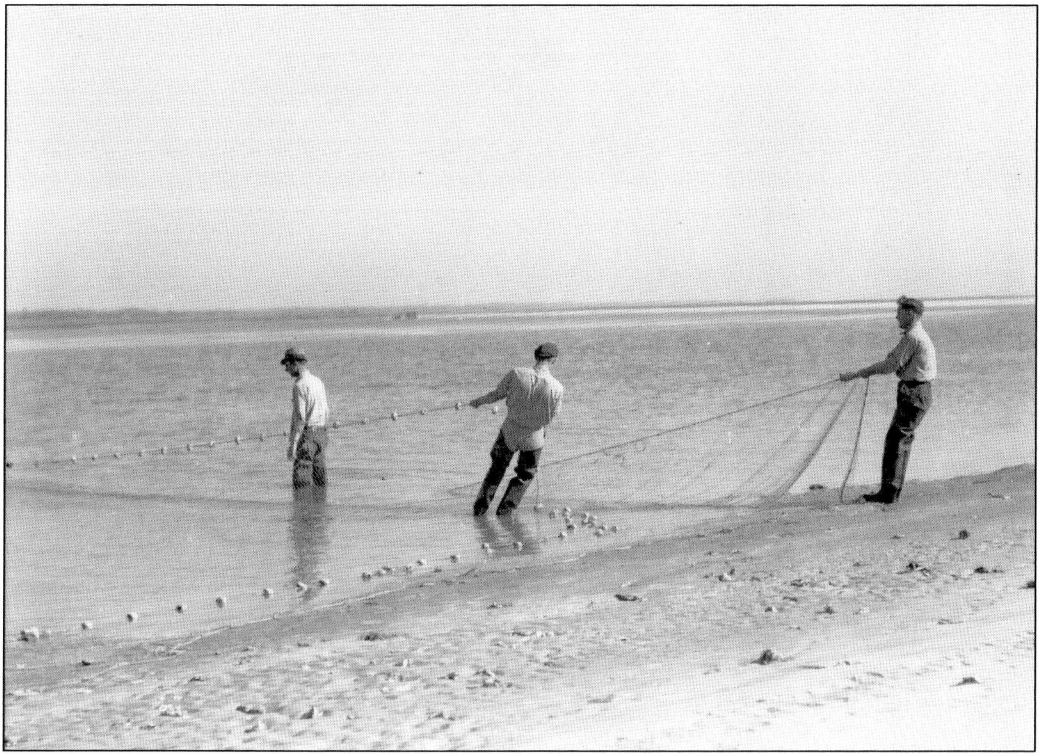

Spot fishing at low tide, fishermen on the beach pull in nets at Gillikin Island in 1938 or 1939. (Courtesy of State Archives of North Carolina.)

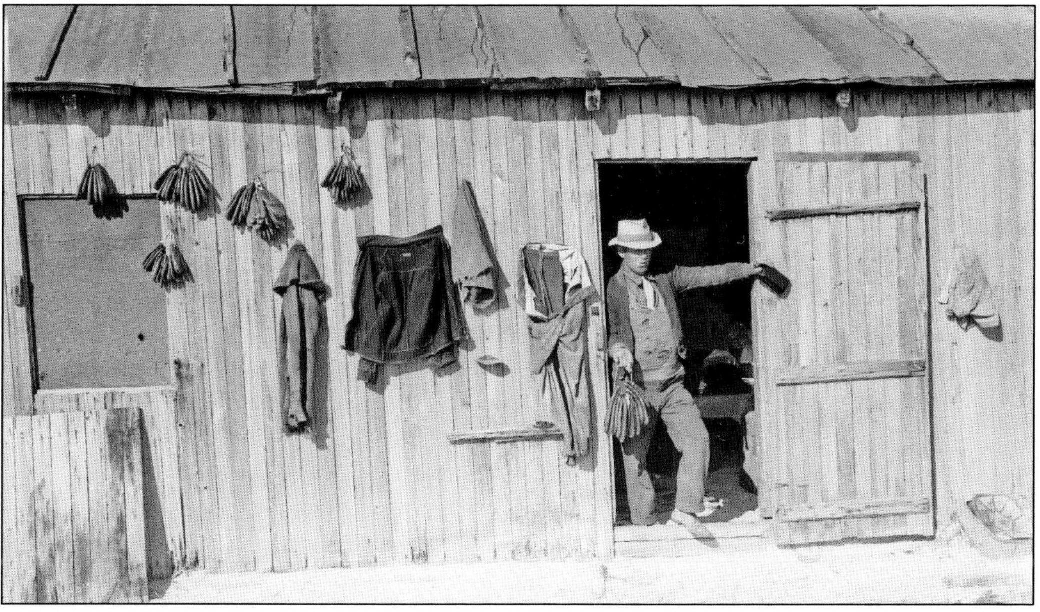

A fisherman poses in the doorway of a fishing shack on Gillikin Island in 1939 after returning from some time on the mainland. He told the photographer, Charles A. Farrell, he wanted to know what he looked like drunk. Note the mullet roe hanging and drying on the walls. (Courtesy of State Archives of North Carolina.)

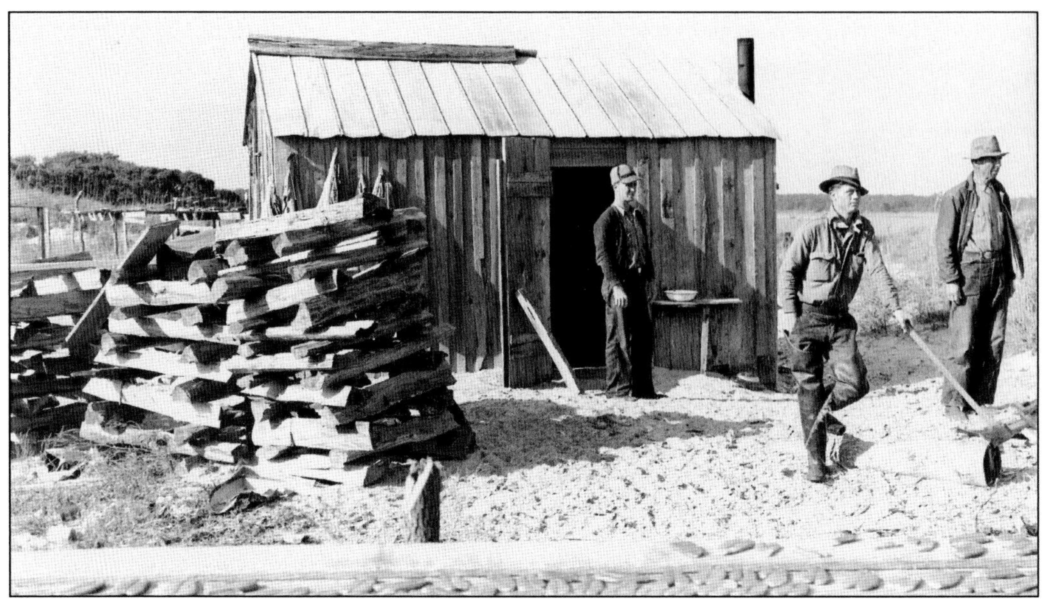

Members of the Gillikin family stand outside one of the fishing shacks in the late 1930s. Firewood is stacked on the left; the man with the axe (for splitting more wood) is probably Leonard Gillikin. (Courtesy of State Archives of North Carolina.)

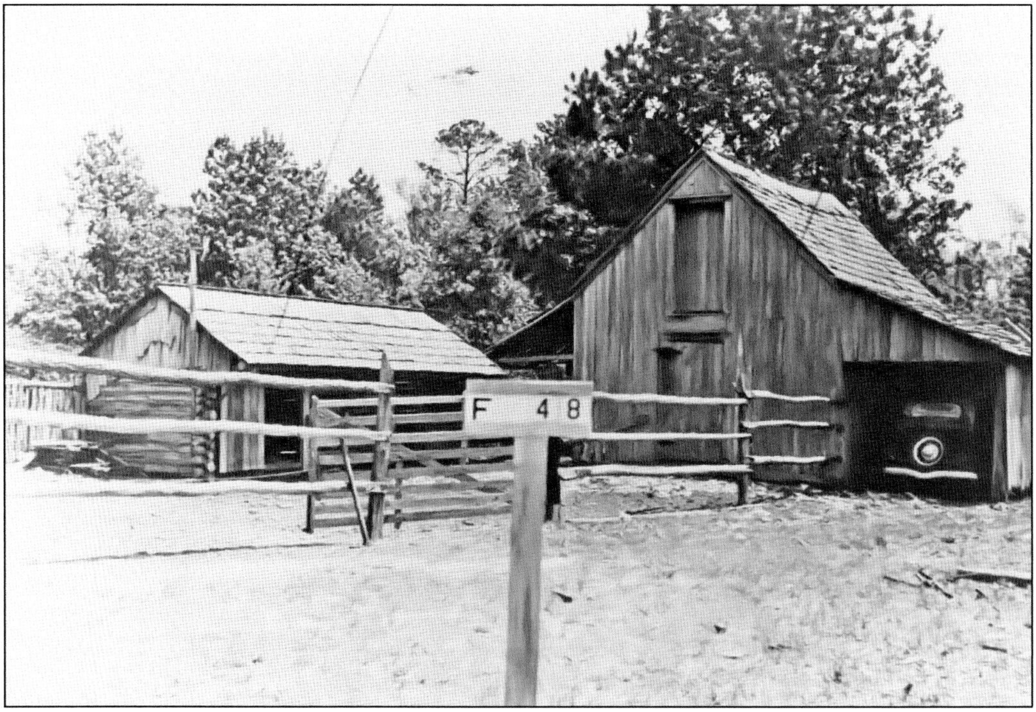

The lives of farmers and fishermen and their families were irrevocably changed by the coming of the military. This image shows the barns on a farm acquired for Camp Lejeune. Note the inventory marker in front. Hundreds of families were required to give up their property; the average price offered was $12 an acre. (Courtesy of Onslow County Museum.)

Two

Cities, Towns, and Communities

From the 18th century onward, Onslow was dotted with a patchwork of small towns and communities situated to utilize abundant natural resources. The establishment of the military bases spurred the steady growth of Jacksonville, while some small family-based communities were obliterated by land acquisition.

A look at old maps and records reveals place-names that have become long-forgotten memories, such as Golden Place, Wolf Pit, Dark Entry, Marines and many more. However, small communities such as Hubert, Verona, and Half Moon survive.

Onslow County is currently divided into five townships: Jacksonville, White Oak, Stump Sound, Swansboro and Richlands. Within these townships are Jacksonville (the county seat) and the incorporated cities of Holly Ridge, Swansboro, Richlands, North Topsail Beach, and a part of Surf City. Sneads Ferry is unincorporated.

The major population center of Jacksonville has grown from a small agrarian community of less than 1,000 in the 1930s to a rapidly growing city—the 13th-largest city in North Carolina, with a population of over 78,000 in 2013.

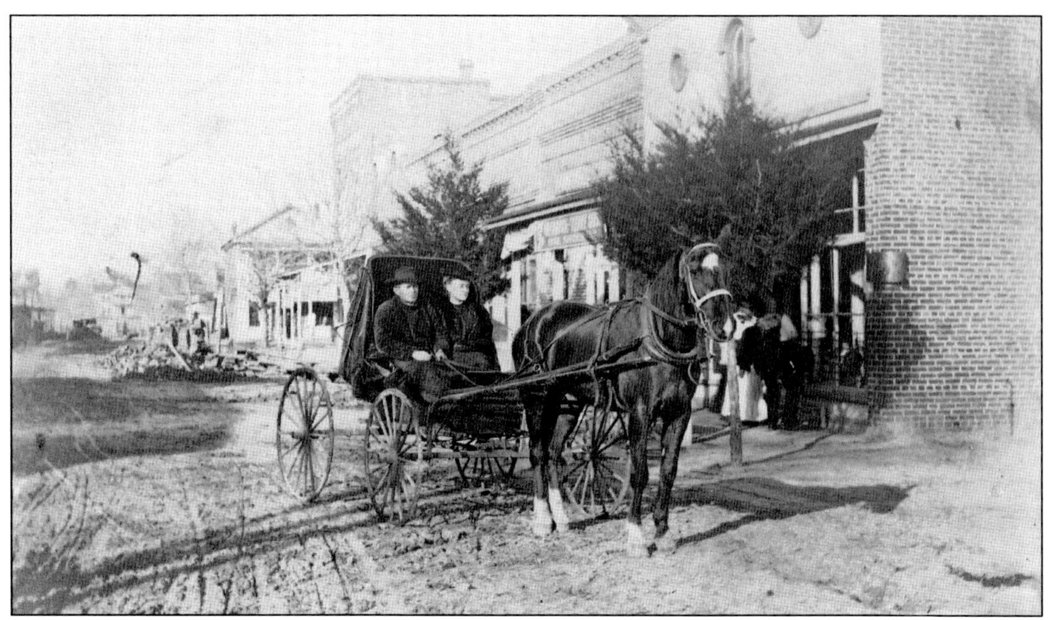

A couple poses with their horse and buggy in early-1900s Jacksonville. The photograph was probably taken on Court Street, where the road remained muddy and unpaved for several more years. (Courtesy of Onslow County Museum.)

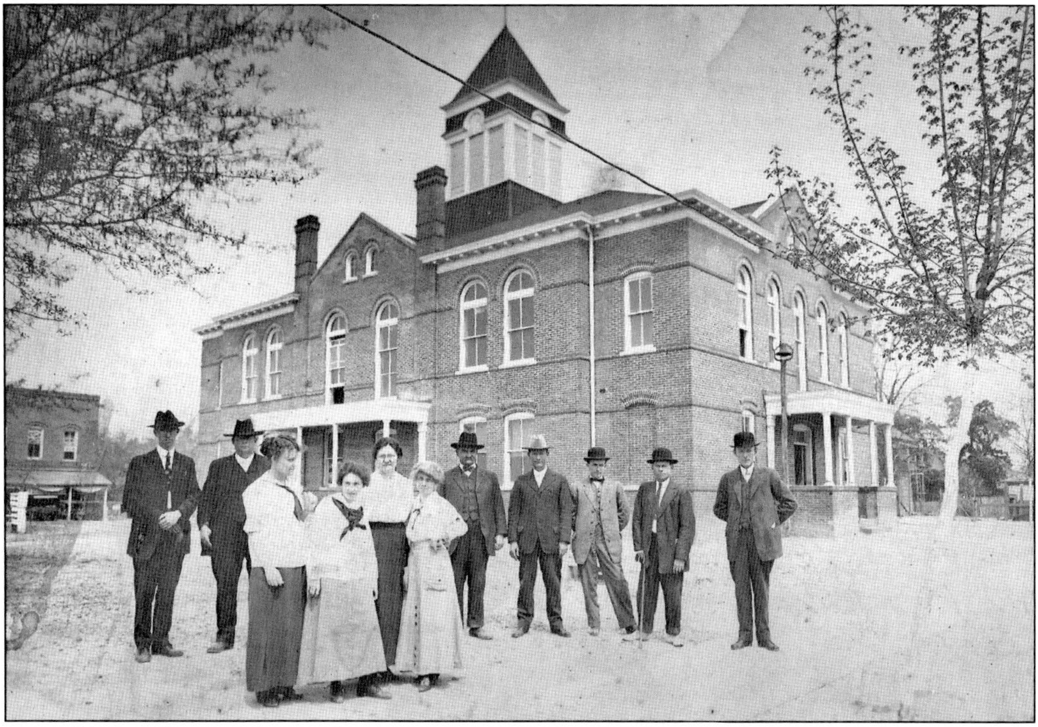

Assembled in front of the Onslow County Courthouse on New Bridge Street in Jacksonville is the courthouse staff in about 1915. This courthouse was built in 1904 by the B.F. Smith Fireproof Construction Company in the Romanesque Revival style and still stands today. (Courtesy of Onslow County Museum.)

Leading citizen John W. Burton held a number of offices in the first part of the 20th century. He served as mayor of Jacksonville, owner and president of the Bank of Onslow, and county commissioner. (Courtesy of Onslow County Museum.)

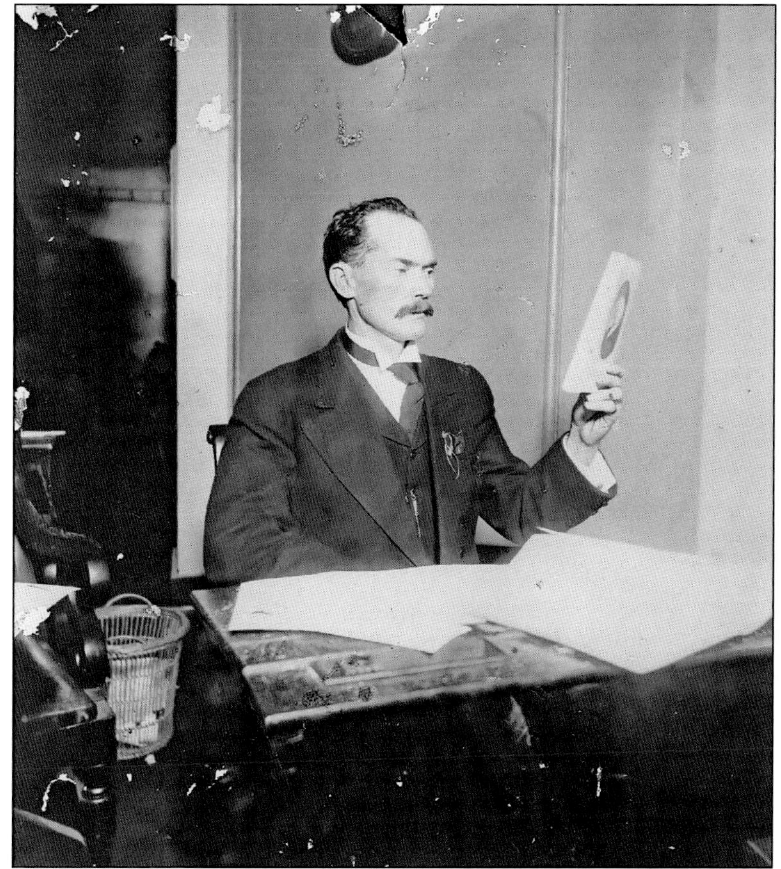

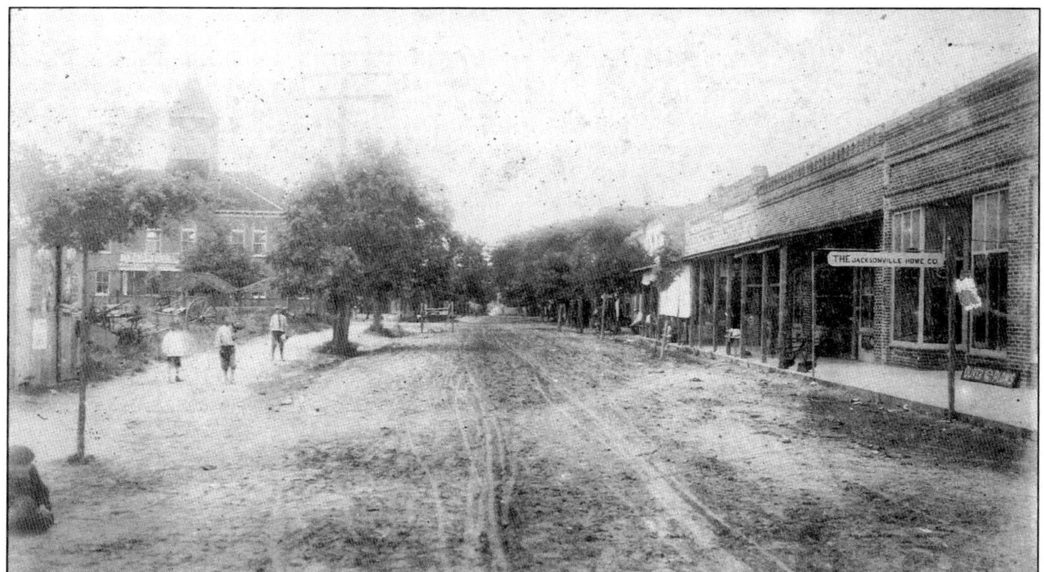

This image was captured in downtown Jacksonville in the 1910s or 1920s. The cupola of the courthouse can be seen in the distance. The unpaved street and plow store to the right reflect the rural nature of the city. (Courtesy of Onslow County Museum.)

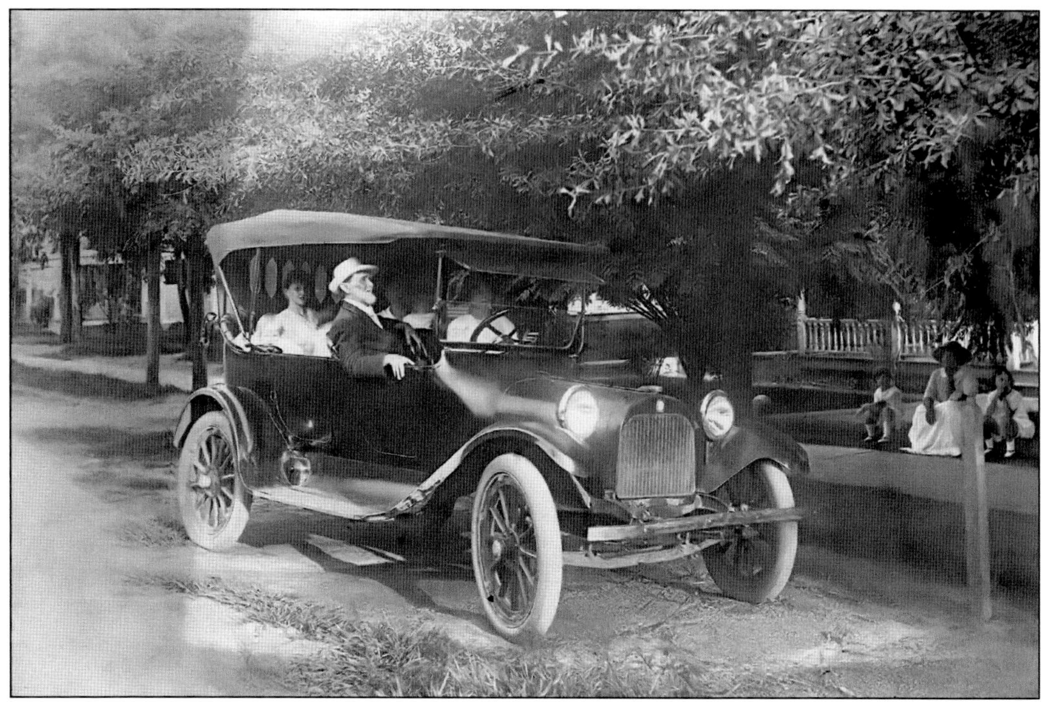

Dr. Richard W. Ward is pictured in one of his many cars. He never drove, claiming that if a man was rich enough to own a car, he was rich enough to hire someone to drive it for him. Dr. Ward was well known in Onslow County; he sold more than 2,600 acres near Town Point to New York financier Thomas A. McIntyre for his Onslow Hall estate. (Courtesy of Onslow County Museum.)

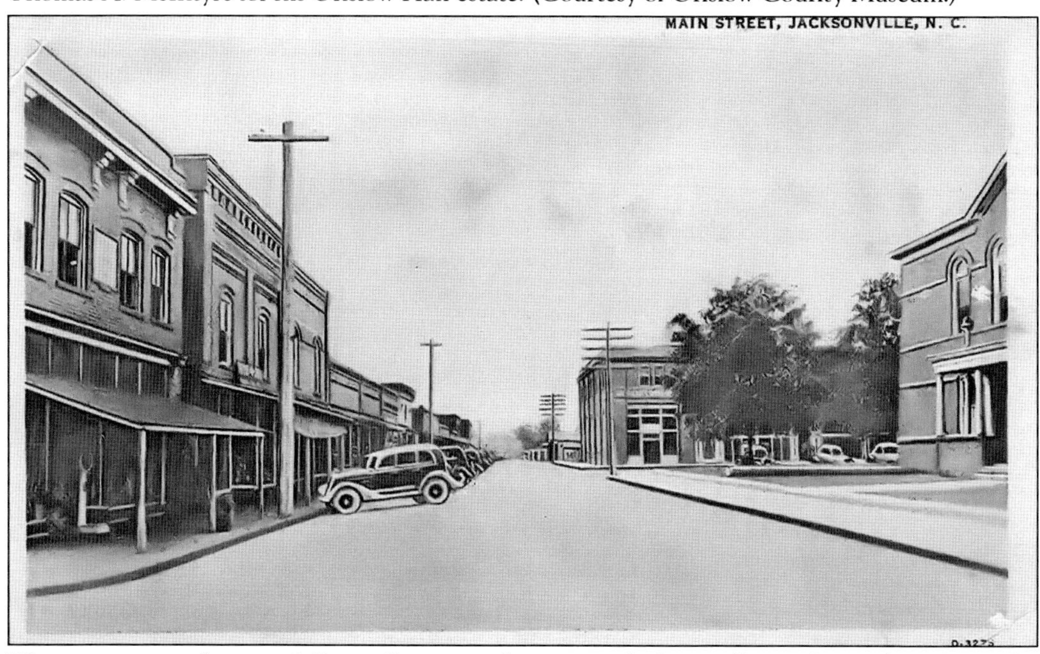

This is a postcard view of Court Street in downtown Jacksonville in the early 1930s. The courthouse can be seen on the right, and the Bank of Onslow is in the distance. (Courtesy of Onslow County Museum.)

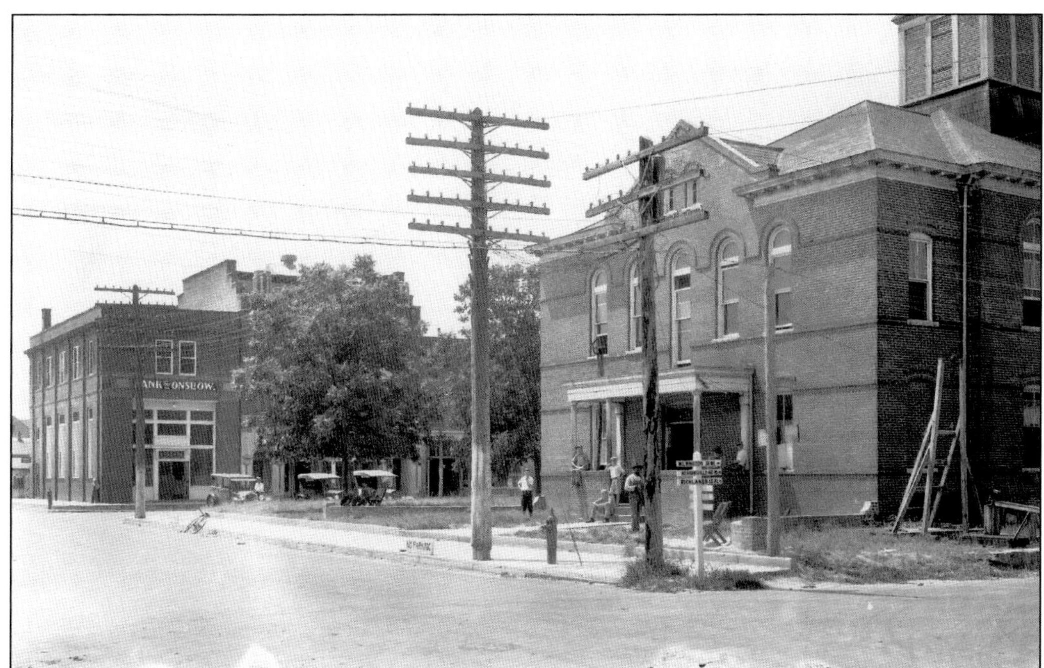

This photographic view of Court Street was probably taken in the late 1930s. As in the postcard view, the courthouse is on the right and the Bank of Onslow is across New Bridge Street, which ran by the front of the courthouse. (Courtesy of Onslow County Museum.)

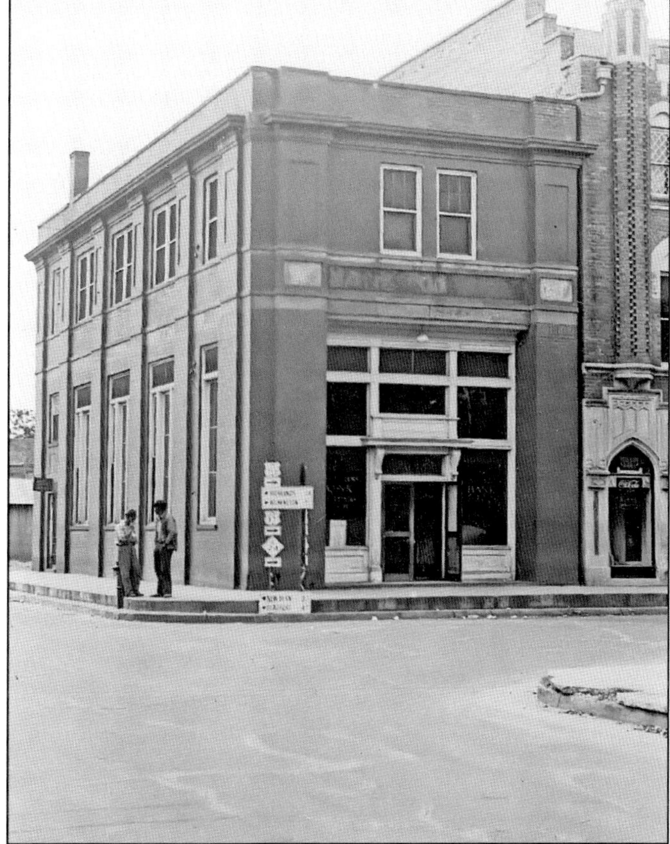

The Bank of Onslow, pictured in the late 1930s on New Bridge Street, was built in 1916. Jacksonville's first bank, it was organized in 1904, and the bank building was designed later to impress customers (Courtesy of Onslow County Museum.)

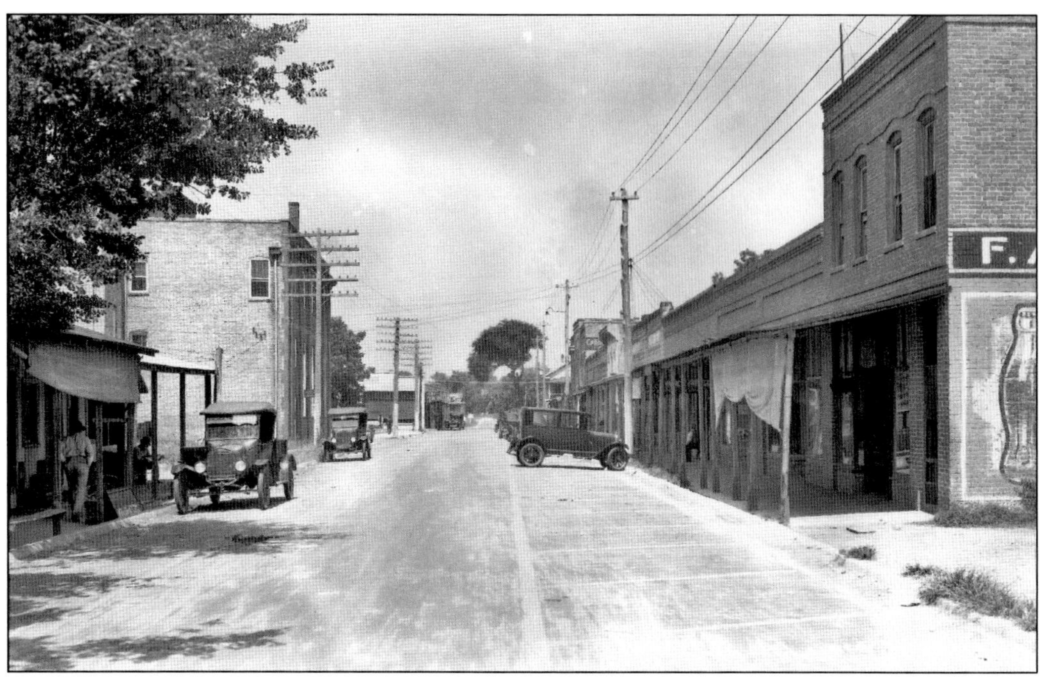

Another view shows downtown Jacksonville in the early 1930s. By this time, the streets were paved and electrical power was available. (Courtesy of Onslow County Museum.)

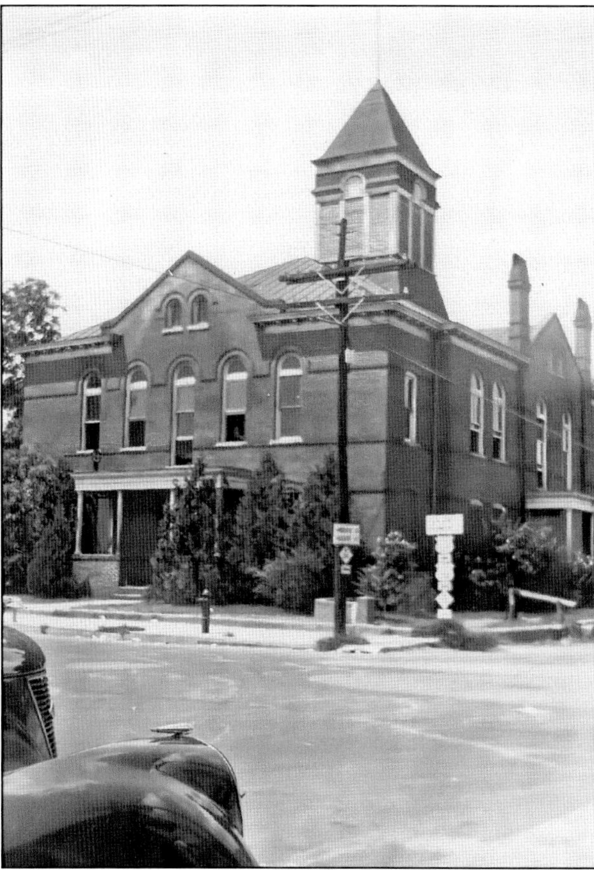

The front exterior view of the courthouse is seen from New Bridge Street about 1939. The courthouse continued to be the hub of activity for the county's residents. At this point, the building was 35 years old and beginning to show signs of its age. (Courtesy of Onslow County Museum.)

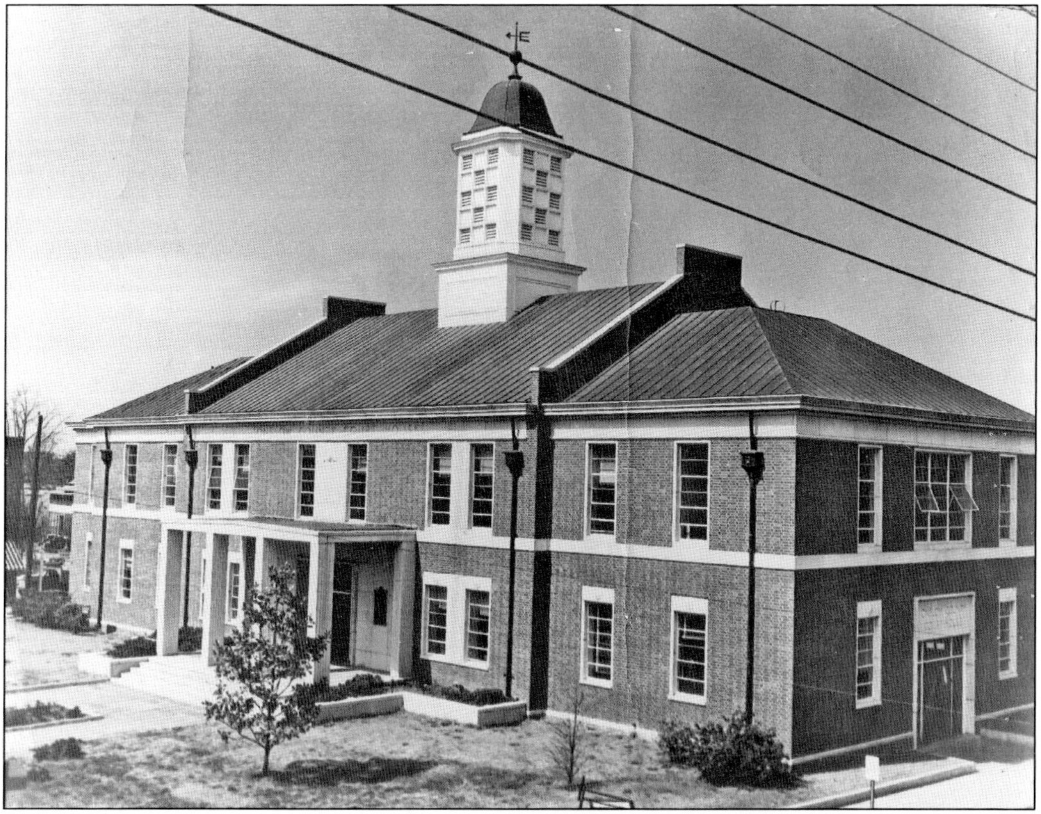

This image of the courthouse was captured at the conclusion of major renovations in 1949. Many of the courthouse's architectural features were altered by the design of Kinston architect John J. Rowland. (Courtesy of Onslow County Museum.)

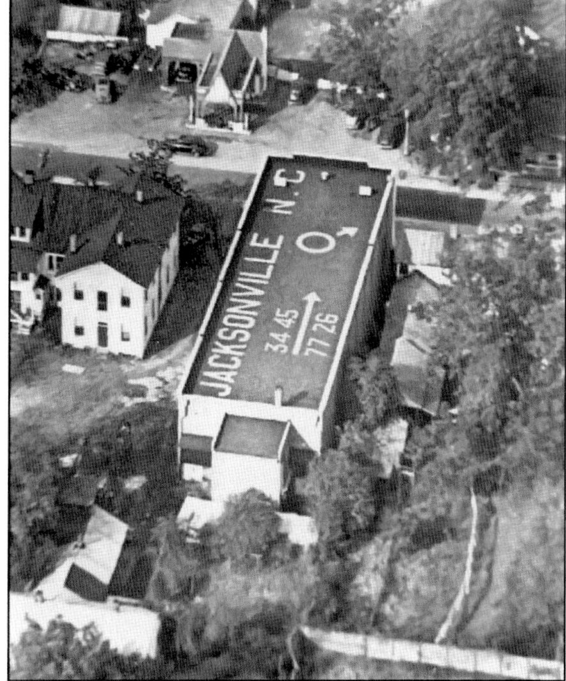

This aerial view shows a portion of downtown Jacksonville in the 1940s. The large rectangular building is the Iwo Jima movie theater on New Bridge Street. (Courtesy of Onslow County Museum.)

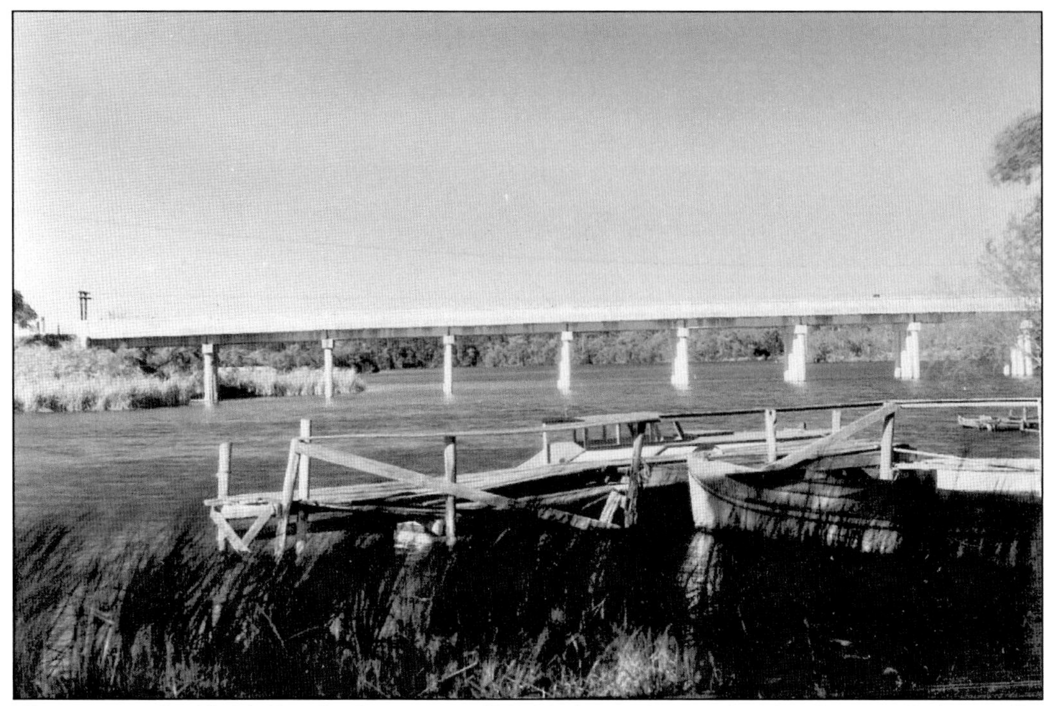

The concrete Buddy Phillips Bridge, a part of US Highway 17 over the New River in Jacksonville, carried untold numbers of people to their destinations for nearly 70 years. A new bridge was finished in 2013, and its size reflects the demographic changes that have occurred over that time span. (Courtesy of Onslow County Museum.)

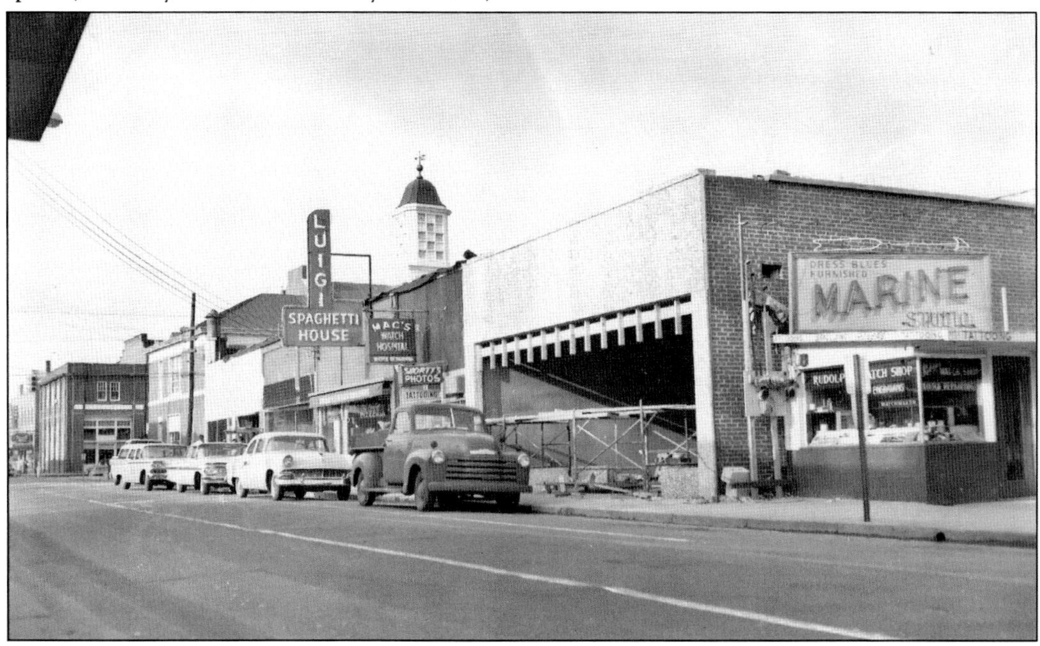

A diversity of businesses came into being as the population increased, as seen in this 1950s shot of Luigi's Spaghetti House, Mac's Watch Hospital, and other businesses located near the courthouse. (Courtesy of Onslow County Museum.)

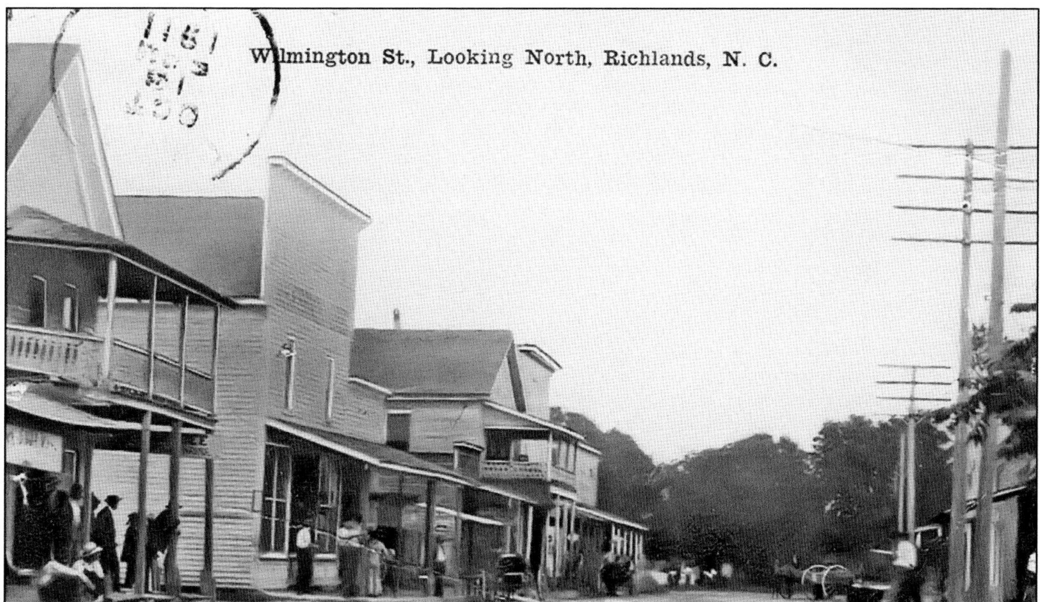

In 1911, Wilmington Street in Richlands was still unpaved, but business flourished in the little town later known for its "perfect water," because of the low iron content of the water obtained from nearby artesian wells. (Courtesy of Onslow County Museum.)

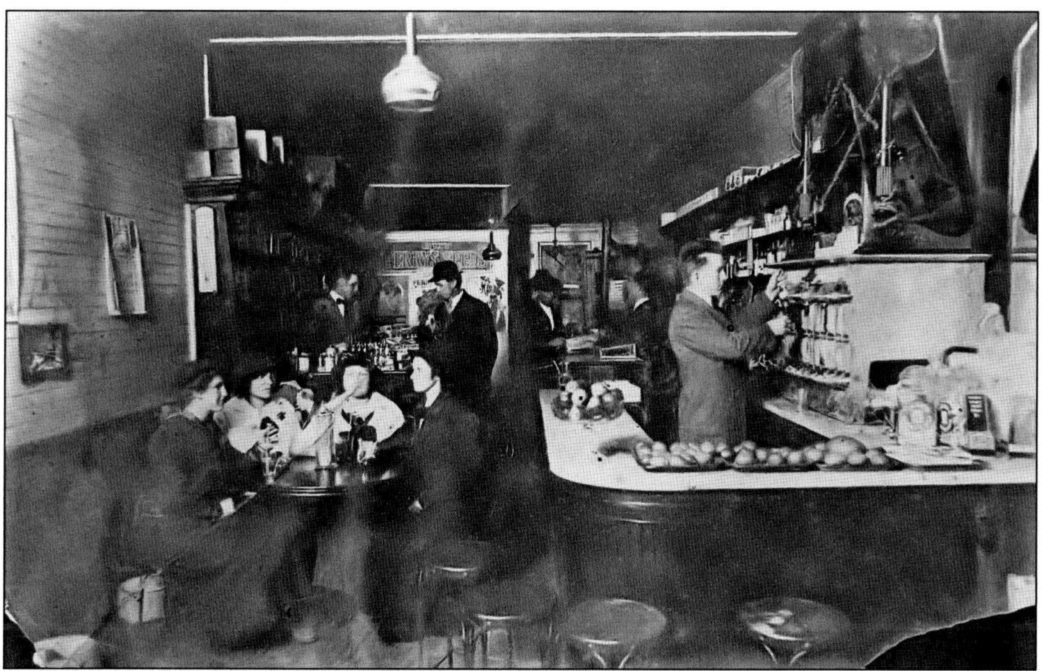

Norwood's Drugstore, owned by Norwood Cox, was a Richlands focal point for socializing and getting a cool drink in the hot summertime. Cox is on the far left behind the counter, and his wife, Hazel, is seated on the right with a group of ladies in about 1915. (Courtesy of Onslow County Museum.)

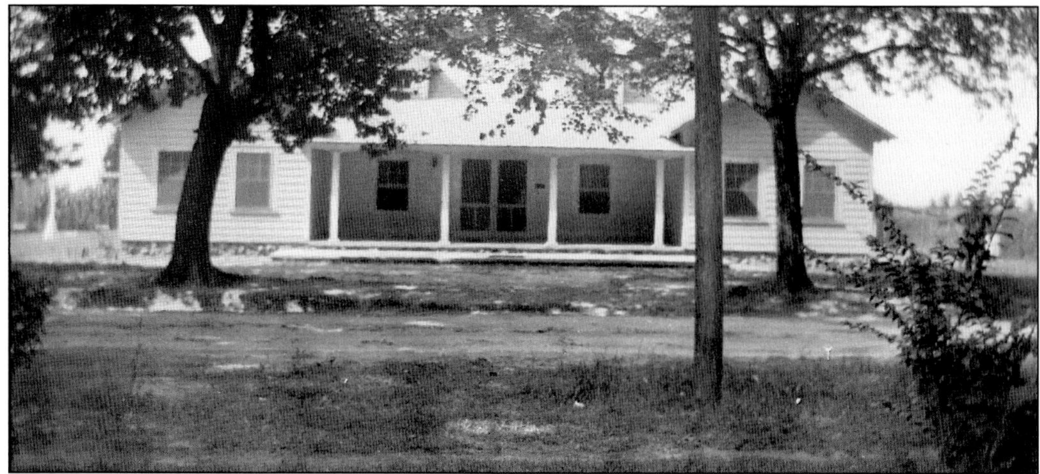

The Works Progress Administration had several projects in Onslow County. This building in Richlands is the last surviving local structure built by the WPA in the late 1930s and served as the first library. It is currently being preserved by the Town of Richlands and used as a community center. (Courtesy of Onslow County Museum.)

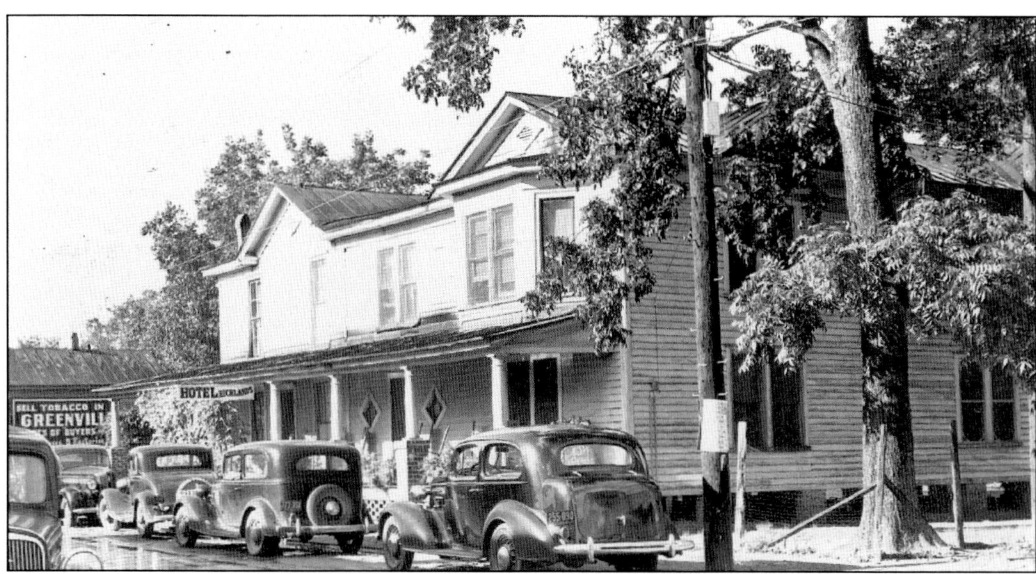

The Hotel Richlands, as seen in this late-1930s image, was originally the 1880s-era Wallace House. It was expanded by the Cox family and known as the Cox Hotel for a time. It is currently a private residence. (Courtesy of the Onslow County Museum.)

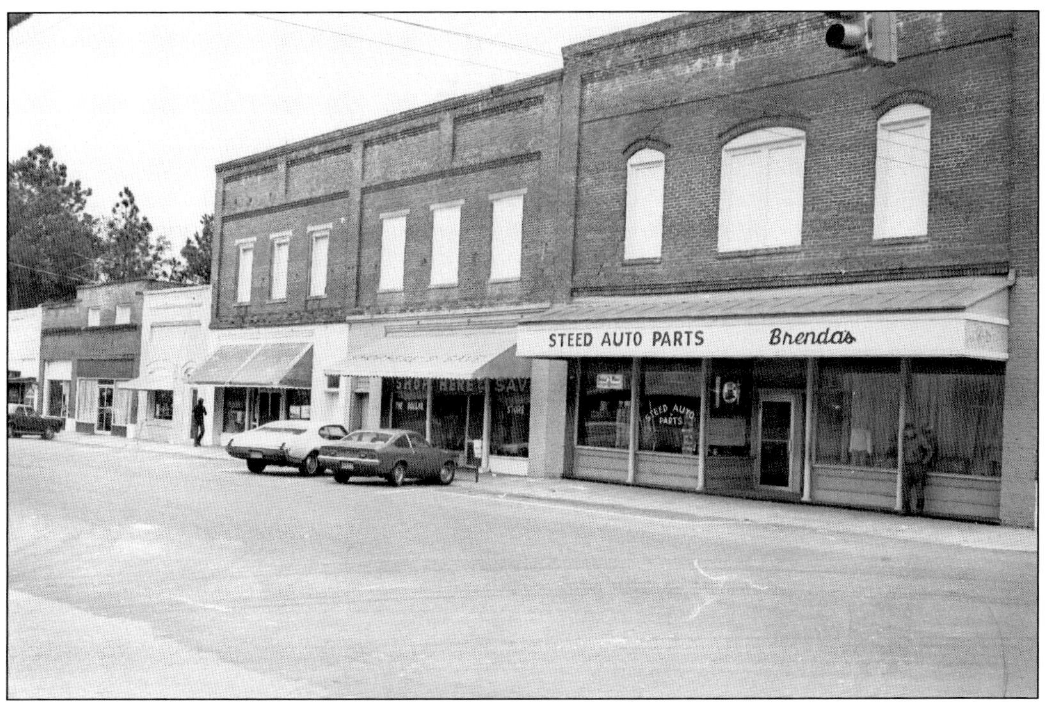

Adaptive reuse continued in the old store buildings along Wilmington Street in 1970s Richlands. (Courtesy of Onslow County Museum.)

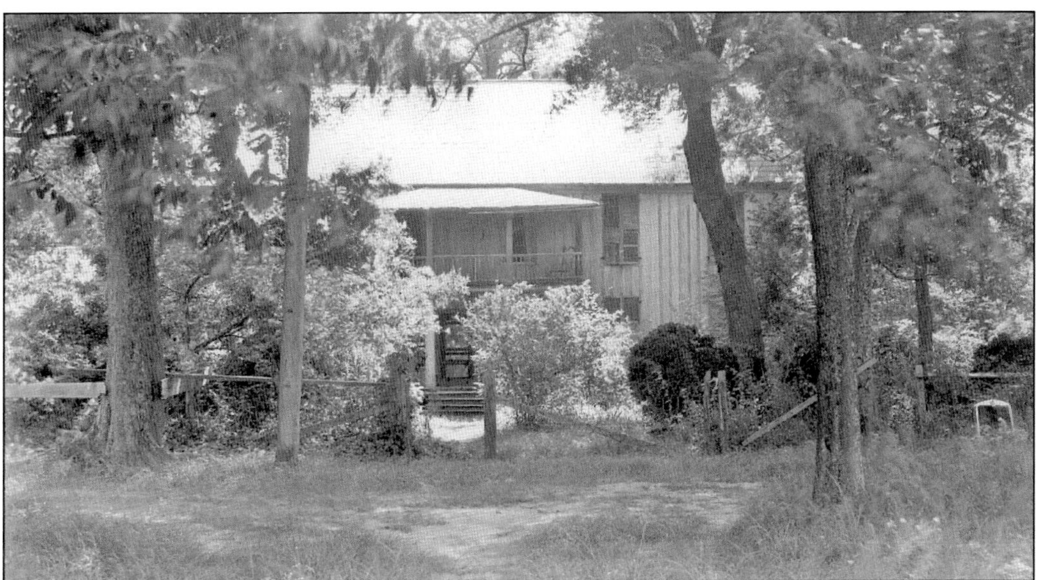
A few miles outside the town on US Highway 258 is the 1851 plantation home of the John A. Avirett family, known as the Avirett-Stephens House, pictured here in 1939. The family owned thousands of acres of land in the mid-19th century and was wealthy enough to own an additional Italianate summerhouse at Catherine Lake. (Courtesy of the Onslow County Museum.)

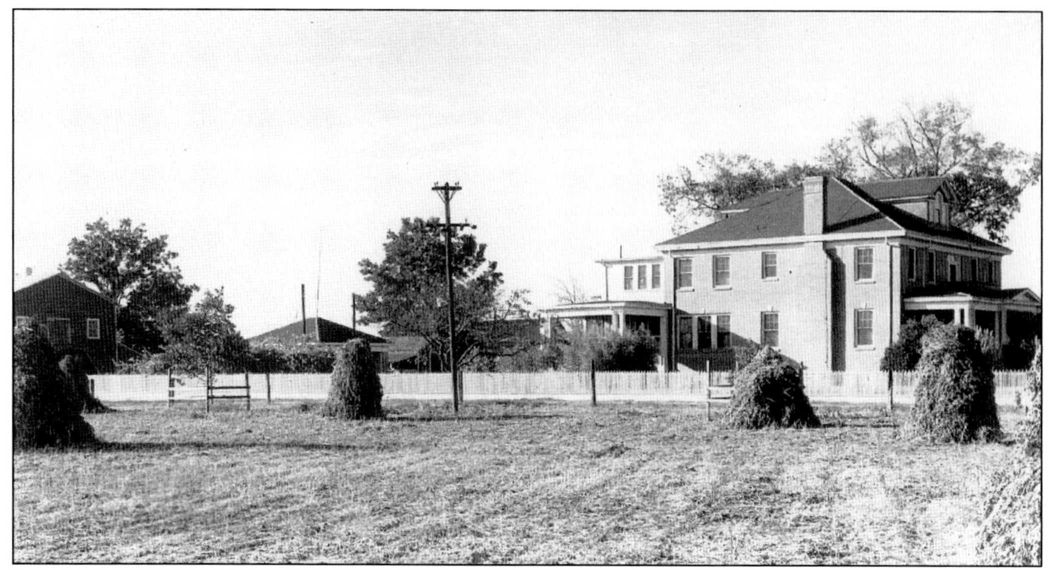

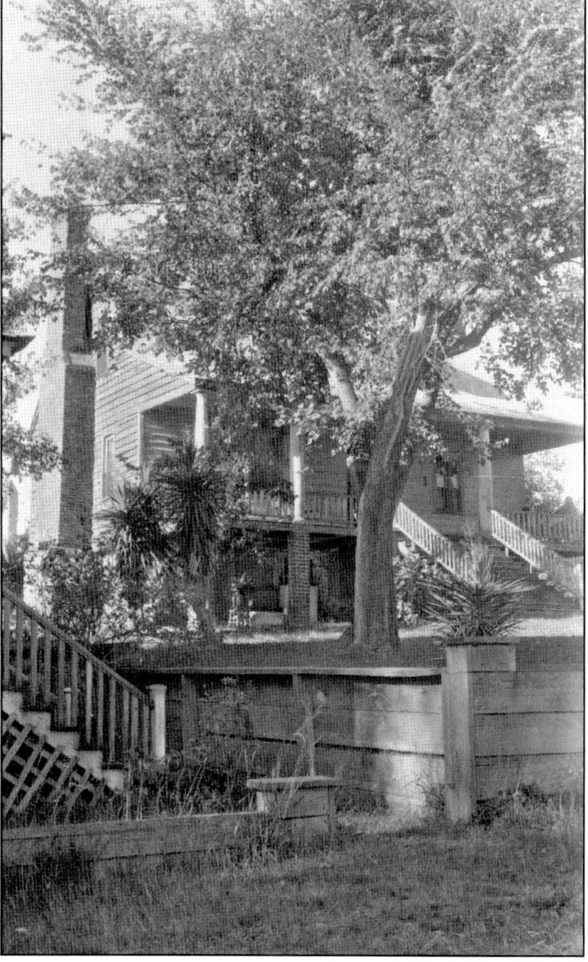

The James Taylor farm was a very successful operation located about a mile from Richlands on the Comfort Road. This late-1930s image shows the large family home and outbuildings; the farm ran the largest dairy in Onslow County in the 1940s. (Courtesy of Onslow County Museum.)

The Jonathan Green House is one of the two oldest houses in Swansboro. Jonathan Green Jr. was probably the builder of the Georgian-style house in the late 18th century. Notable features are the ballast stone foundation and Flemish bond brick pattern on the east chimney. (Courtesy of State Archives of North Carolina.)

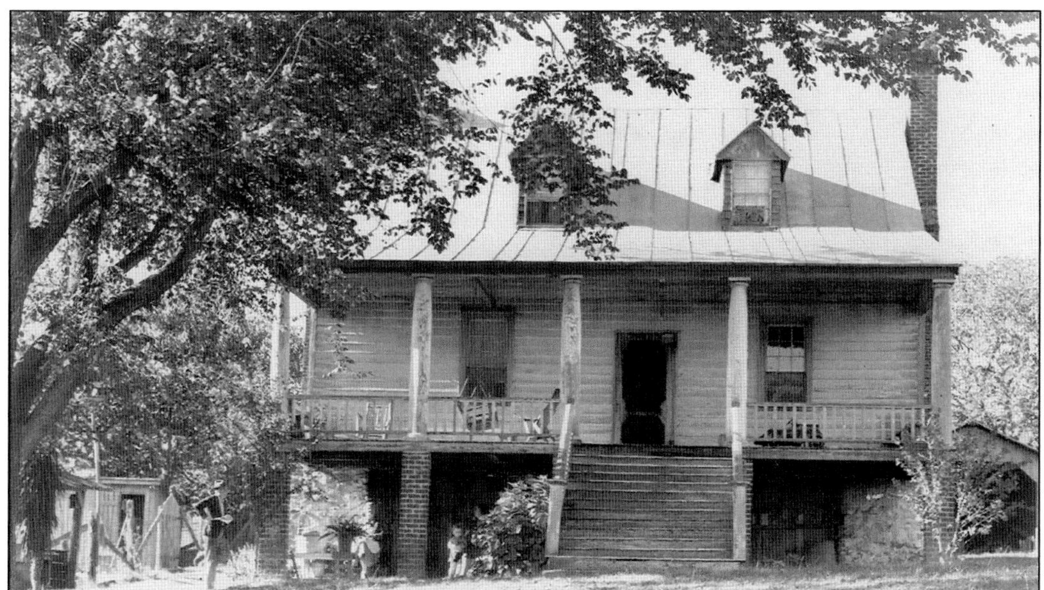

This 1938 view shows the Jonathan Green House before the underside of the porch was closed in. Mary P. Underseth and her children can be seen here, near the washing machine on the far left. It is believed that the columns were acquired at some point from the old Swansboro Graded School. (Courtesy of Onslow County Museum.)

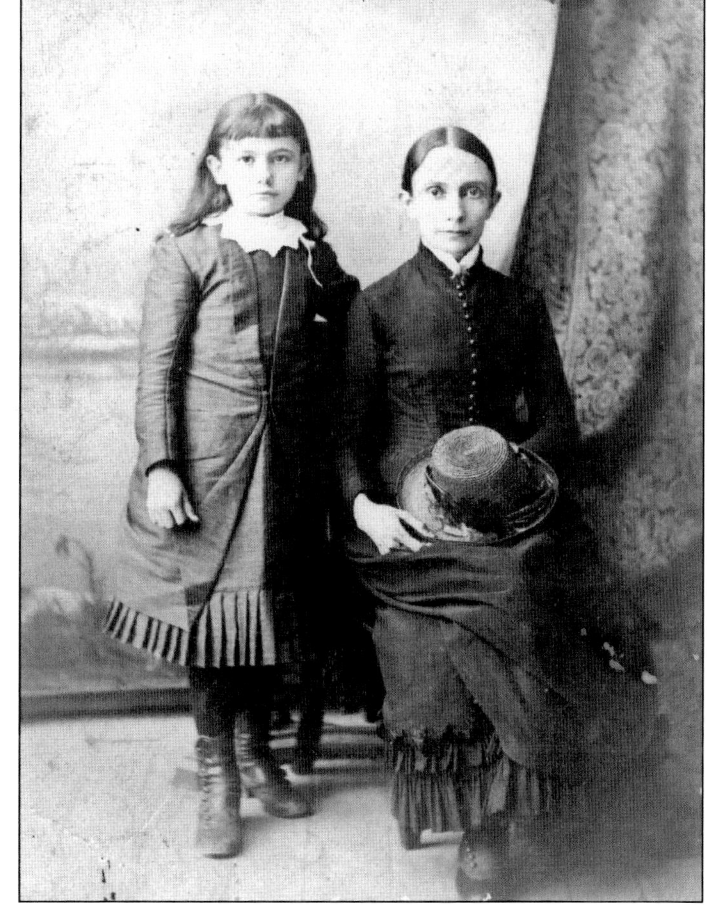

Hester Gibson Ward was considered the local "medicine woman" in the Swansboro area after the Civil War. She is seen here in about 1872 with her daughter Minnie. (Courtesy of State Archives of North Carolina.)

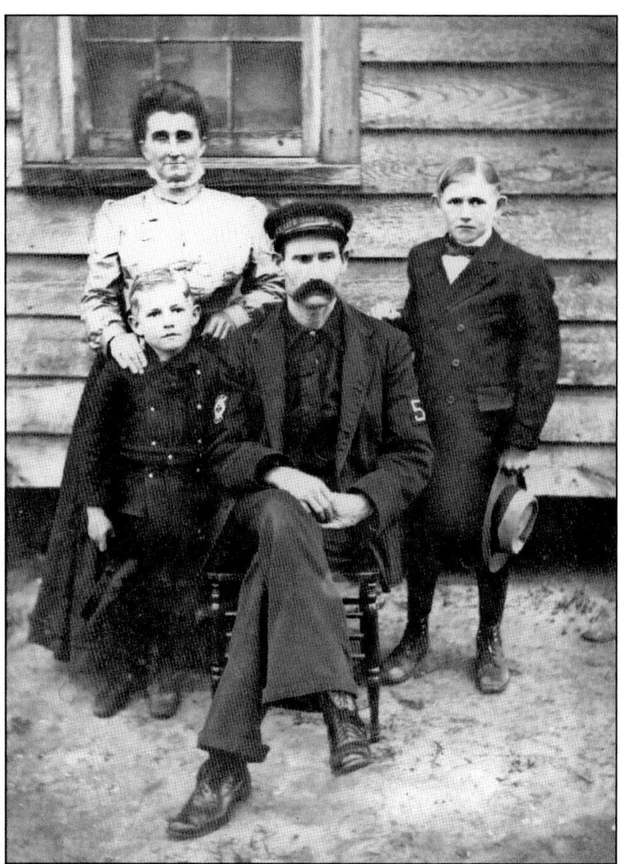

William Henry Hill Sr. is pictured in about 1908 with his wife, Lena Jones Hill, and sons William H. Hill Jr. (left) and Robert Hill. Hill Sr. was a local shipwright and one of the original crewmen of the US Life-Saving Service at Bogue. His arm patch indicates that he is surfman no. 5. (Courtesy of State Archives of North Carolina.)

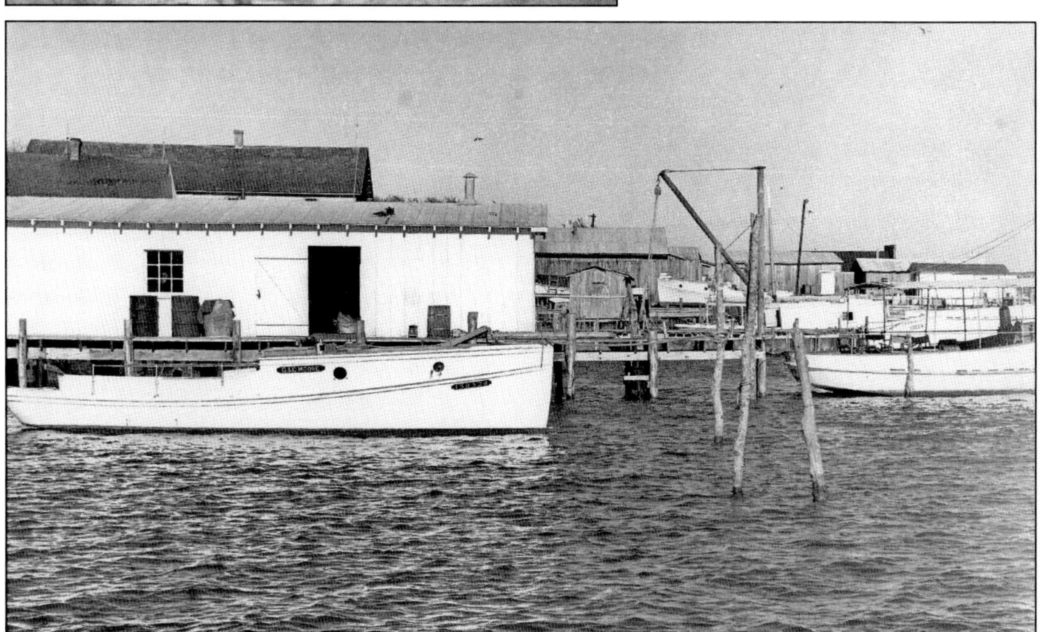

Swansboro's waterfront with its boats and fish houses is seen here in 1939. (Courtesy of Onslow County Museum.)

Conchita Riggs poses in the middle of Front Street in 1950s Swansboro; pedestrians had few worries in the "friendly town by the sea." (Courtesy of Onslow County Museum.)

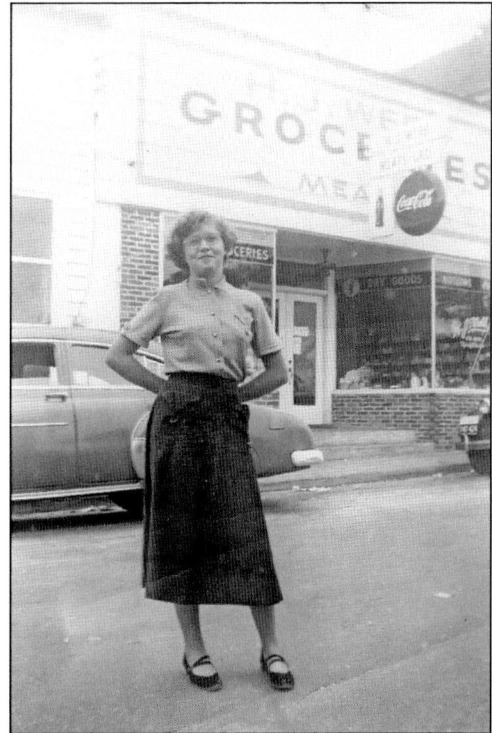

Cars were still being taken across the river on the Sneads Ferry in 1938 before the WPA bridge was opened in 1939. There had been a ferry there since the mid-18th century. Jack Prescott was the last in a long line of ferrymen when the last ferry ran in 1941. (Courtesy of Onslow County Museum.)

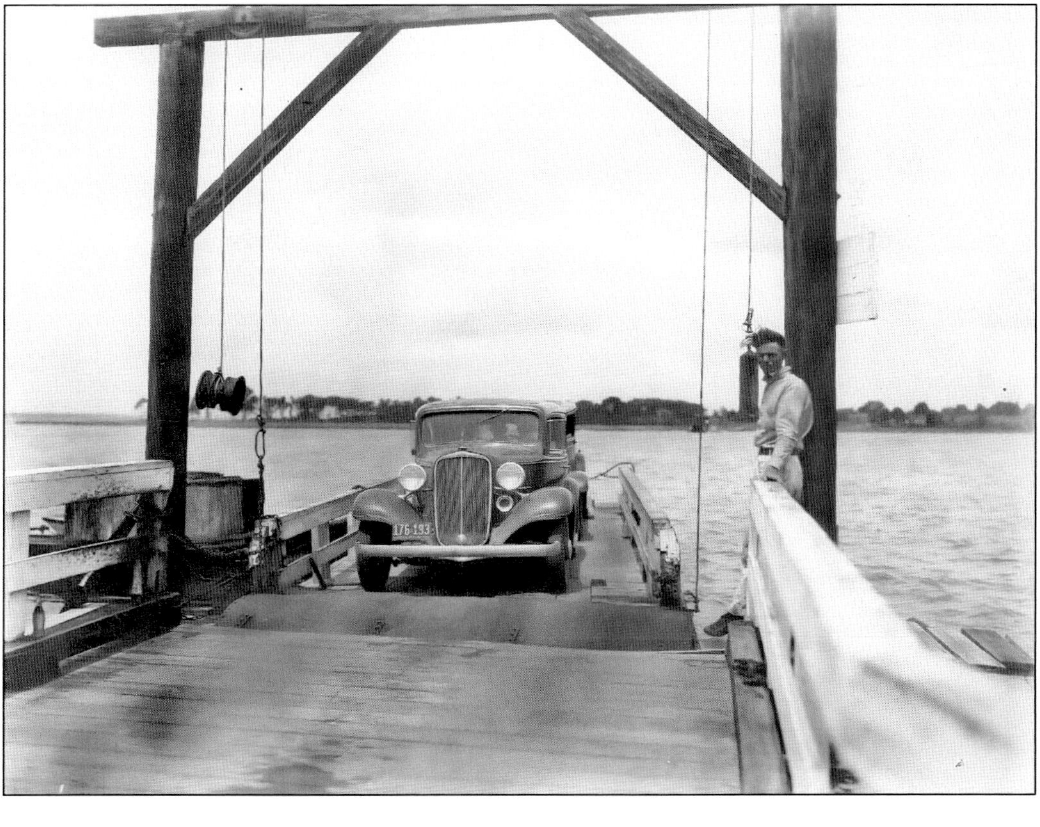

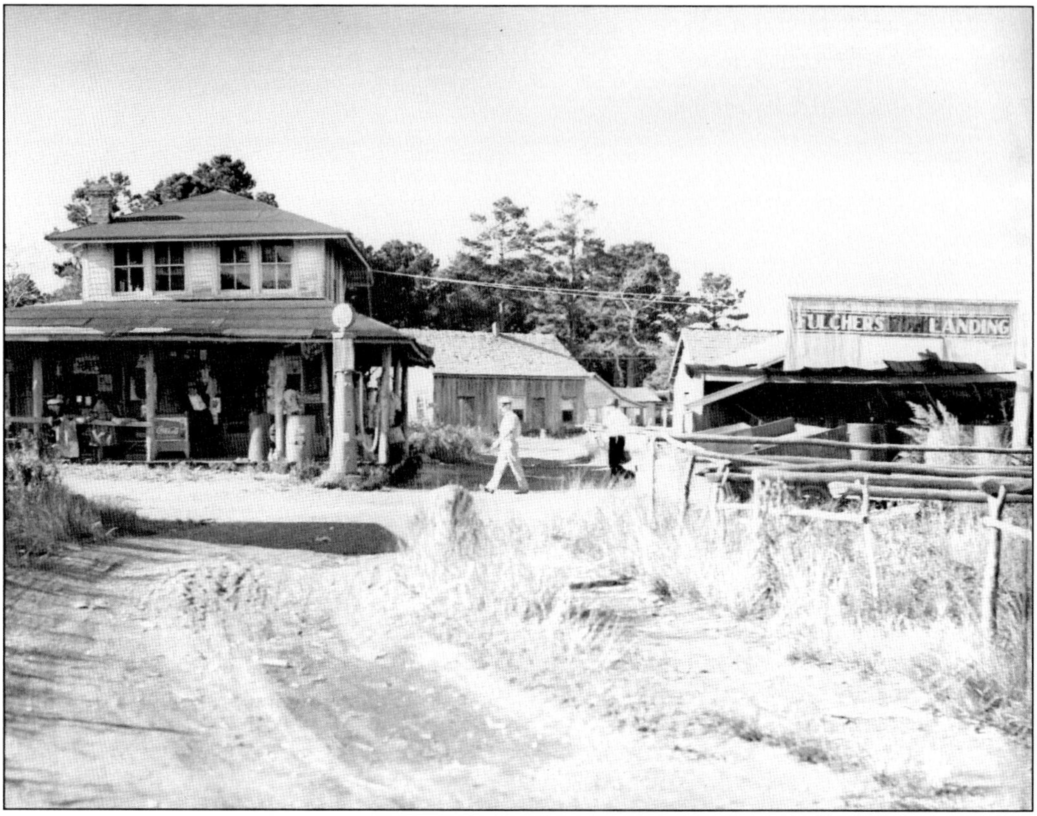

Fulcher's Landing was a small but thriving part of Sneads Ferry in the late 1930s. The dirt road led to the store and filling station on the left, a good place for the locals to sit and talk. (Courtesy of State Archives of North Carolina.)

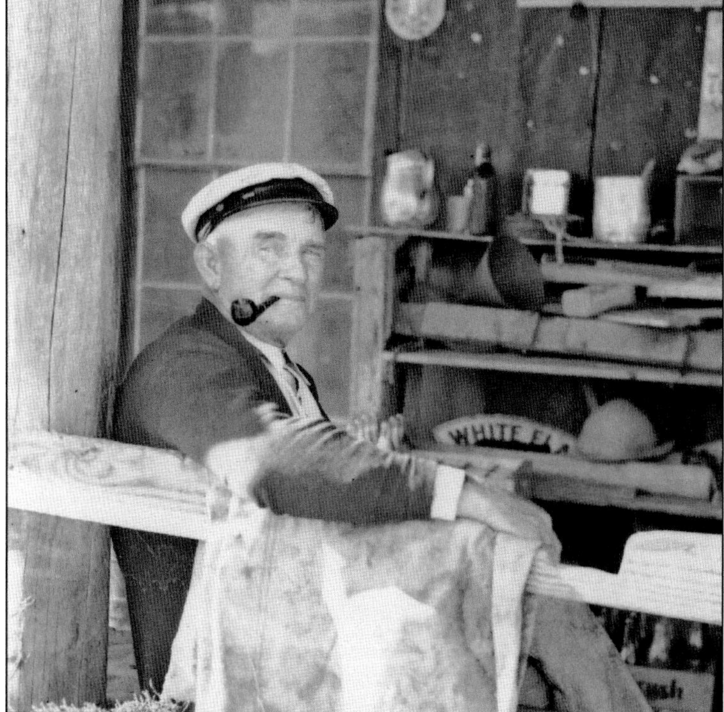

Capt. Ramp Jones whiles away the hours at Fulcher's Landing in the late 1930s. He was one of the early members of the Bogue Life-Saving crew. (Courtesy of State Archives of North Carolina.)

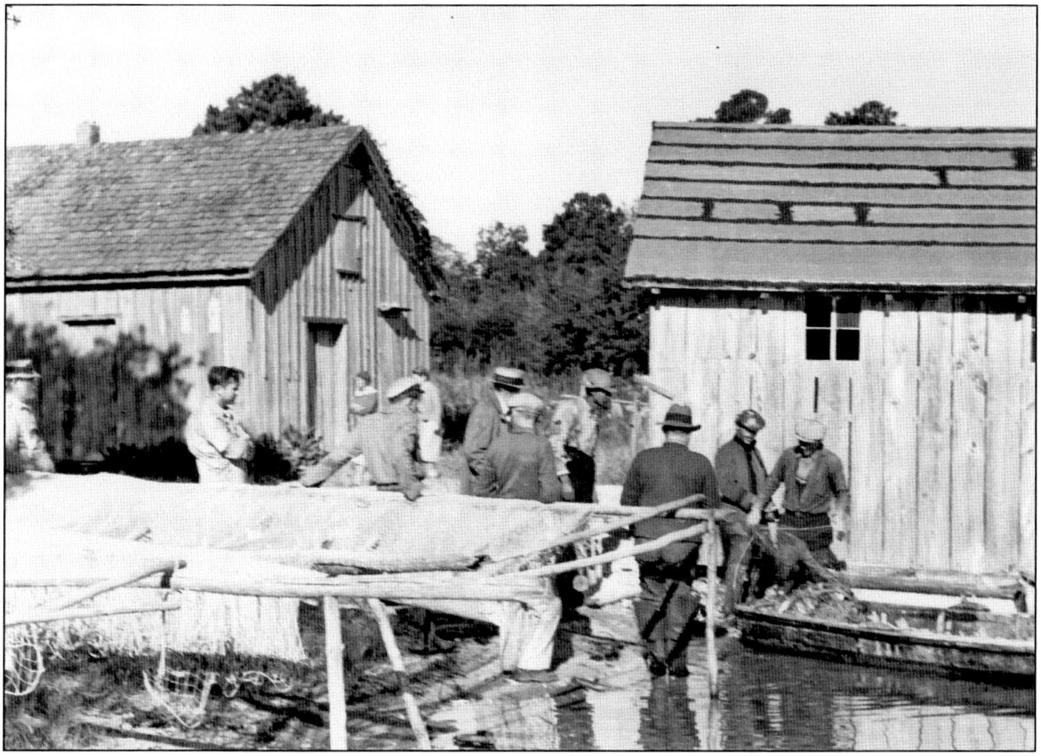

A group of Sneads Ferry fishermen unloads a catch at Fulcher's Landing in the late 1930s. Their cotton nets are drying on the net spreads to the left. (Courtesy of State Archives of North Carolina.)

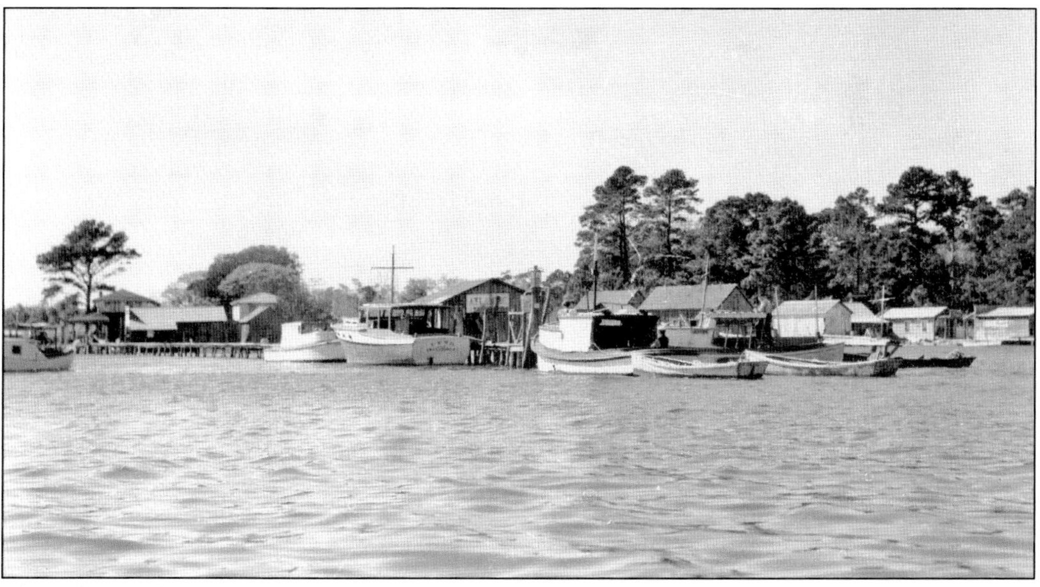

The village of Marines was across from Fulcher's Landing on the New River, as seen here in 1939. The area was originally settled by the Zorobabel Marine family and their descendants. This ironically named community was entirely engulfed by the US Marine base in 1941. (Courtesy of State Archives of North Carolina.)

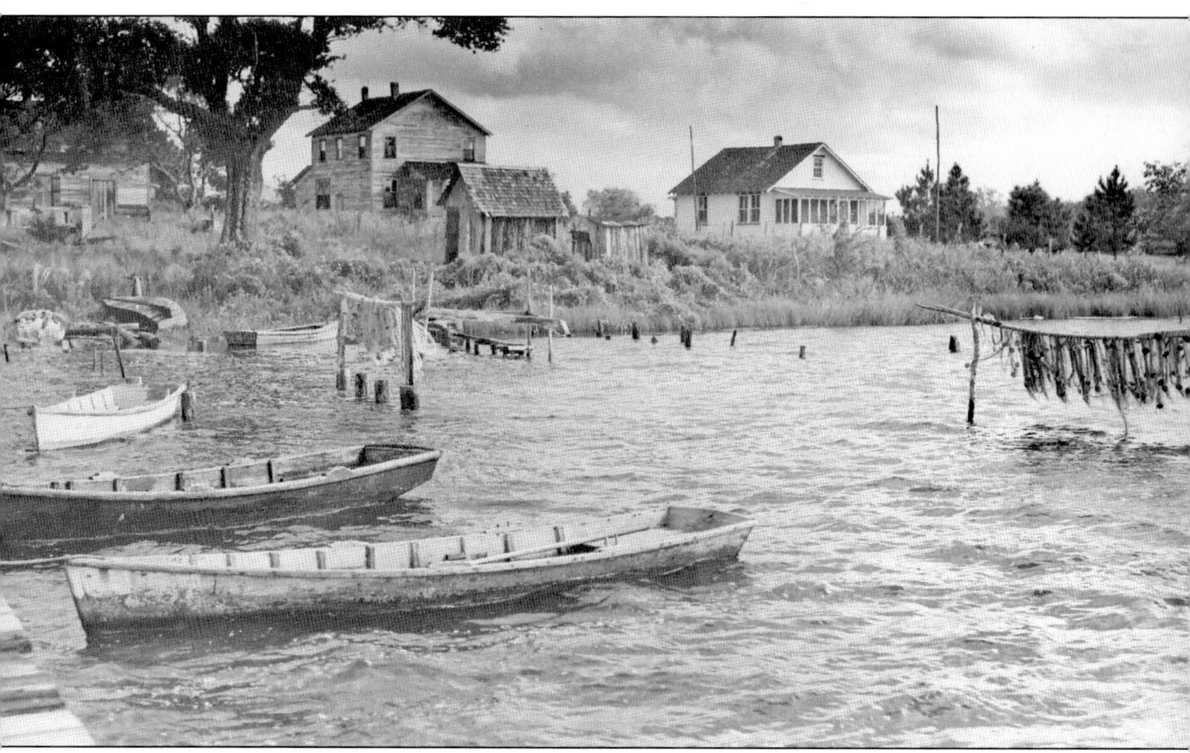

Some residences at Marines can be seen in this late-1930s image of the village. The clouds gathering in the sky, the net spreads, and tethered fishing boats recall the last days of the small community. (Courtesy of Onslow County Museum.)

Three

Local Economy

Onslow County has a long history of business and commercial pursuits; industries dotting the landscape in the 1880s reflected the rural nature of Onslow, such as turpentine distilleries, lumber mills, cotton gins, and gristmills. Shipbuilding ventures, common in the Swansboro area, began to decline during the 19th century. Others business pursuits included blacksmithing, cooperage, and wheelwrighting. Onslow also had its share of the growing hospitality industry, beginning with taverns and ordinaries in the 18th century and progressing to boardinghouses and hotels into the 20th century. Considered part of the backwater of eastern North Carolina, Onslow County still managed to attract business investors in the late 19th century. It was known throughout the state for its bountiful natural resources. Lumber mills and sawmills were established in Swansboro and Jacksonville, utilizing the New River, the White Oak River, and, by 1891, the railroad for transportation. Commercial fishing also continued to play an important role in local economy.

The business climate was permanently altered by the coming of the military in the 1940s. Along with the influx of military personnel was the arrival of civilians looking for work. The civilians needed not only work, but also shelter for their families and places to shop. Jacksonville and Holly Ridge soon became boomtowns, with their small rural populations suddenly increasing from hundreds to thousands. Businesses sprang up quickly to support the tide of humanity calling Onslow County home. Downtown Jacksonville changed from a slow-paced center of local government to a fast-paced home of retail businesses, law offices, and, later, havens of entertainment for the troops, such as the venerable USO (United Service Organizations), and the less respectable nightclubs on Court Street.

Growth continued steadily through the 1950s with the coming of the New River Shopping Center in Jacksonville in 1953. Shopping centers were the newest idea as old downtown areas faded in importance. A number of locally memorable stores were located there, until it too began to decline in favor of the enclosed shopping mall. The Jacksonville Mall opened in 1981 to great fanfare and featured 70 retail businesses.

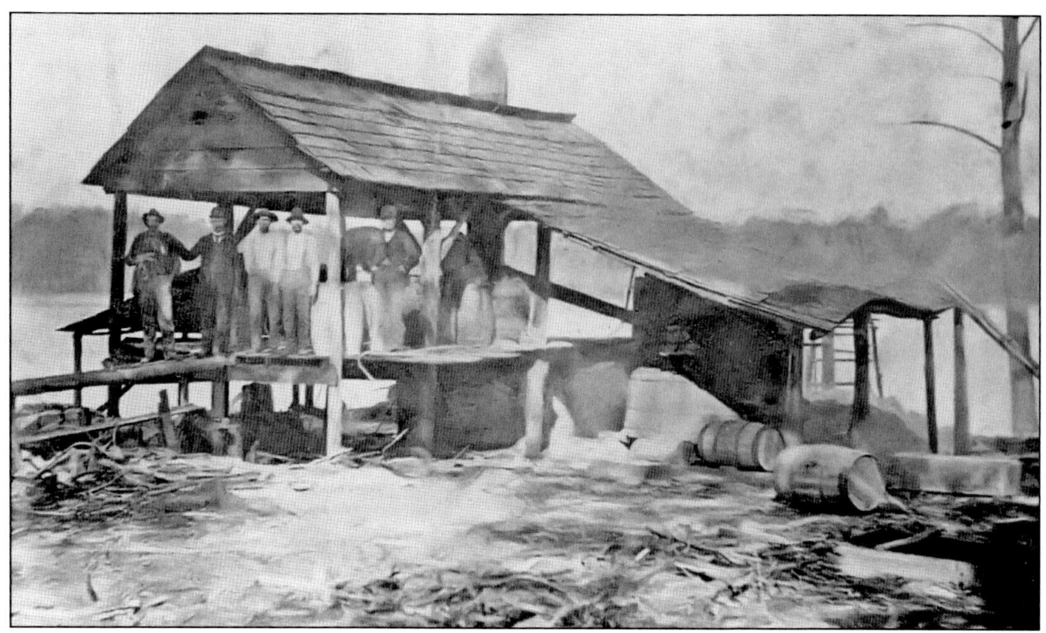

One of the earliest enterprises in Onslow was naval stores, or the turpentine business, as it was commonly known. From colonial times through the 19th century, vast acres of longleaf pine trees provided resin for the manufacture of products such as tar for ship maintenance and turpentine. The overharvesting of the longleaf pine caused the demise of the industry by the early 20th century. This late-19th-century distillery was located at Catherine Lake. (Courtesy of Onslow County Museum.)

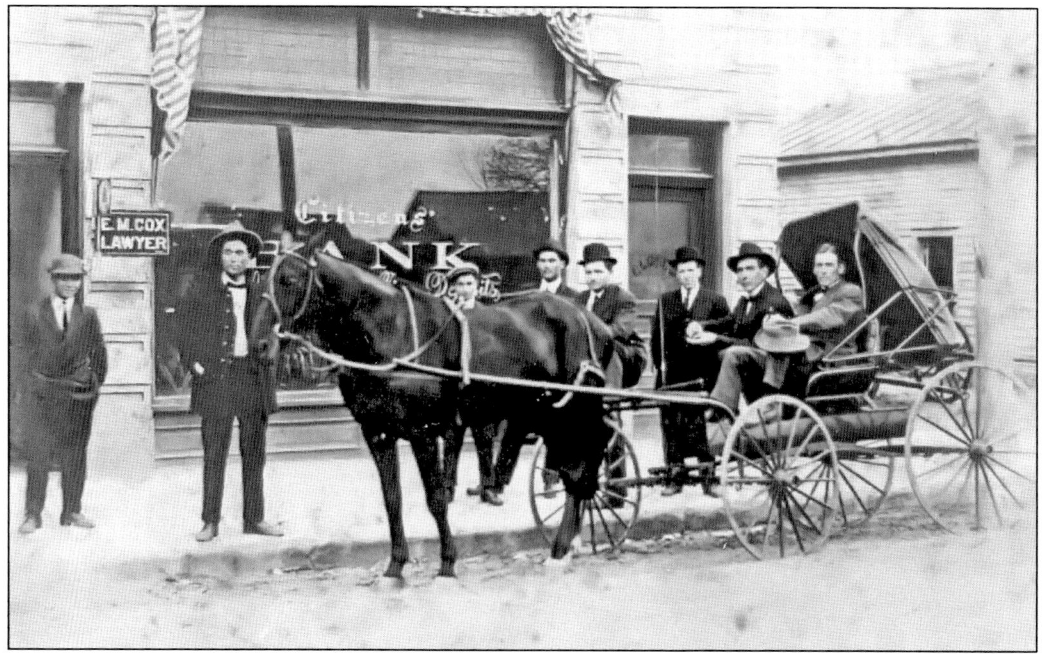

In Richlands, members of the Cox family gather in front of the Citizens Bank and the law office of E.M. Cox in about 1905. The bank financed local farmers and other enterprises. (Courtesy of Onslow County Museum.)

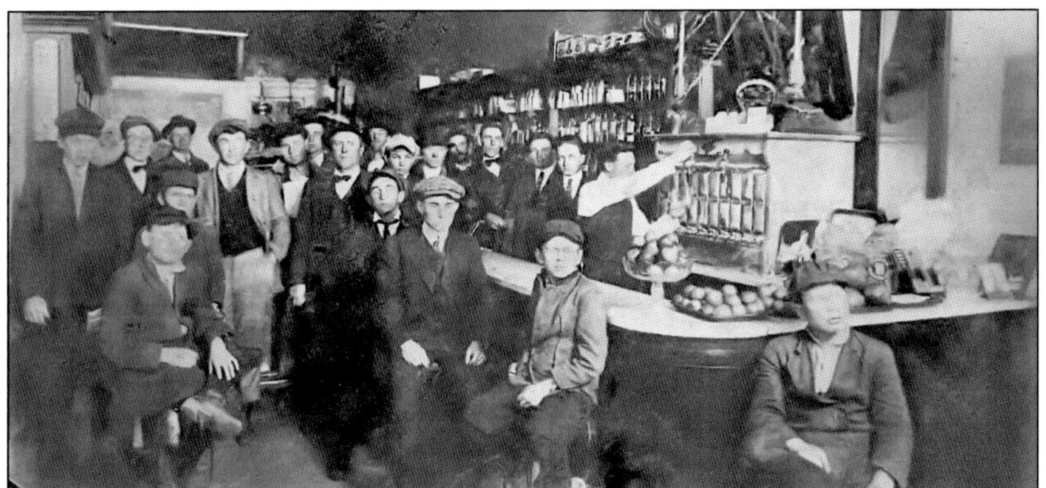

Norwood's Drugstore in Richlands was a well-liked place for the locals to meet and share news and gossip. Here, in about 1910, local men and boys gather around the marble-topped counter. Norwood Cox, the owner, is behind the bar. (Courtesy of Onslow County Museum.)

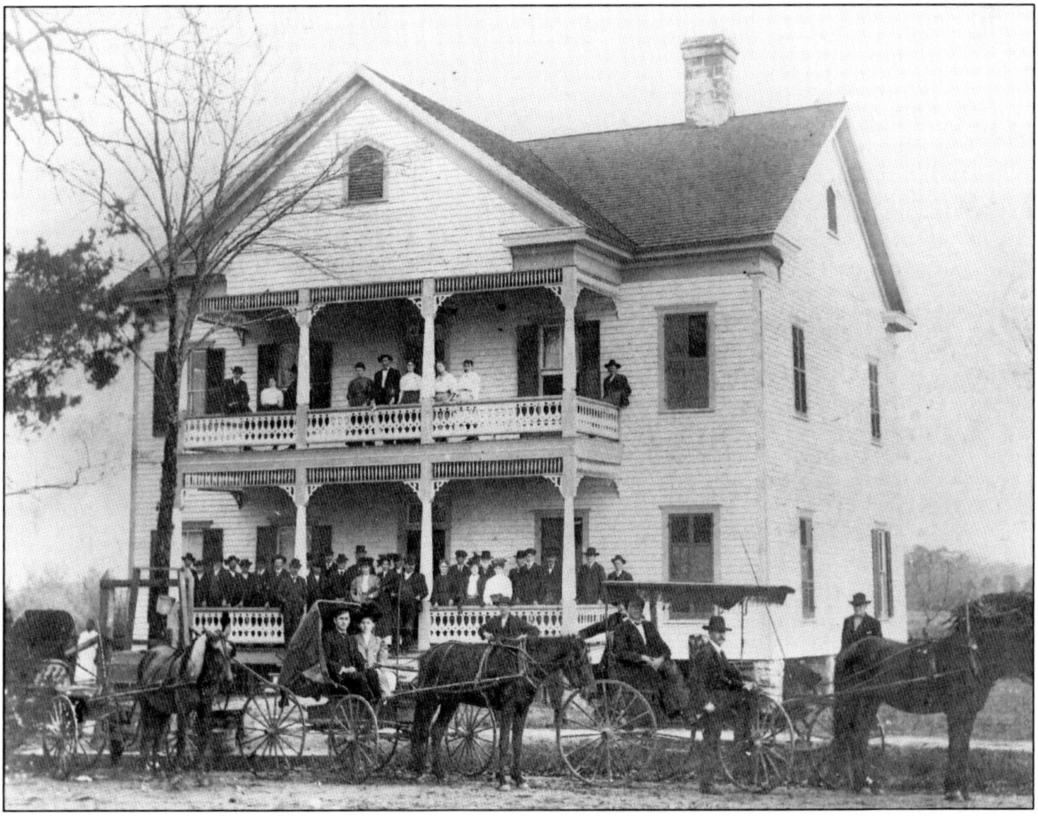

The Dover & Southbound Railroad connected in Richlands in 1906; the Hardy Hotel was a popular place for travelers to rest since it was not far from the depot. The hotel sent buggies out to pick up guests, as seen in this image from about 1910. Located on North Wilmington Street, the c. 1890s residence is now known as the Miller-Venters House. (Courtesy of Onslow County Museum.)

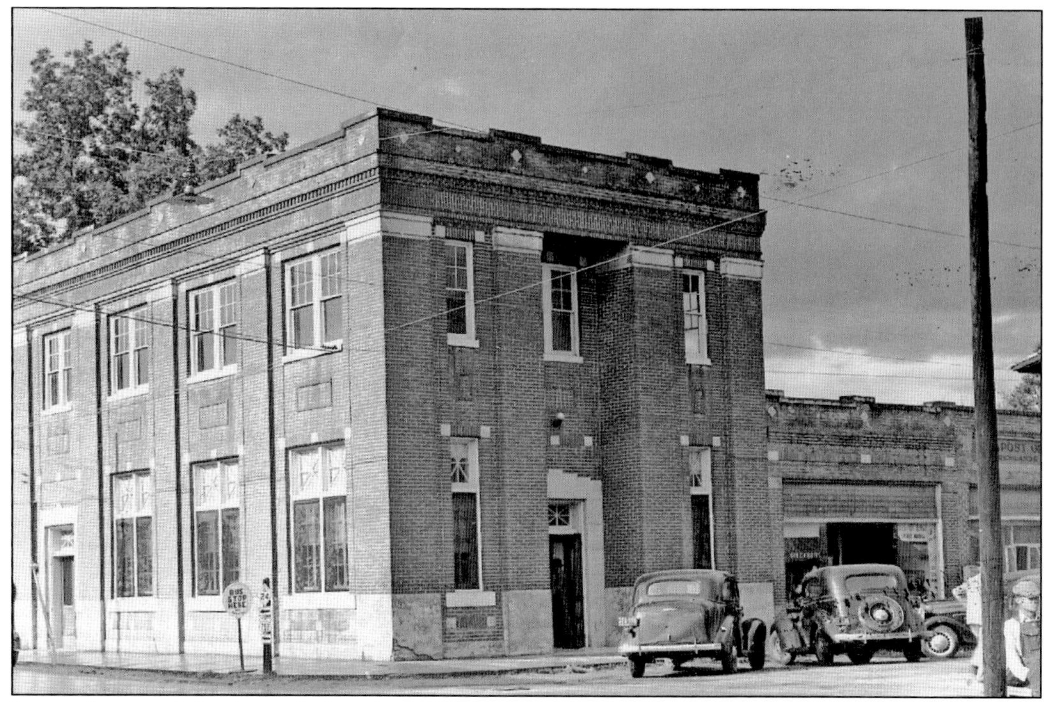

Later, the town's bank resided in this 1927 brick building on Wilmington Street, also known as the Bank of Richlands. The building still stands and has served a number of functions, including as an office space for the Onslow County Museum from the 1970s to 1990s. (Courtesy of Onslow County Museum.)

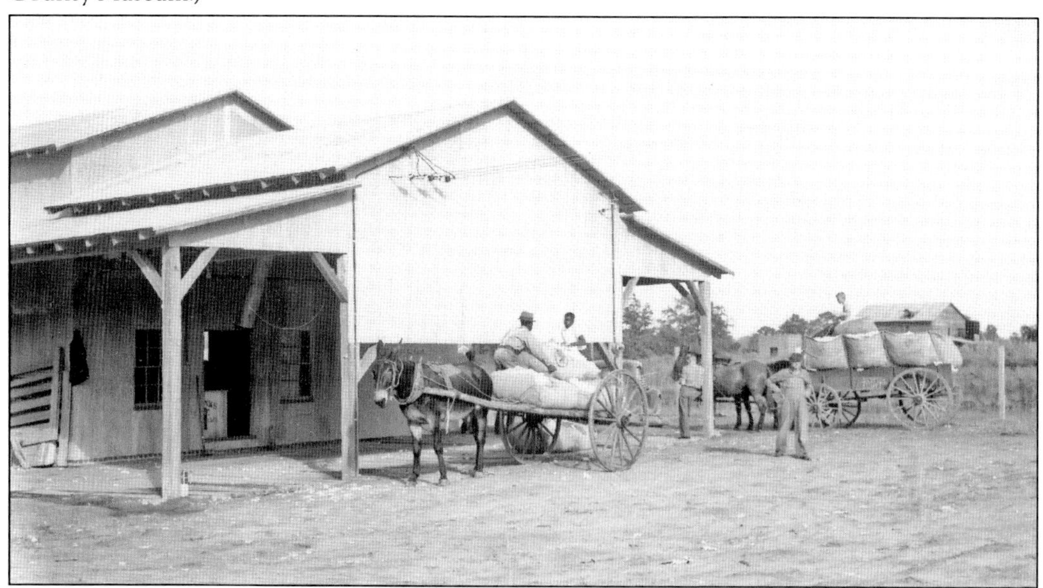

According to the agricultural census of 1940, a total of 906 acres of farmland were planted in cotton in 1939, when this photograph was taken. Farmers had switched to tobacco that year, with over 10,000 acres planted, nearly 4,000 acres more than reported in 1934. This cotton gin in Richlands remained a busy place; in Onslow, 1,882 bales of cotton were produced in 1939. (Courtesy of State Archives of North Carolina.)

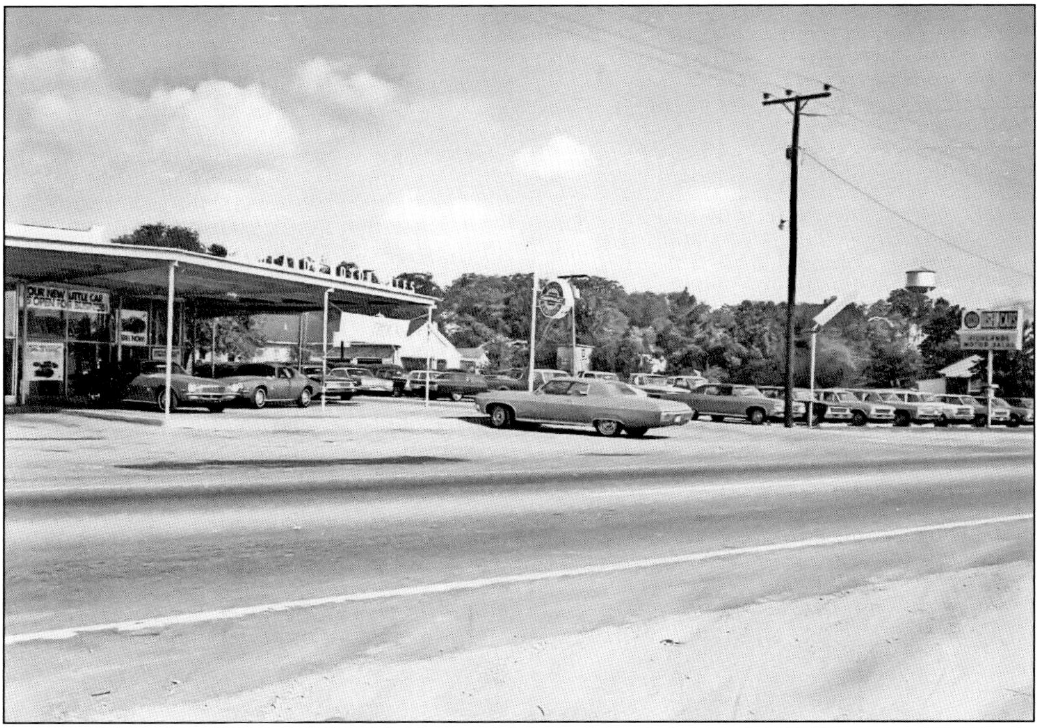

Richlands Motor Sales, in Richlands on Highway 24, was the go-to dealership in the Richlands area for a number of years. Richlands' old water tower can be seen in the distance. (Courtesy of Onslow County Museum.)

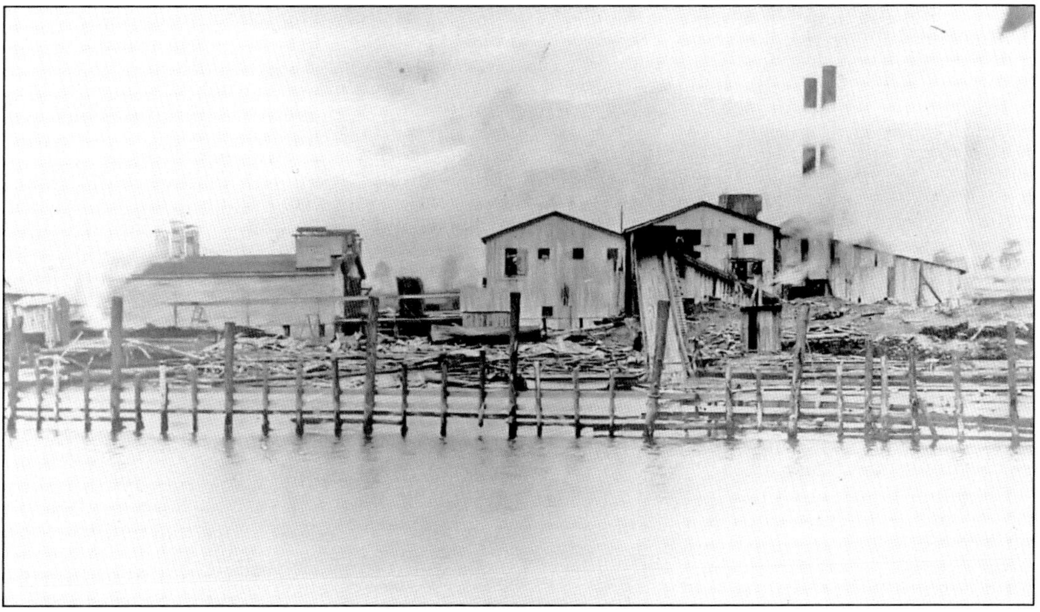

The small hamlet of Swansboro was revitalized by the presence of the Swansboro Land and Lumber Company, seen here in the early 20th century. The population increased as more people were employed by the mill, and a number of new homes were built by local shipwrights and carpenters, such as Robert Lee Smith. (Courtesy of Onslow County Museum.)

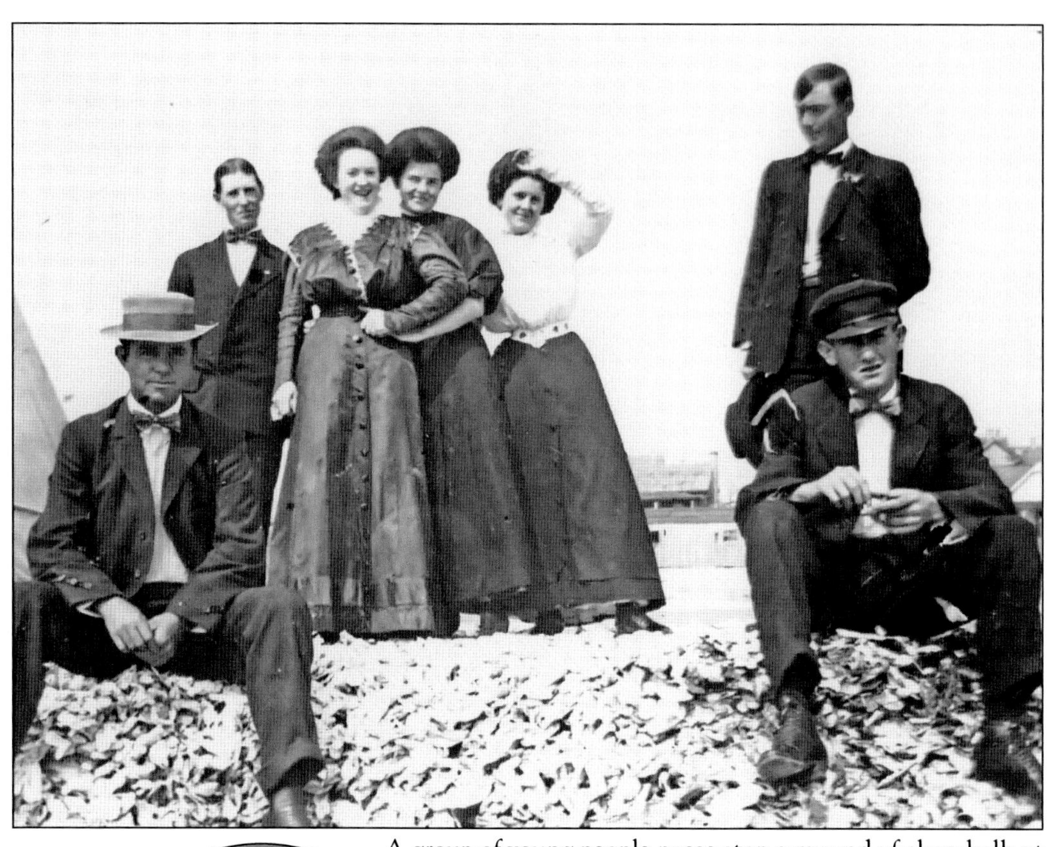

A group of young people poses atop a mound of clamshells at the Swansboro location of the Beaufort Little Neck Clam Company in about 1900. Onslow's bountiful supplies of shellfish attracted several business ventures. (Courtesy of State Archives of North Carolina.)

Daniel A. Hargett is believed to have been the first registered pharmacist in Onslow County. He worked out of the pharmacy located in the Old Brick Store in Swansboro. He is pictured here with an unidentified lady in the early 20th century. (Courtesy of State Archives of North Carolina.)

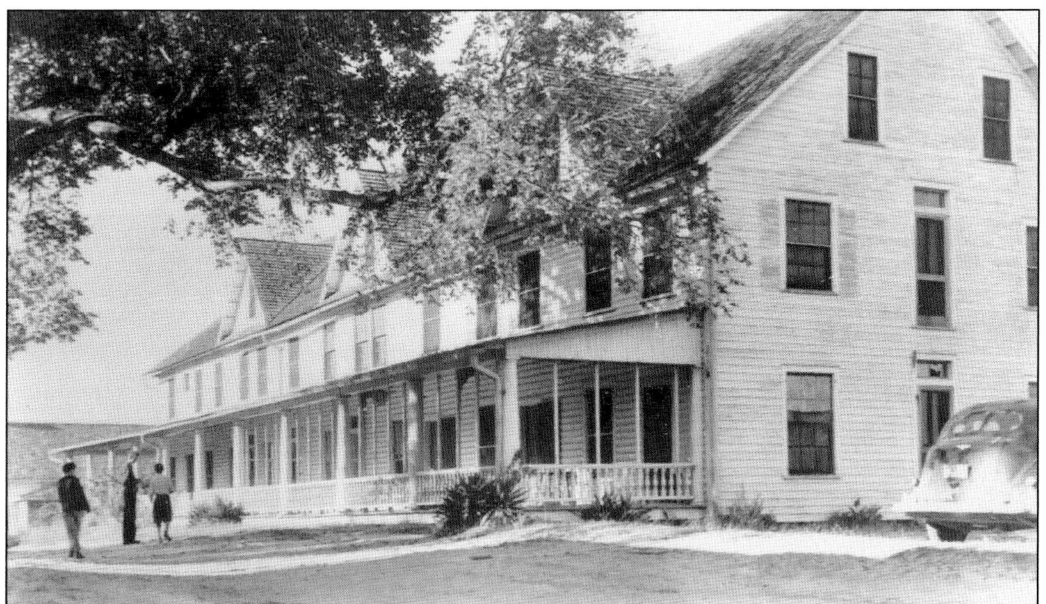

Swansboro's Tarrymore Hotel was built by Robert Lee Smith around 1910 for William J. Moore, who had owned a similarly named hotel in Wrightsville Beach. The hotel was a hub of social activity for a couple of decades until World War II. (Courtesy of Onslow County Museum.)

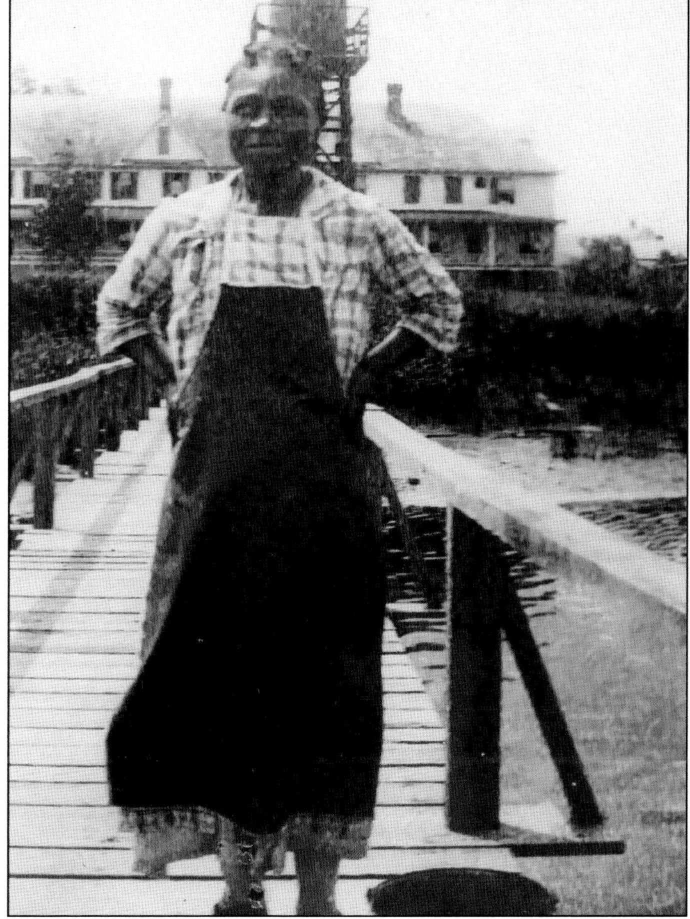

Charity Hargett worked for many years at the Tarrymore Hotel in Swansboro. She is pictured here about 1930 on the pier; the hotel can be seen in the background. (Courtesy of State Archives of North Carolina.)

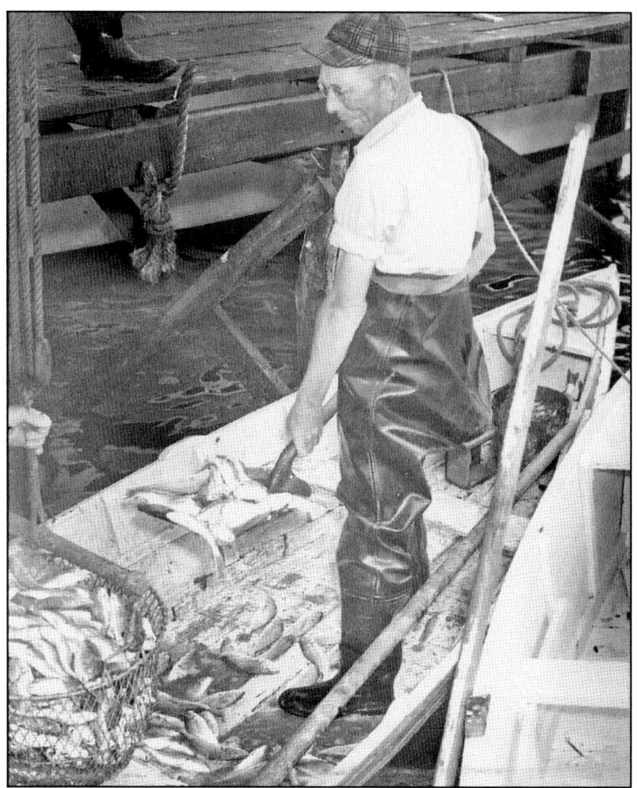

Richard Cordell Littleton (1900–1964) of Swansboro unloads a catch of spot at the pier. The Littletons made their living from the sea and waterways for generations in Onslow. Richard's grandfather George is listed as a sailor in the 1880 census. (Courtesy of State Archives of North Carolina.)

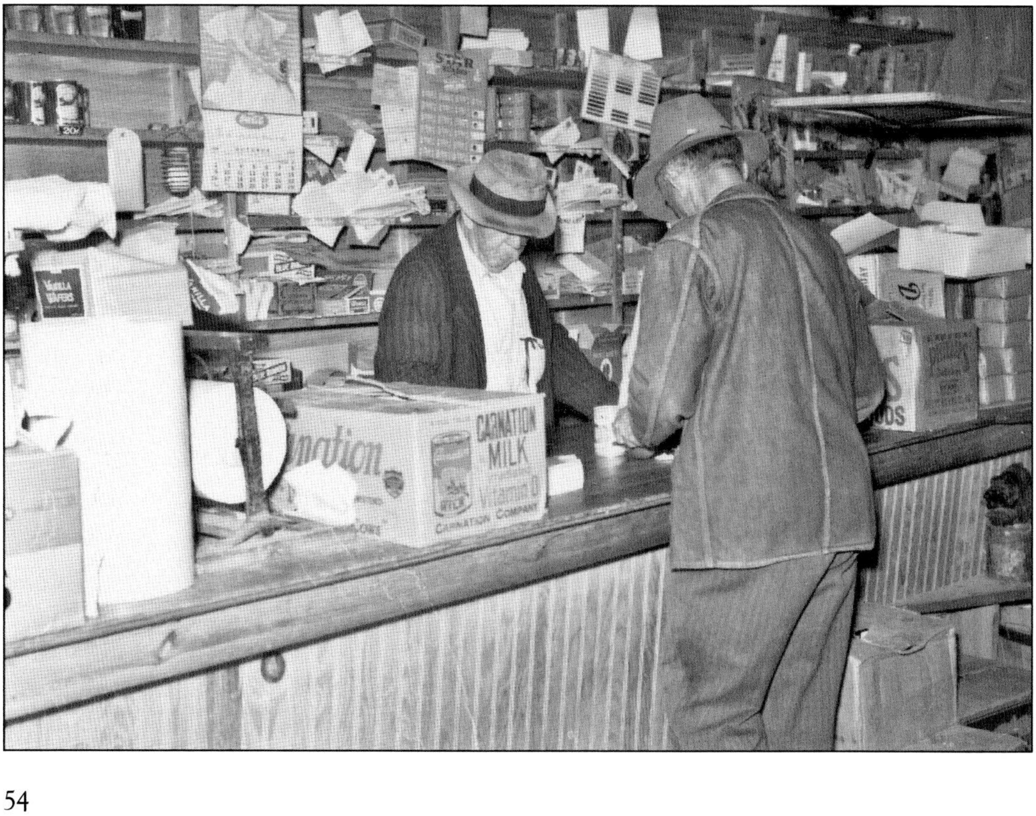

Conducting business at the Fulcher's Landing Store is Jim Fulcher, also known as "Old Man Fulcher." Residents could buy a number of products from the crowded inventory. Most families would make a shopping trip to Wilmington or New Bern only once or twice a year. (Courtesy of State Archives of North Carolina.)

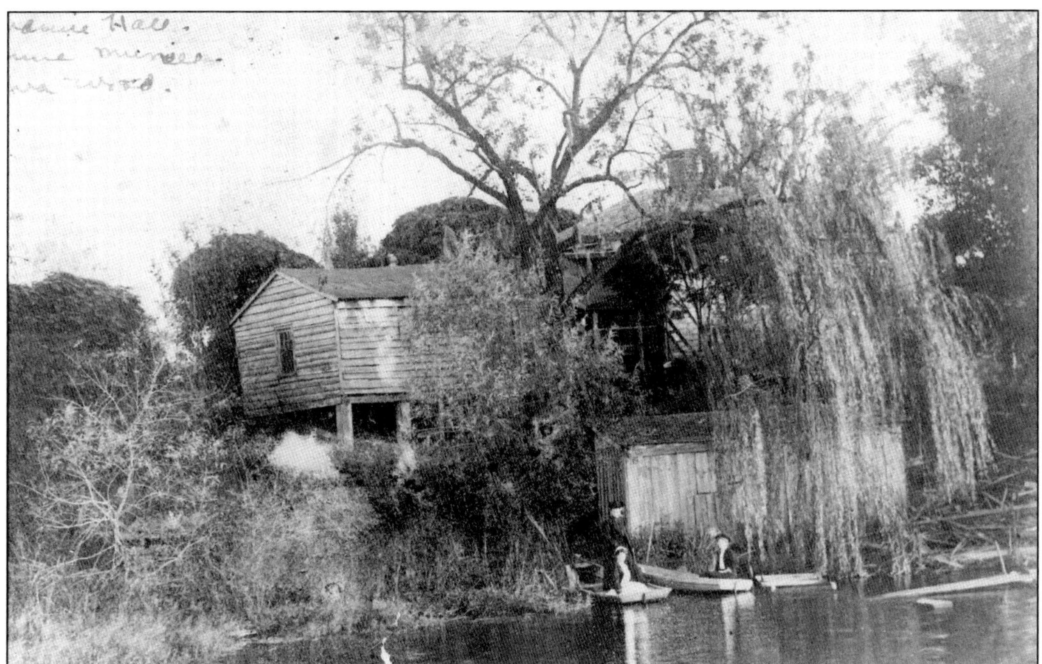

The 1850 Pelletier House, seen here on the banks of the New River in about 1900, served as the law office of Rufus Pelletier. It is the oldest surviving structure in Jacksonville. The two ladies seated in the boats are Anne Murrill (left) and Eva Ward Loy. The woman standing on the bank is unidentified. (Courtesy of Onslow County Museum.)

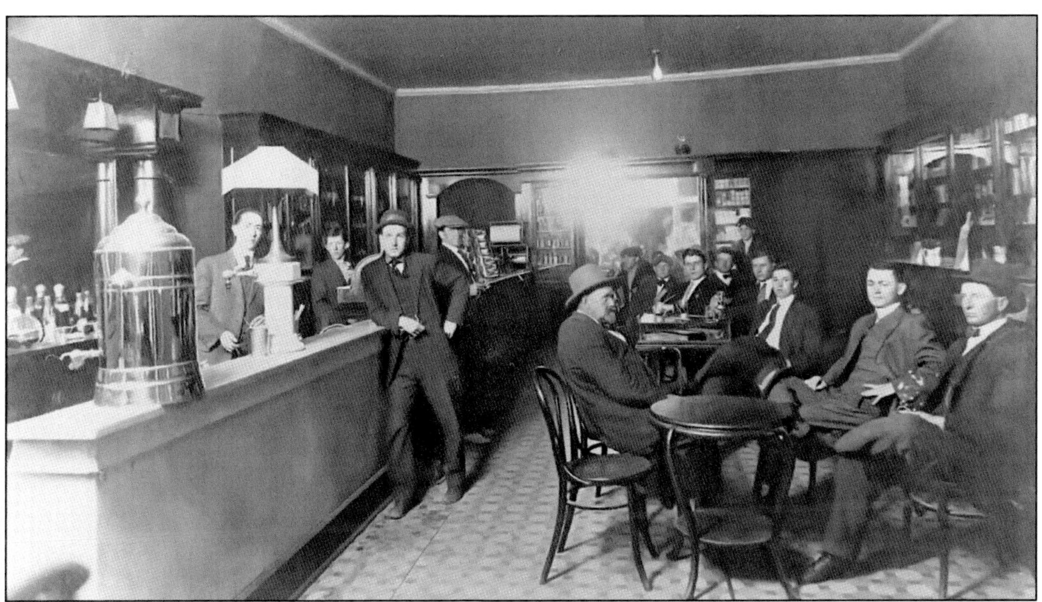

Ketchum's Drugstore in downtown Jacksonville was a well-known gathering spot in the early 20th century. (Courtesy of Onslow County Museum.)

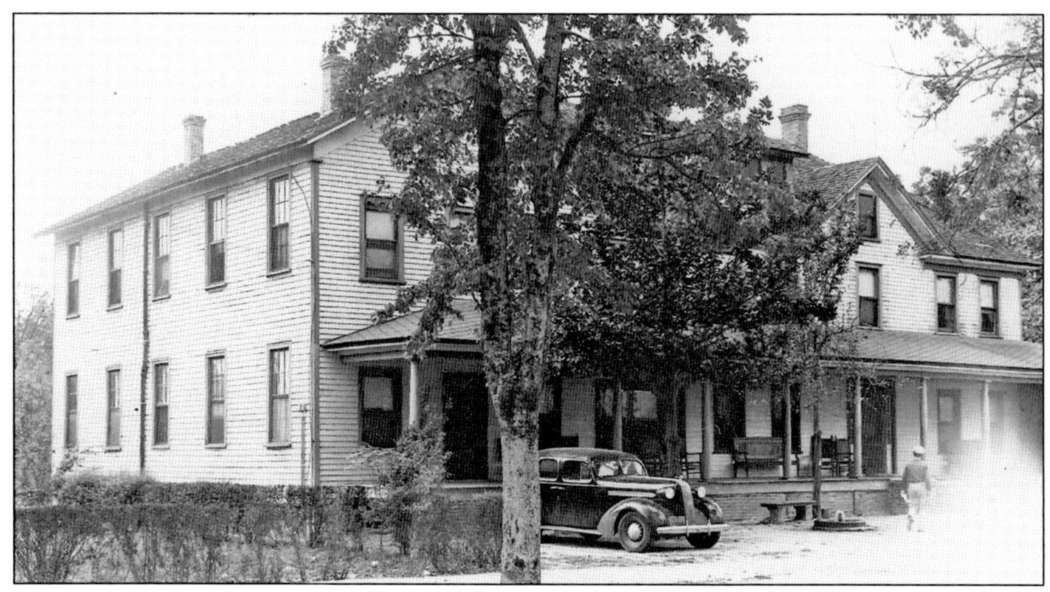

Weary travelers found respite at the Riverview Hotel in Jacksonville. A number of hotels sprang up with the coming of the military bases in the early 1940s. (Courtesy of Onslow County Museum.)

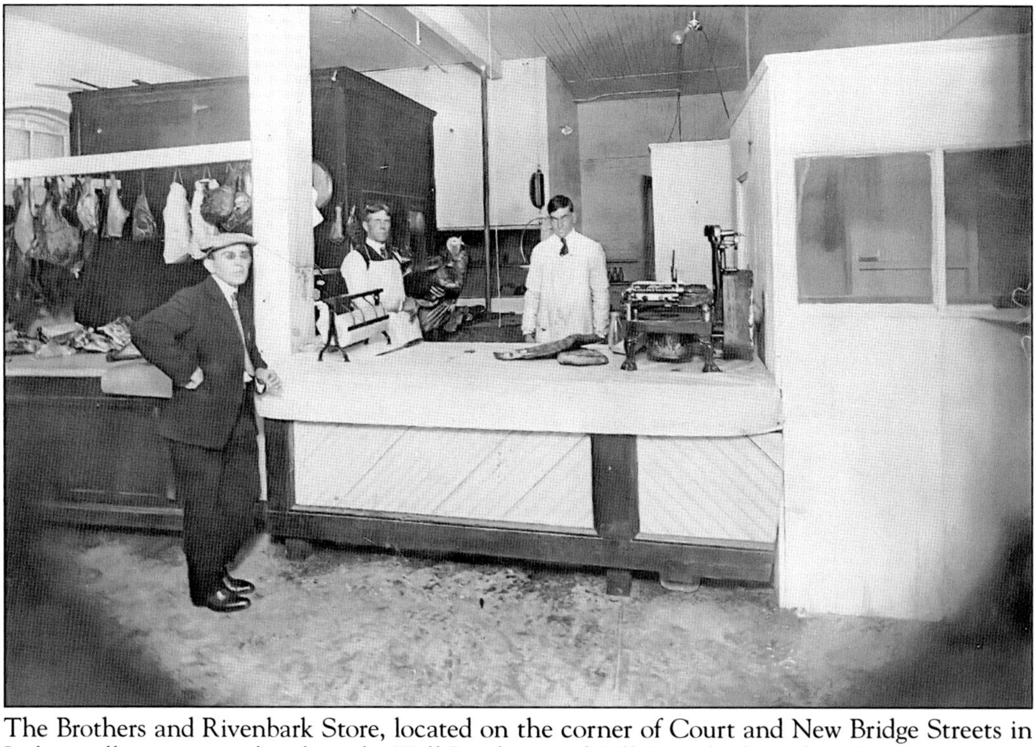

The Brothers and Rivenbark Store, located on the corner of Court and New Bridge Streets in Jacksonville, was owned and run by Will Brothers and Bill Rivenbark in the 1920s. This image shows the butcher shop area of the store. (Courtesy of Onslow County Museum.)

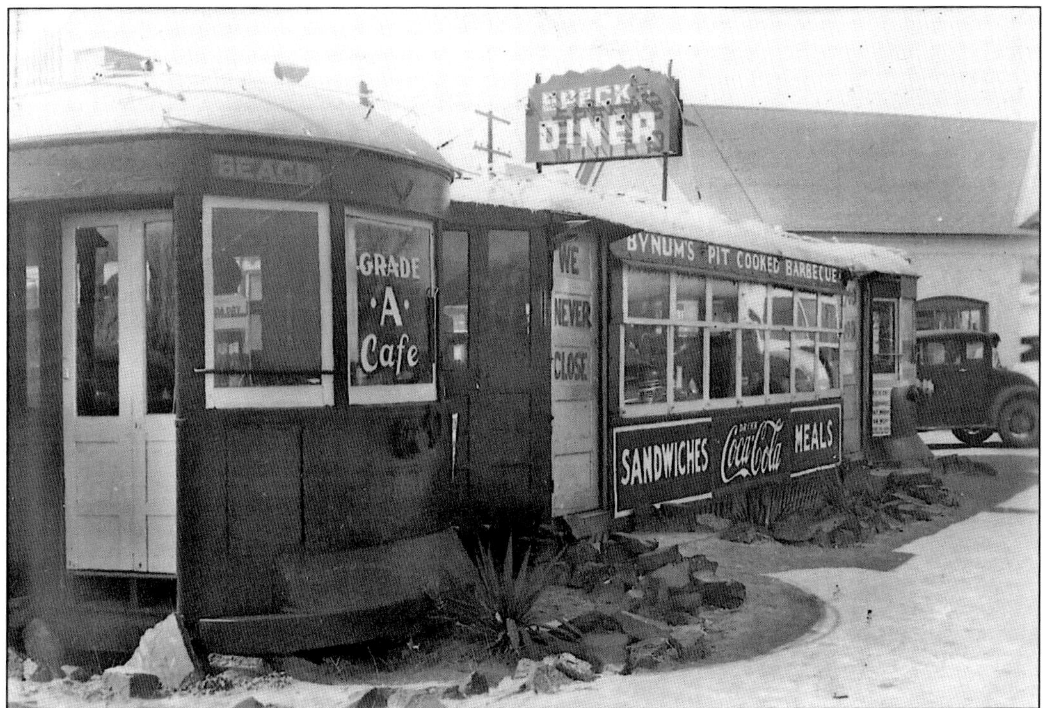

Speck's Diner in Jacksonville was owned and operated by Coleman Bynum and served the public a variety of meals, including his pit barbecue in this old trolley car adapted for reuse as a restaurant. The name was later changed to Coleman's Diner. (Courtesy of Onslow County Museum.)

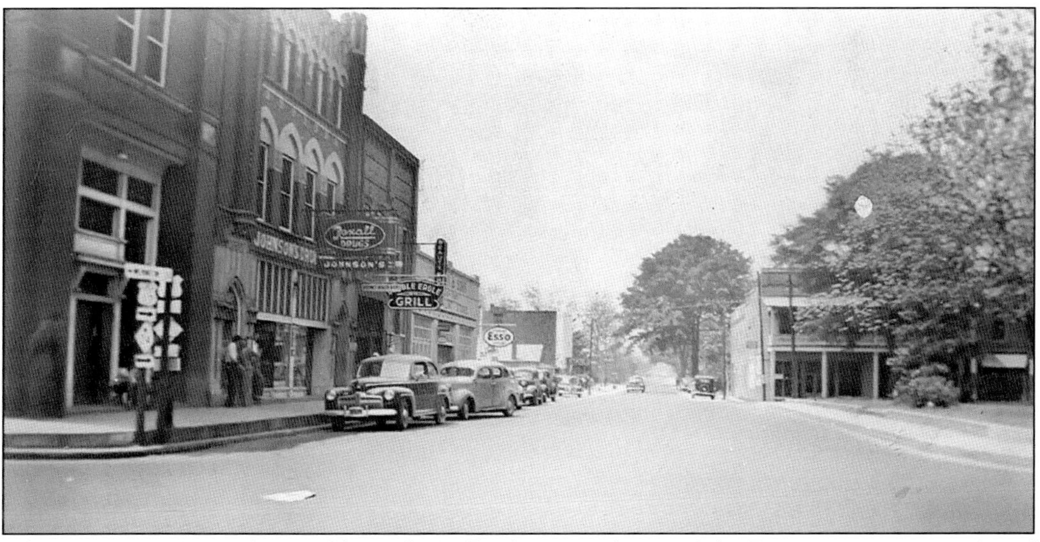

Johnson's Drug Store, the Double Eagle Grill, a beauty salon, and the Esso gas station are a few of the businesses seen in this view looking down Jacksonville's New Bridge Street in the late 1940s. Johnson's, established in 1933 by Graham Johnson, was located in the old Masonic Temple building, constructed in 1919 for Lafayette Lodge No. 83. (Courtesy of Onslow County Museum.)

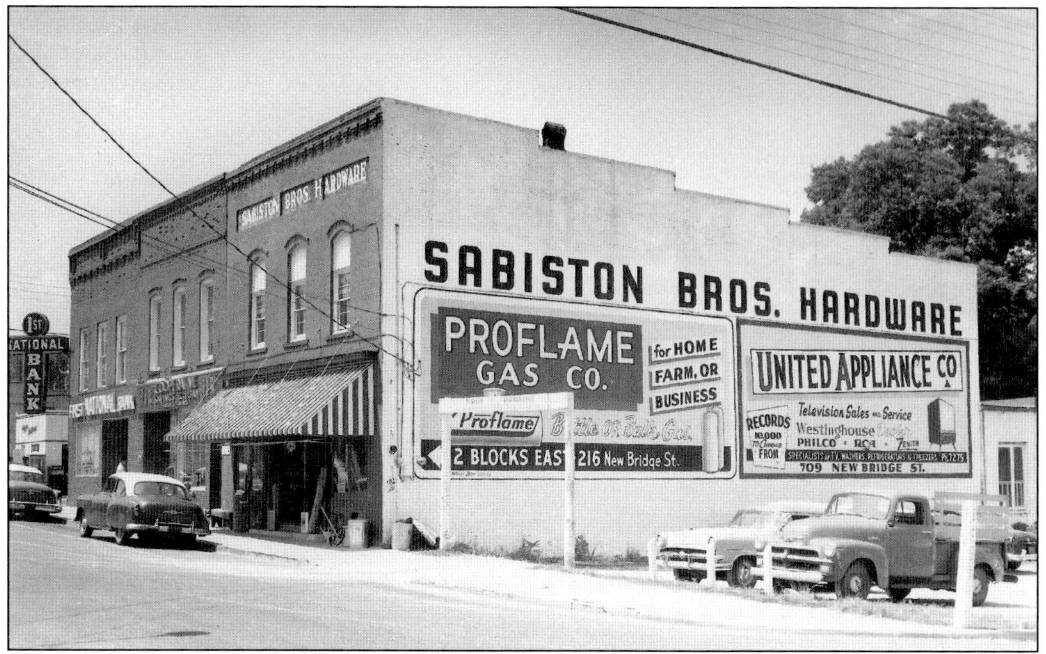

Businesses were thriving in 1950s Jacksonville. Pictured here are the First National Bank and Cooperative Savings and Loan the left, and Sabiston Brothers Hardware Store. Advertising signs painted on the side of the store encourage additional shopping down the way on New Bridge Street. (Courtesy of Onslow County Museum.)

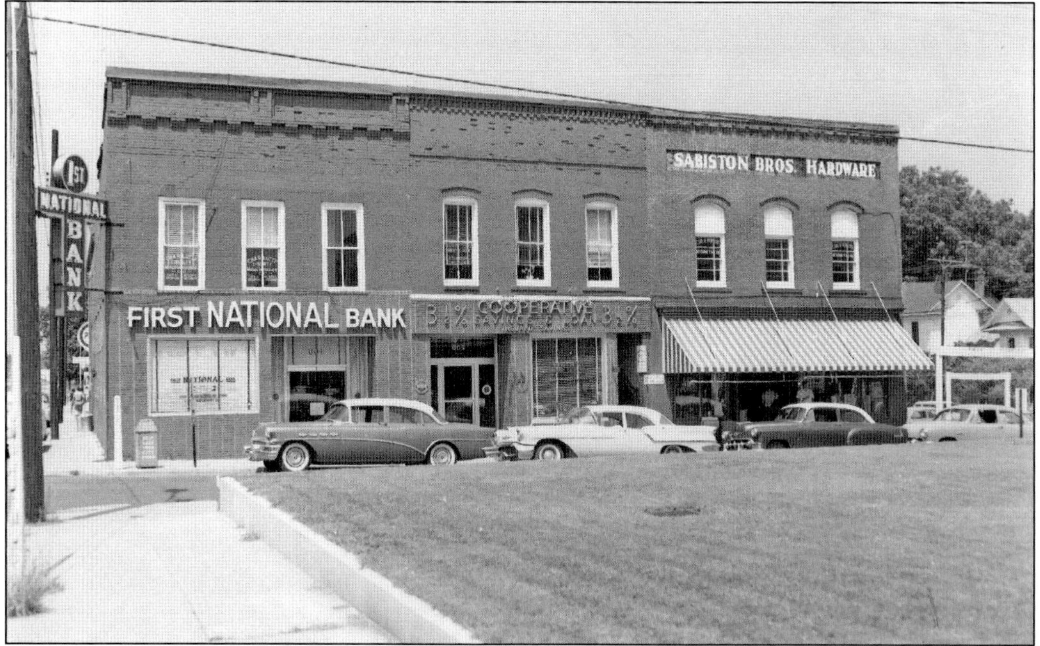

This is a frontal view of the First National Bank, Cooperative Savings and Loan, and Sabiston Brothers Hardware in the 1950s. Charlotte Liberty Mutual Insurance Company had offices above the bank, and Carl V. Venters's law office was located above the hardware store. (Courtesy of Onslow County Museum.)

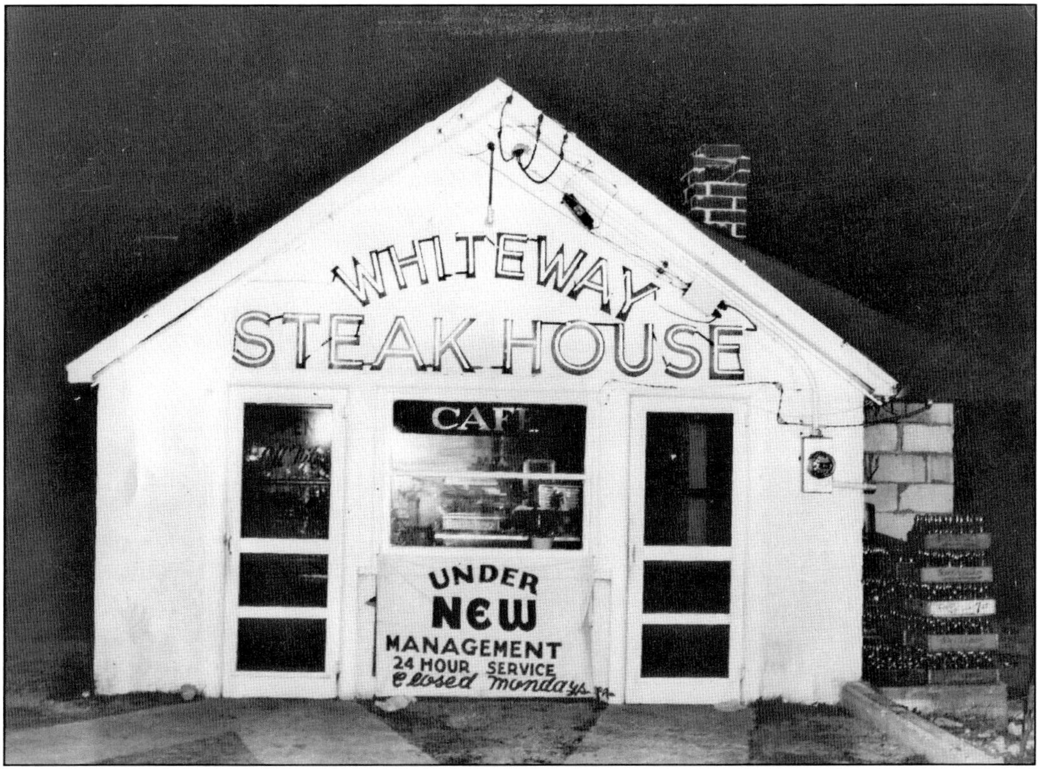

Under new management at the time, the Whiteway Steakhouse Café in Jacksonville was ready for business in the 1950s with stacks of bottled 7Up and Dr. Pepper near the entrance. (Courtesy of Onslow County Museum.)

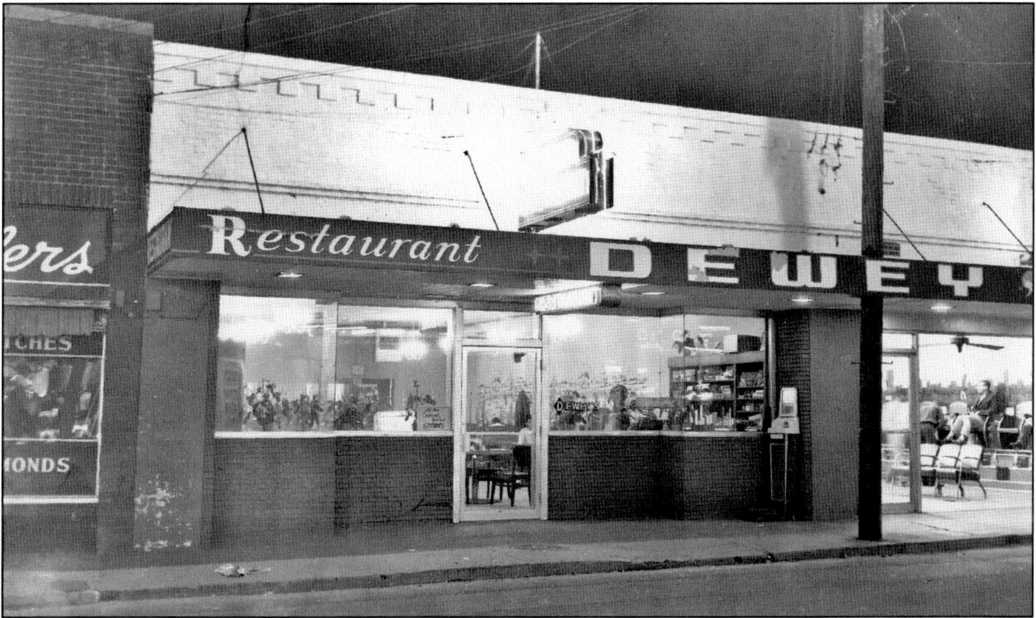

Dewey's Restaurant, featuring charcoal-broiled steaks, was located in downtown Jacksonville in the 1950s. A shoeshine shop was next door on the right. (Courtesy of Onslow County Museum.)

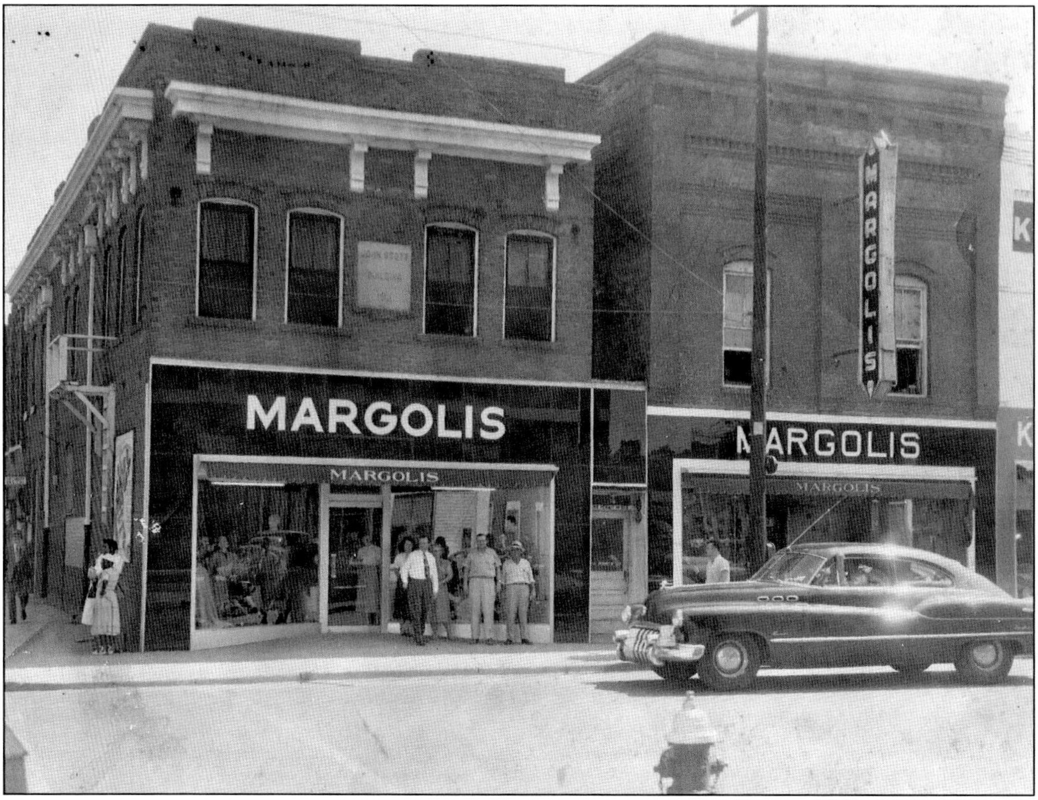

In the 1950s, Margolis Store encompassed both the John Scott building and the Clayton Petteway building on Court Street, erected in 1910 and 1913, respectively. The store was a fixture in the community for a number of years; men's and women's clothing and shoes were the main items sold. (Courtesy of Onslow County Museum.)

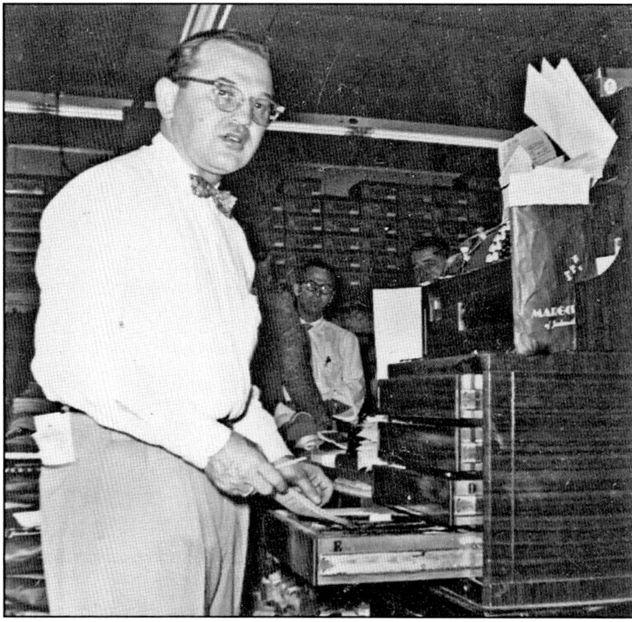

Leon Margolis, owner of Margolis Store, is seen at the cash register of his establishment in Jacksonville in the 1950s. Note the name printed on one of the store's shopping bags on the right. (Courtesy of Onslow County Museum.)

Leon Margolis is pictured on the sidewalk near his store on Court Street. Leon's parents, Max and Fannie Margolis, emigrated to the United States from Russia in 1912. (Courtesy of Onslow County Museum.)

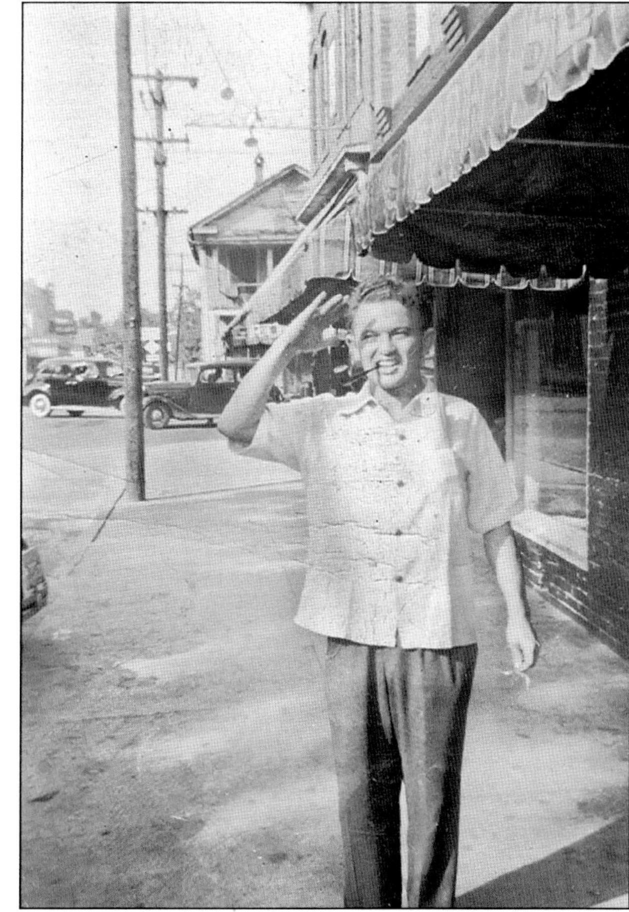

The John Scott and Clayton Petteway buildings on Court Street are pictured in the late 1980s after Margolis Store had moved to another location in Jacksonville. The store is still in operation as the Margolis Men's Store. (Courtesy of Onslow County Museum.)

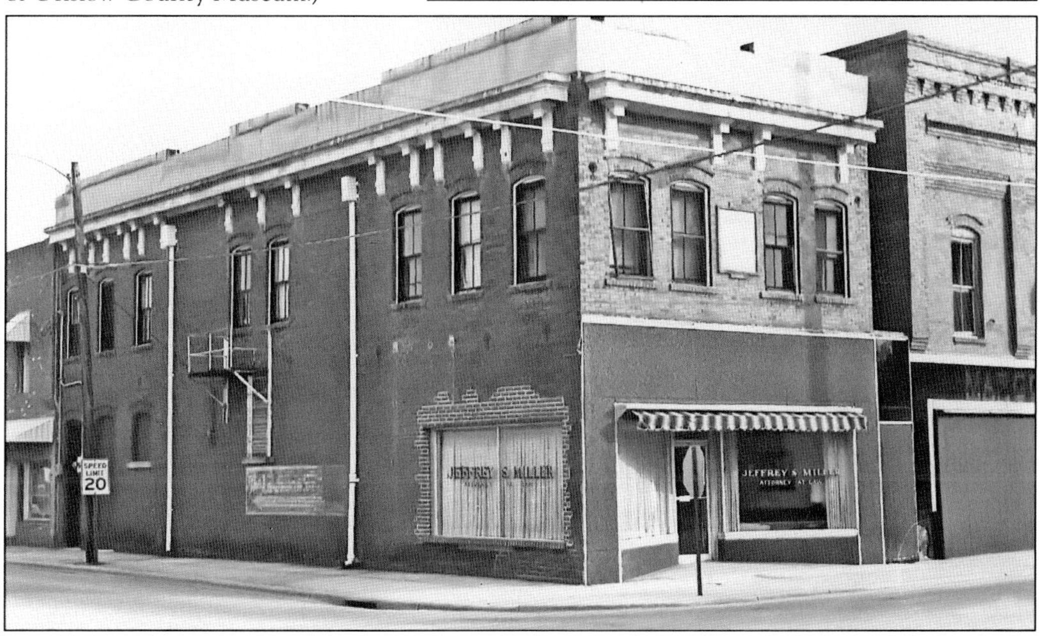

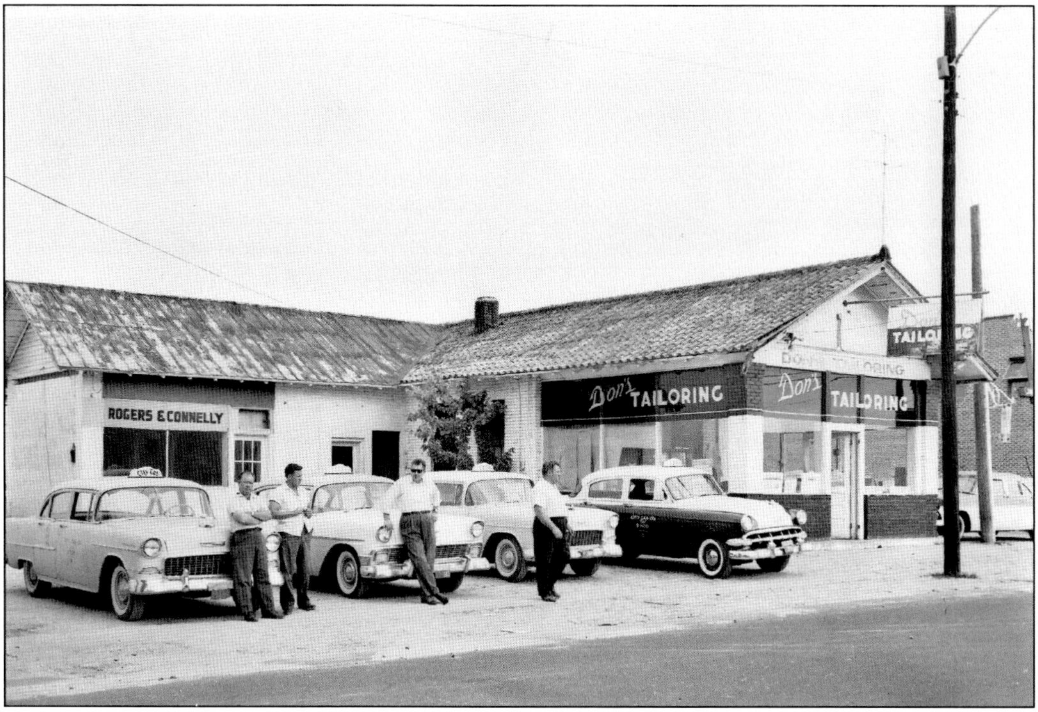

In downtown 1950s Jacksonville, taxi drivers working for Rogers and Connelly wait for customers to call. Next door is Don's Tailoring Shop. (Courtesy of Onslow County Museum.)

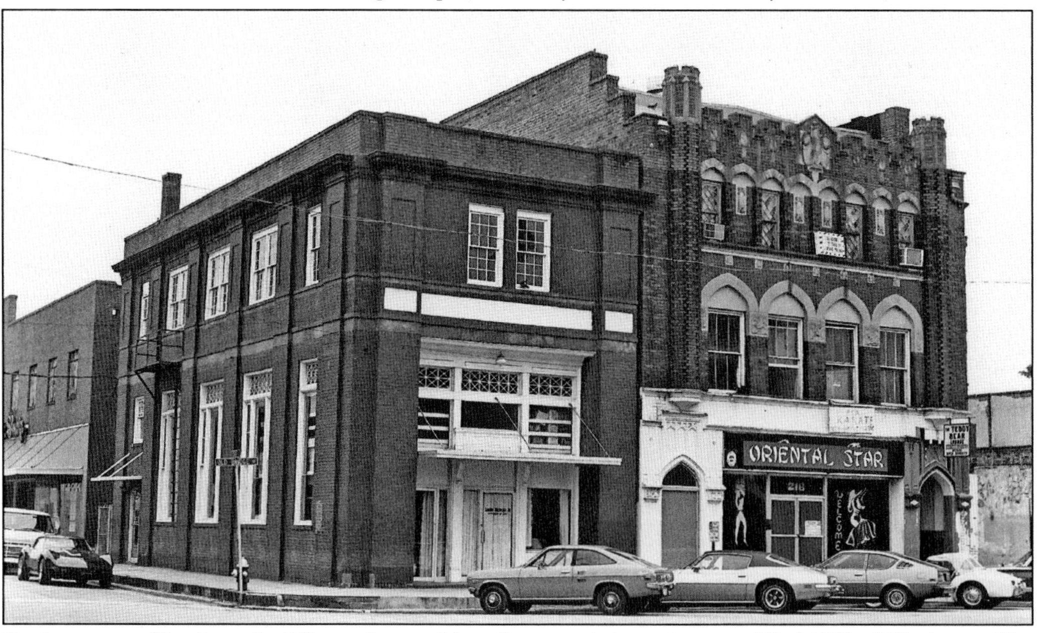

Businesses and business buildings changed hands several times in post–World War II Jacksonville. The area around the courthouse became a somewhat wild and unsavory place on weekends, leading some traditional businesses to move elsewhere. In the late 1980s, the Masonic Temple building had become the Oriental Star and Teddy Bear Lounge. By the next decade, revitalization was the goal of the city. (Courtesy of Onslow County Museum.)

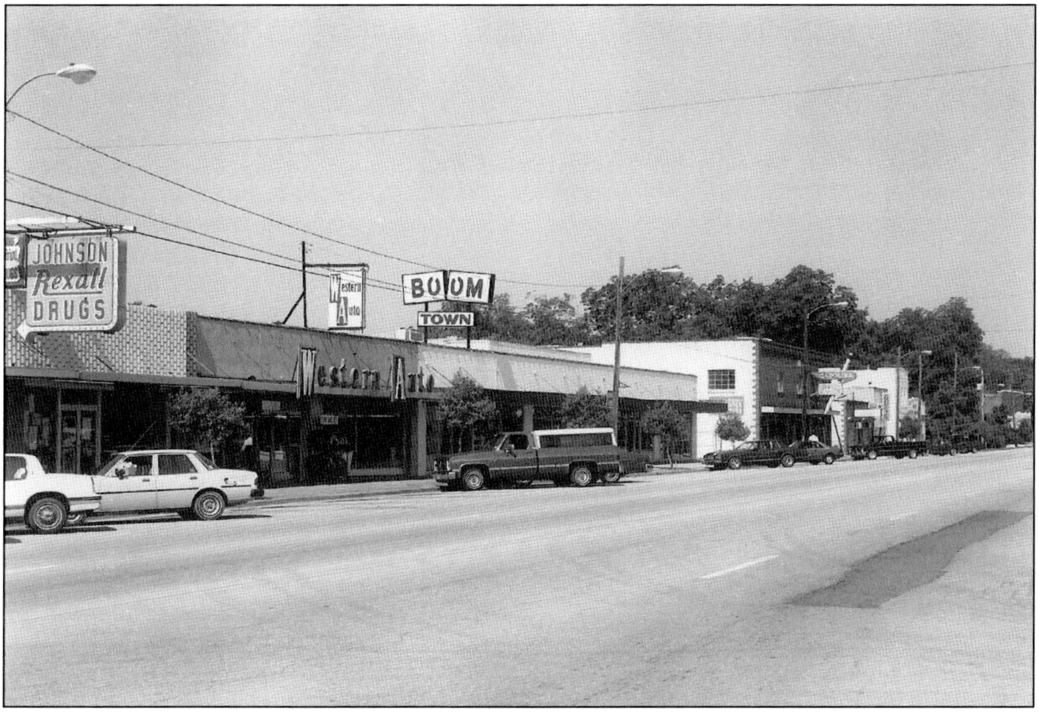

Johnson's Drug Store, formerly located in the Masonic Temple, served its longtime customers on New Bridge Street in the late 1980s, along with Western Auto, Boomtown Furniture, and Carolina Office Supply. Johnson's is one of the oldest locally owned pharmacies in eastern North Carolina. (Courtesy of Onslow County Museum.)

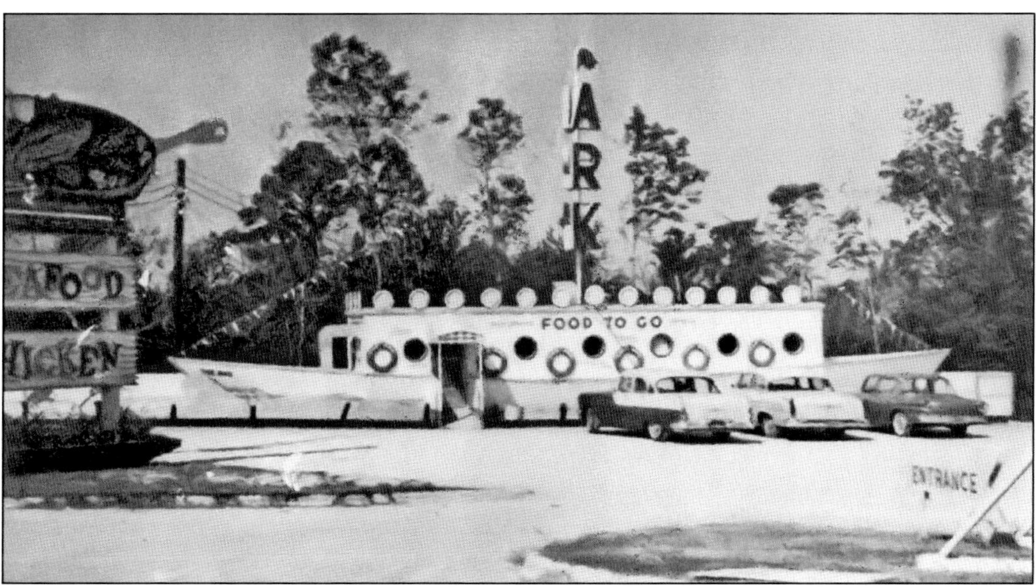

The Ark Restaurant is a familiar landmark in Jacksonville. Opened in 1960 by Eddie and Bunky Bynum, the nautically themed restaurant and takeout is known for its fried chicken and hush puppies. Seen in this 1963 image, the establishment suffered a fire in 1992 but was rebuilt and is a still a friendly sight on South Marine Boulevard. (Courtesy of Onslow County Museum.)

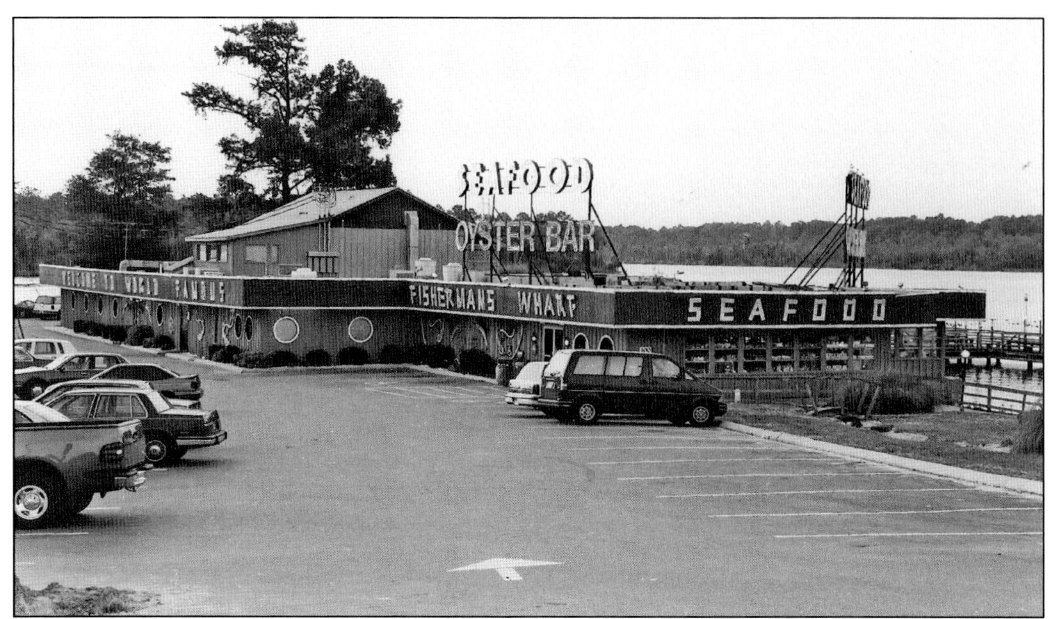

The Fisherman's Wharf, also owned by the Bynum brothers, served locals and visitors its "world famous" seafood from the mid-1970s to its closing and eventual demolition in the early 2000s. Its location, directly on the New River at the bridge, made it a popular destination. (Courtesy of Onslow County Museum.)

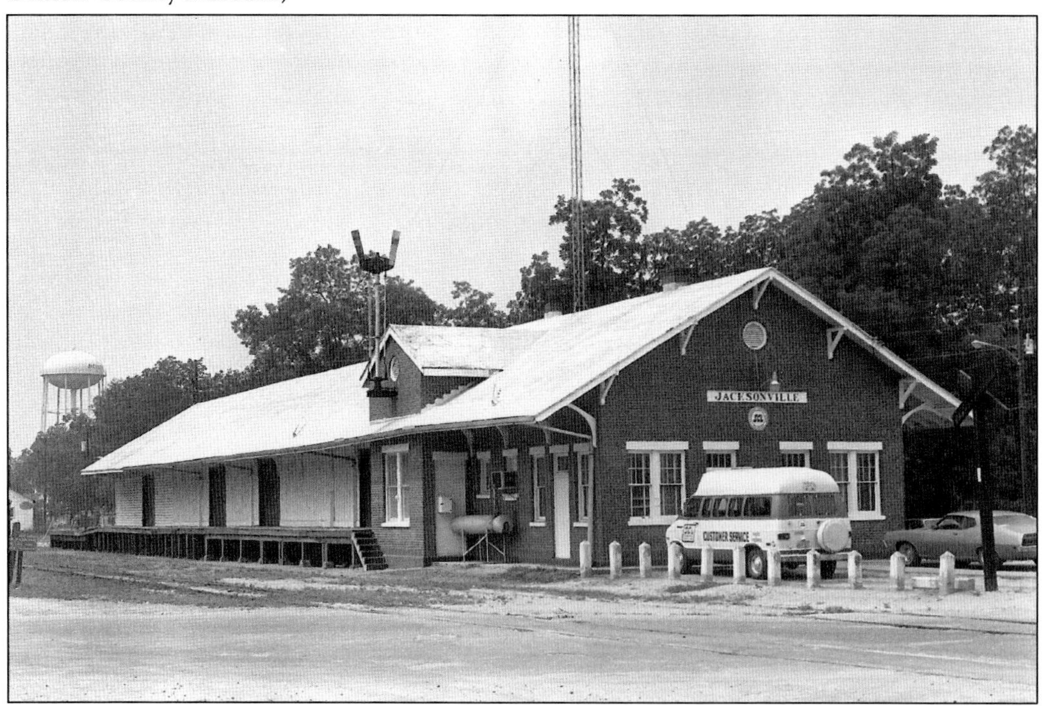

The railroad was a long time coming to Jacksonville, not connecting from Wilmington until 1891. Sometime after 1925, the original depot was replaced by a brick station that served its patrons faithfully until 1984, when all rail service was suspended. This image shows the freight wing extending from the south gable. (Courtesy of Onslow County Museum.)

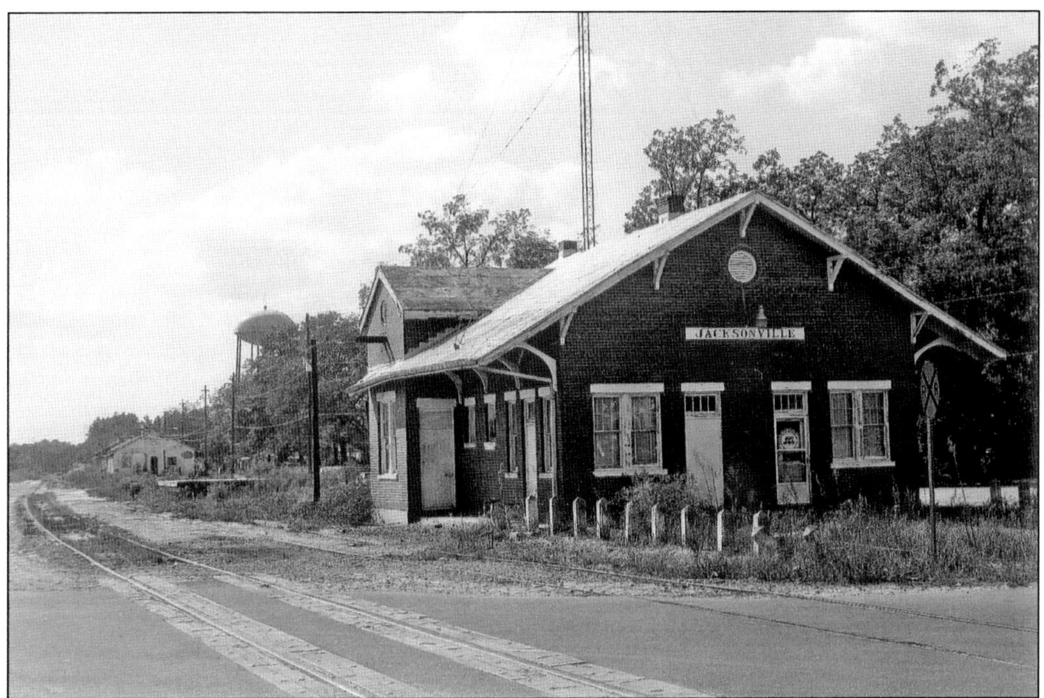

This view of the Jacksonville Train Depot was taken in October 1984, after the freight wing had been removed, and the building was essentially abandoned. Since then, the old depot has been revitalized and is an integral part of the city's beautiful Riverwalk Park. (Author's collection.)

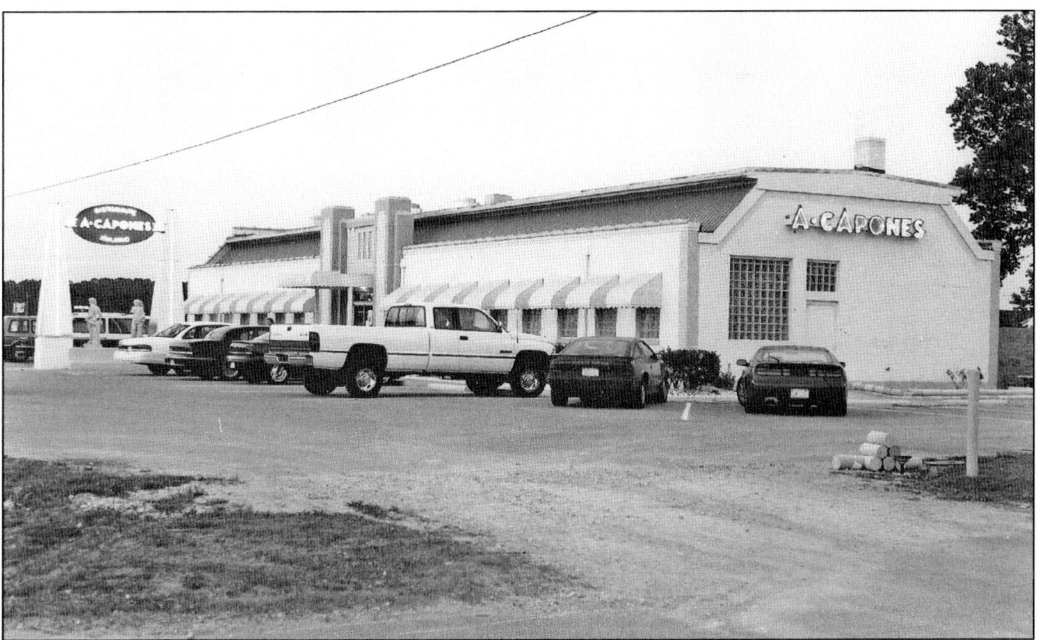

Formerly A. Capone's Italian Restaurant on US Highway 17, this structure has also served a number of other purposes, including a prison camp for convict road workers and an early-1960s location of Coastal Carolina Community College. (Courtesy of Onslow County Museum.)

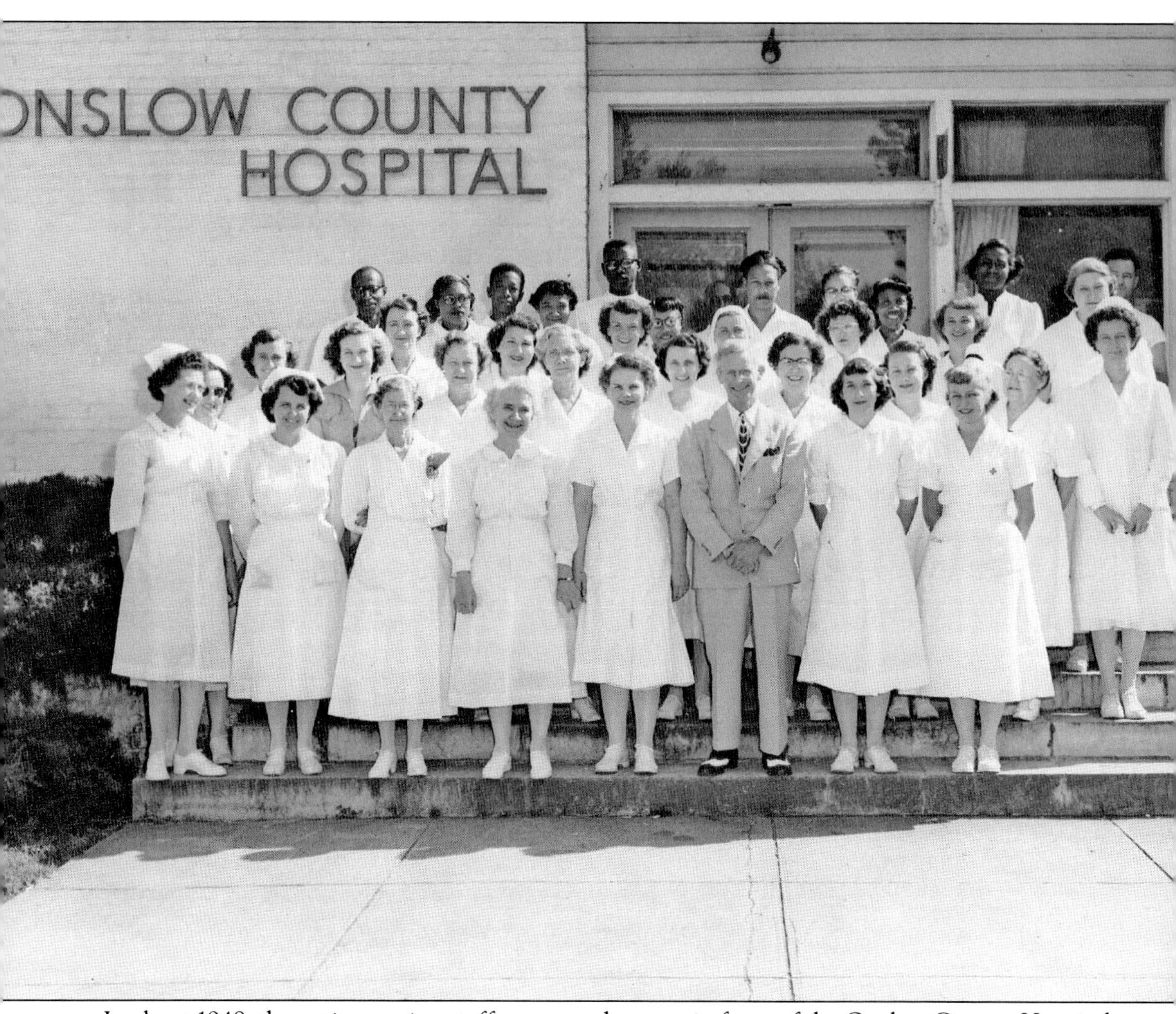

In about 1948, the entire nursing staff poses on the steps in front of the Onslow County Hospital, which was then located on College Street. (Courtesy of Onslow County Museum.)

Four

Places of Worship

Onslow County was officially established in 1734, and at about the same time, an Anglican religious district was also founded, called St. John's Parish. Church wardens were appointed and visiting ministers made the rounds in Onslow, but there is no evidence that there was ever a church built. According to contemporary accounts, the people of Onslow were more open to the Baptist movement by the mid-18th century. The latter part of the century brought Methodism, with Bishop Francis Asbury as its untiring proponent.

Following the Civil War, newly freed slaves enthusiastically established a number of churches. Most were Methodist or Baptist, such as the earliest black church, Sandy Run Baptist, which was organized at least by the mid-1860s and is still in existence today, followed by Blooming Hill Missionary Baptist in Richlands, St. Thomas AME in Swansboro, and several others.

Prohibition of liquor in Onslow County was a major concern for many of Onslow's church members from the late 19th century to the enactment of Prohibition with the Eighteenth Amendment. But there remained a market for liquor, as evidenced by the many stills confiscated during the time. Though Prohibition was repealed in 1933, local churches continued to preach against the evils of liquor in the home.

The founding of Camp Lejeune brought diversity in beliefs to the area. A small number of Jewish families had lived in Onslow since the early part of the 20th century; they attended synagogue in Wilmington until 1957, when a small brick building on Wardola Street in Jacksonville was designed and built for use as a Jewish worship and meeting place. When Camp Lejeune was built, it included not only a Protestant chapel but also a Roman Catholic chapel—St. Francis Xavier. The Roman Catholic church in Jacksonville, now Infant of Prague, and Swansboro's St. Mildred were established in the mid-1940s.

Well over 100 churches exist in Onslow County today; the majority are Christian—primarily evangelical Protestant, mainline Protestant, and Roman Catholic.

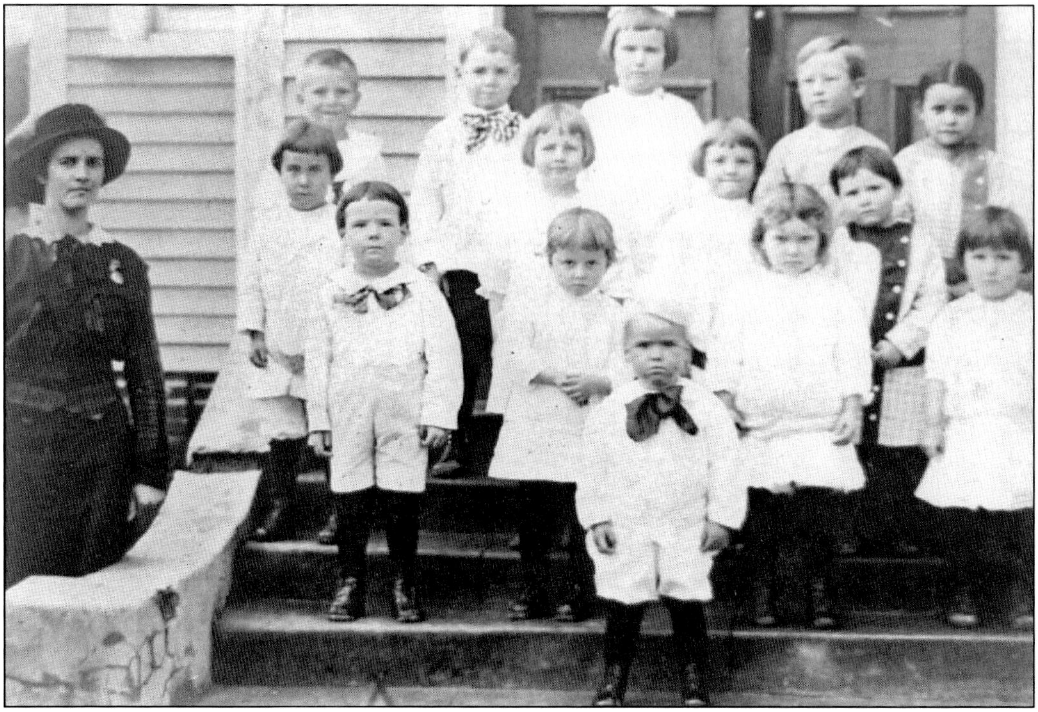

As it is today, Sunday school was an intrinsic part of going to church and learning about the Christian faith. Hazel N. Cox is seen here on the left, with her young charges in front of the Richlands Methodist Church in about 1915. (Courtesy of the Onslow County Museum.)

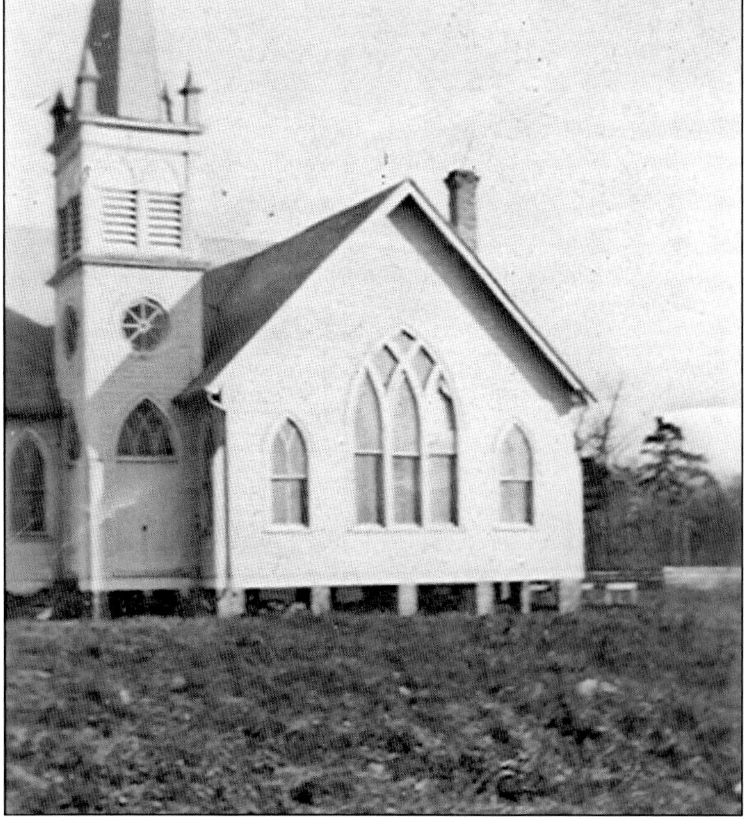

The Richlands area has been a seat of Methodism since 1791. This image of the current Richlands United Methodist Church was taken in the late 1930s, shortly after it was built on the same site as the church in the previous photograph. (Courtesy of Onslow County Museum.)

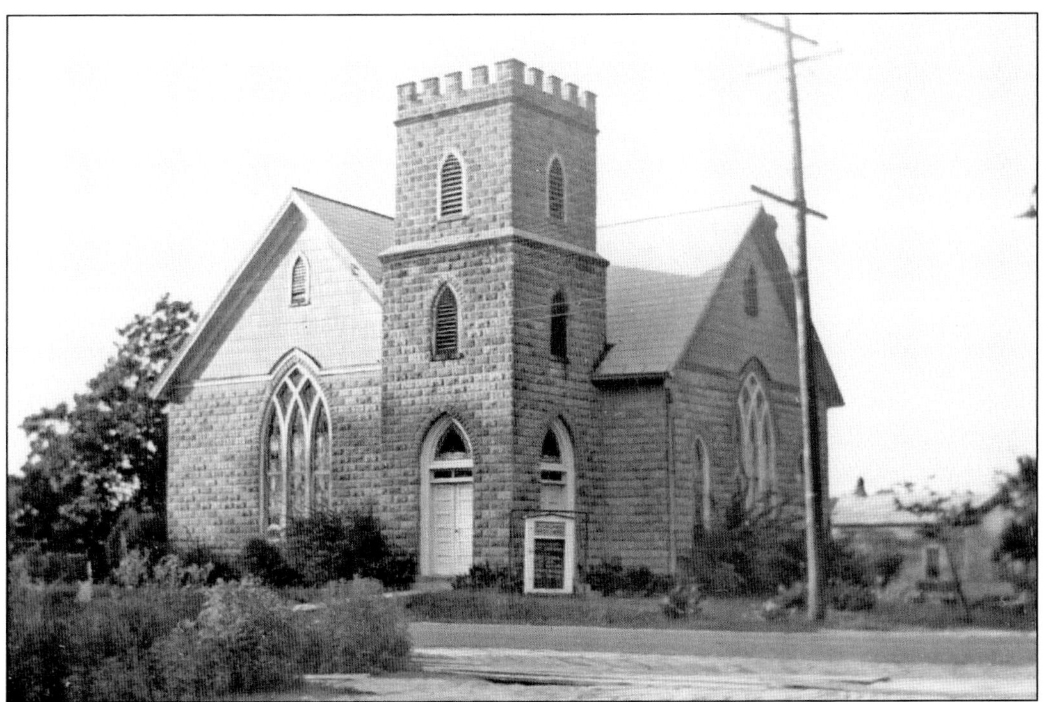

Located on Hargett Street in Richlands, this early-20th-century church was commonly known as "Emma's Chapel," after Emma C. Nicholson, an early supporter of the Baptist church then housed there. The First Baptist congregation now worships elsewhere; this Gothic-inspired structure is now home to another Christian denomination. (Courtesy of Onslow County Museum.)

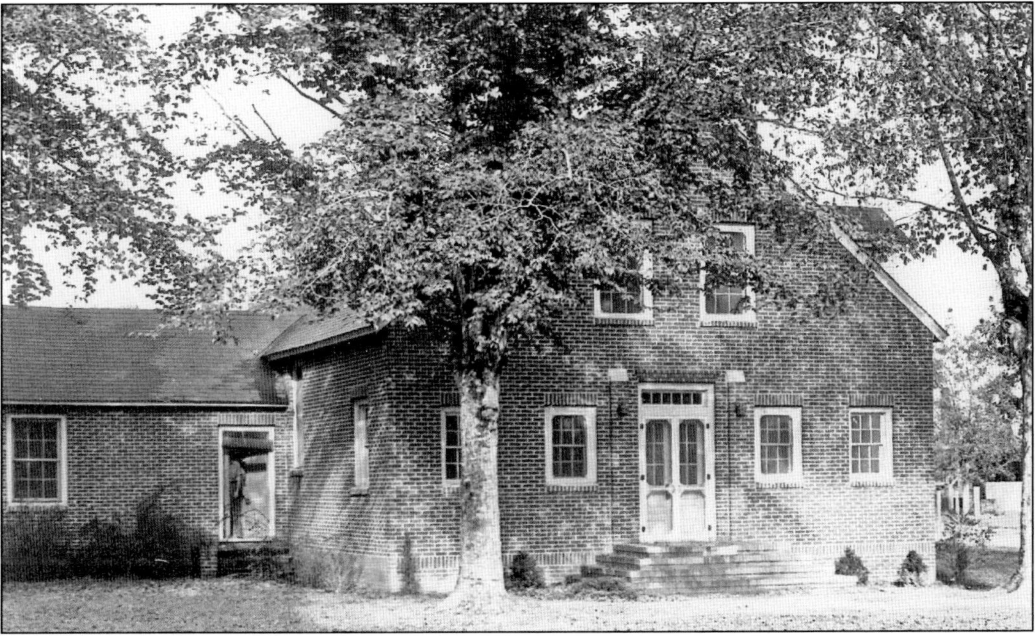

The brick-veneered Richlands Christian Church is pictured in about 1939, three years after it was dedicated in August 1936. It replaced the frame chapel that had stood on that site since 1882. The Richlands Church of Christ is currently located there. (Courtesy of Onslow County Museum.)

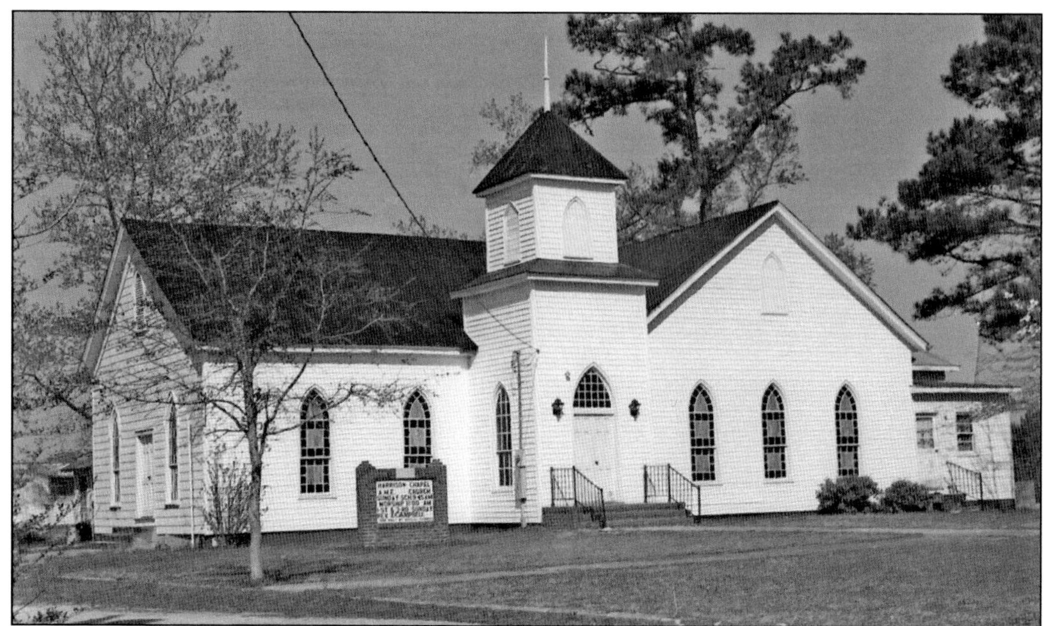

Harrison Chapel AME Zion Church was built about 1903 on Dreadnaught Road in Richlands. The church's exterior is enhanced by subtle Gothic elements, while the interior features a beautiful curved altar rail. (Courtesy of Onslow County Museum.)

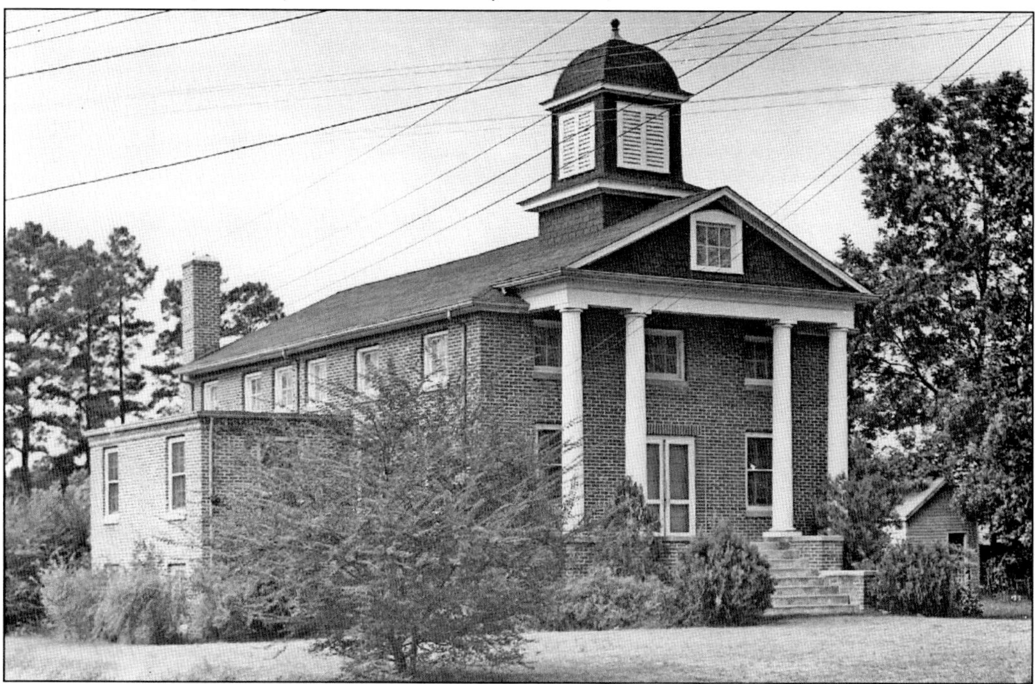

This 1930s-era Baptist church was located on Anne Street in downtown Jacksonville. The chapel in the picture was torn down and rebuilt as Bethany Baptist Church in the Nine Mile community. Another First Baptist Church was built on the same lot in 1950. Since then, the First Baptist congregation has expanded and is now in a large complex on Gum Branch Road. The Anne Street church is now the Jacksonville Bible Church. (Courtesy of Onslow County Museum.)

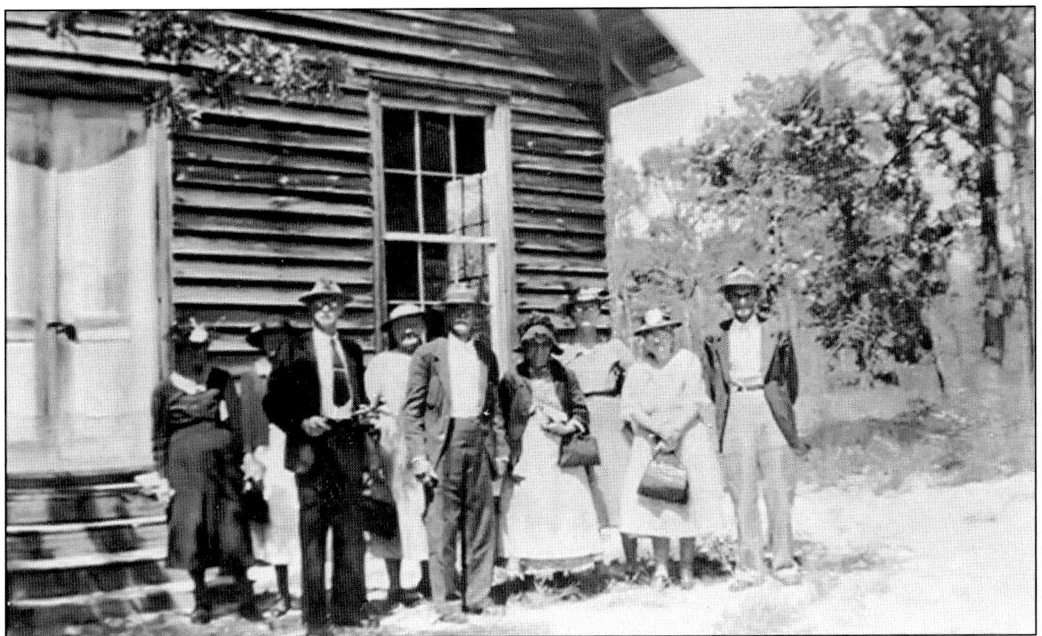

Growing from an early Baptist congregation, Ward's Will Church was constructed on land donated by Edward Ward. The church was later relocated to a lot near Marines Post Office. The people in front of the church are members attending the last service held there in 1941, when they gave up their church as part of land acquisition by the federal government. (Courtesy of Onslow County Museum.)

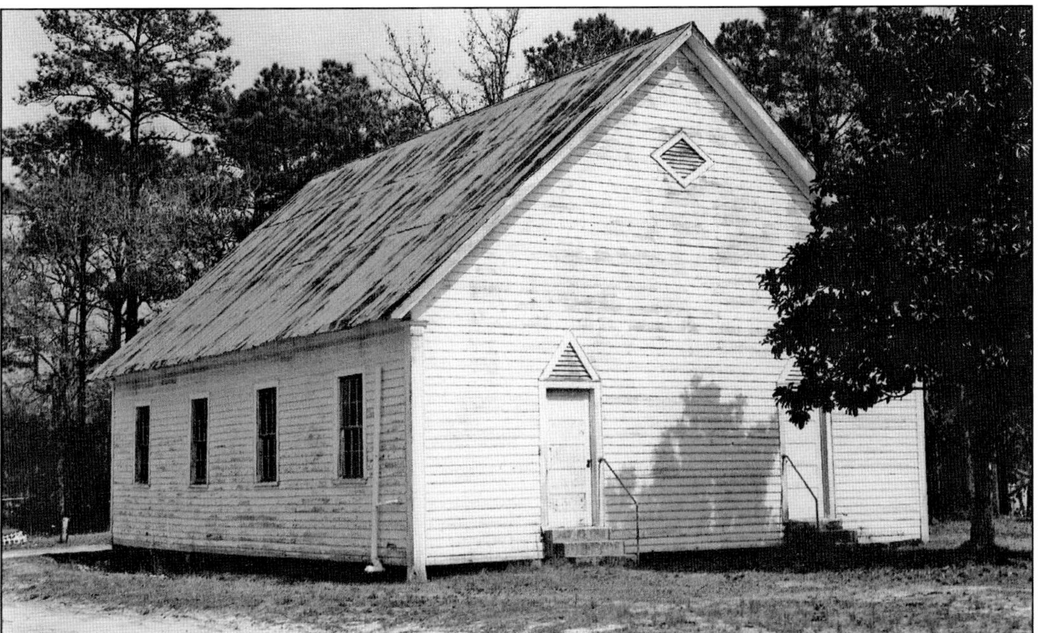

In the Sneads Ferry vicinity, Primitive Baptists' seat of worship was at Yopp's Meeting House, erected in the late 19th century in the nave plan. The two entrances reflect the Primitive Baptist practice of men and women sitting on opposite sides of the church. African Americans also sat in a separate section. (Courtesy of Onslow County Museum.)

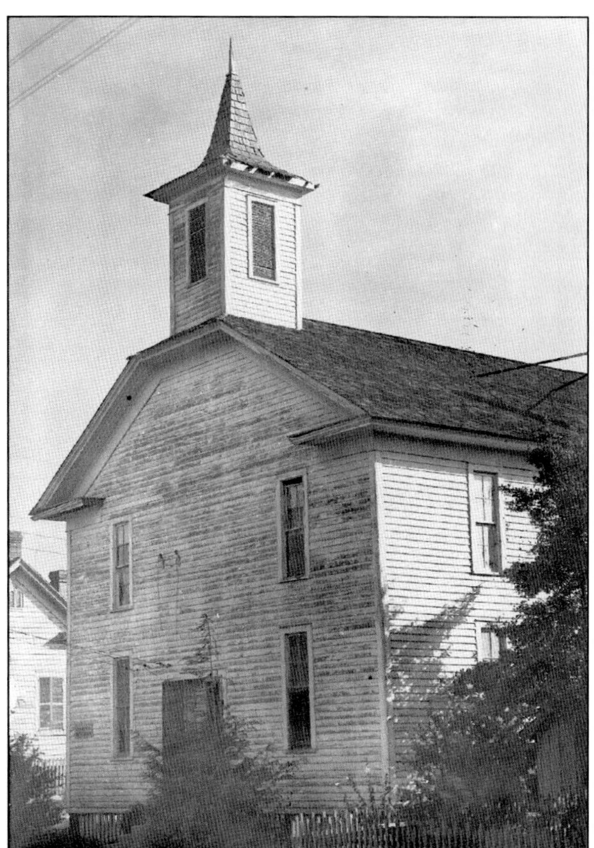

Swansboro's Baptists formed their own congregation in the late 1890s, erecting this two-story church on Main Street. This image was taken in 1939, and the belfry was removed sometime after that. (Courtesy of Onslow County Museum.)

The Southwest Primitive Baptist congregation is one of the oldest in Onslow County. Well before the mid-19th century, this pleasingly simple church was built in the meetinghouse style, which had an entrance on the long side of the structure. It has since been modified to include entry on the ends, a more common arrangement. (Courtesy of Onslow County Museum.)

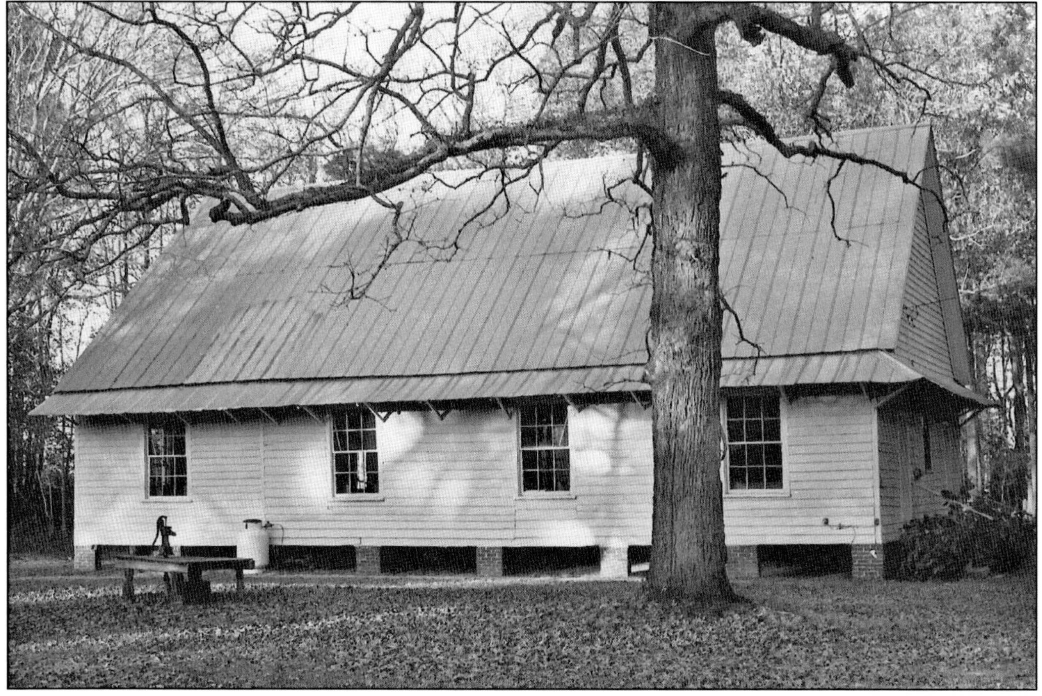

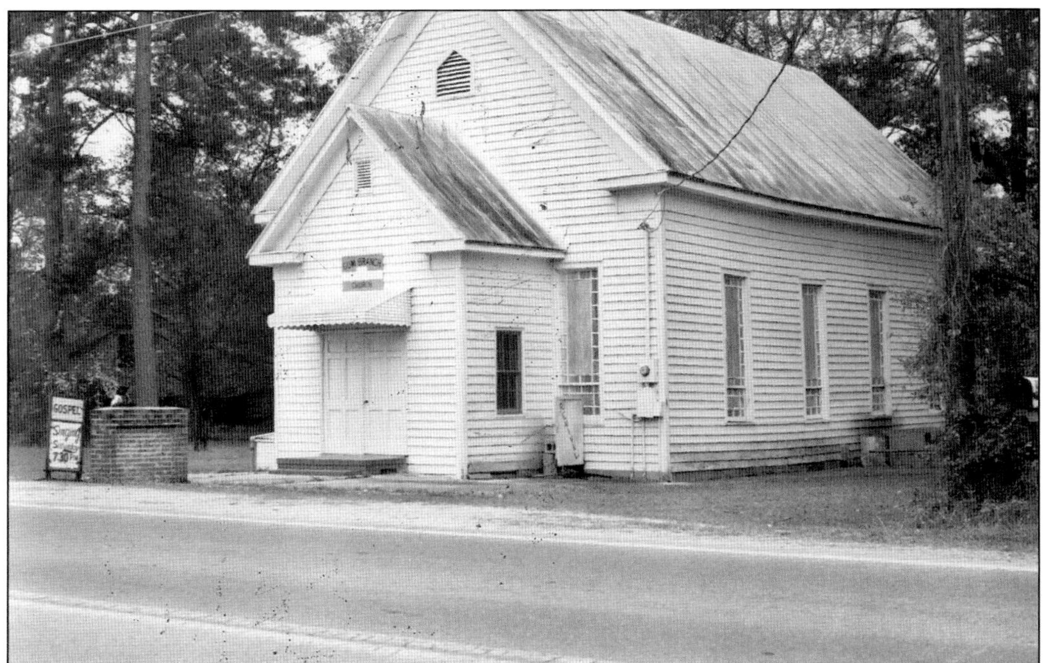

Originally functioning as Gum Branch Baptist Church, this small church has been located on Gum Branch Road near Richlands since the early 20th century. Its charming belfry and milk-glass window panes are a familiar sight to most Onslow residents; the church is still in use as a house of worship. (Courtesy of Onslow County Museum.)

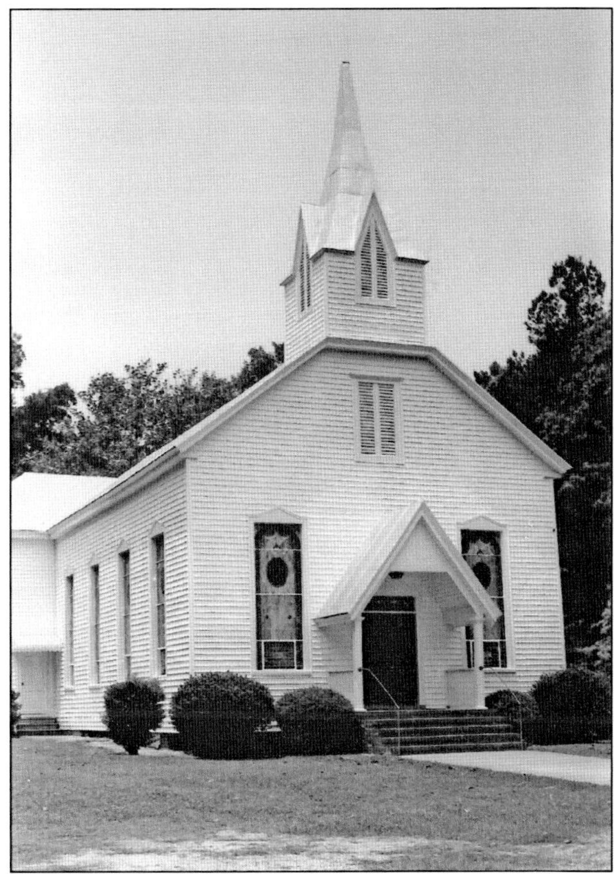

Methodism was embraced in Onslow in the first half of the 19th century. After a series of brush arbor revivals, a congregation was formed near Palo Alto Plantation on the Belgrade-Swansboro Road. It is traditionally thought that David W. Sanders gave money to ensure that his slaves could go to the church, hence the original slave galleries, which have since been removed from the current Tabernacle United Methodist Church. (Courtesy of Onslow County Museum.)

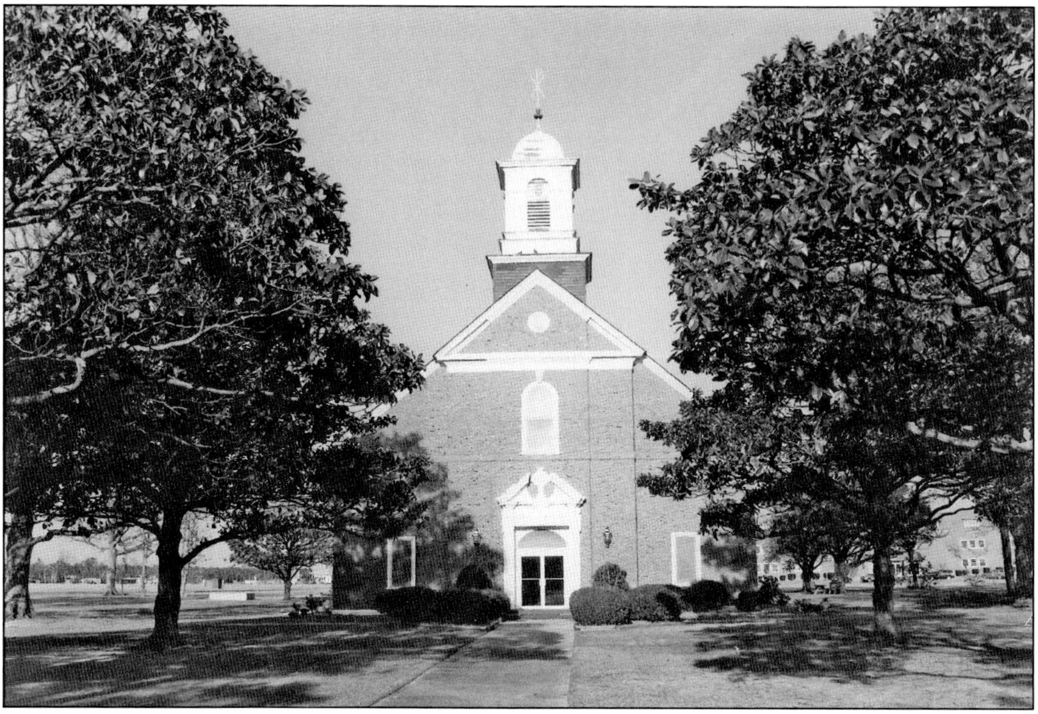

The Protestant Chapel on Camp Lejeune, built in 1942, is known for its beautiful stained-glass windows, designed by Katherine Lamb Tait and produced by Lamb Studios. Each of nine side windows depicts an archangel, flanked by historical scenes from US Marine Corps history; the 10th window features the figure of Victory. (Courtesy of Onslow County Museum.)

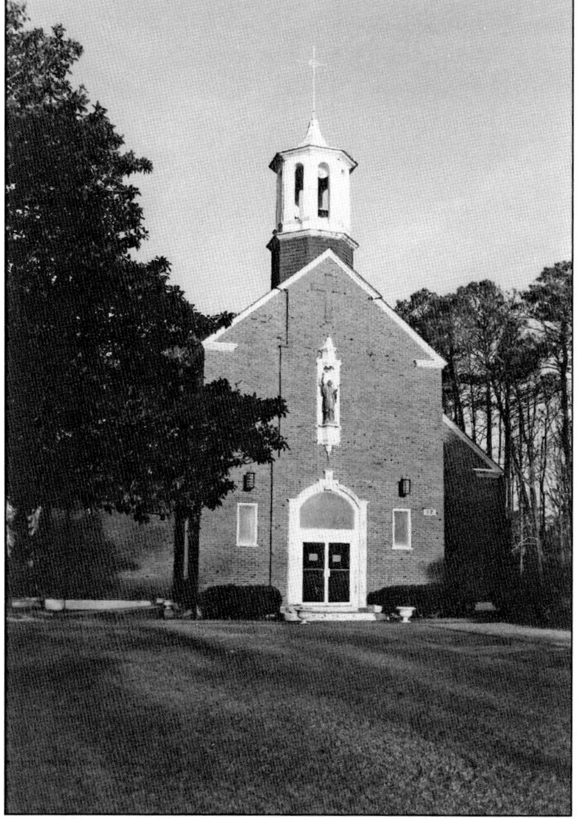

Camp Lejeune's St. Francis Xavier Catholic Chapel was built concurrently with the Protestant chapel. It also features stained glass by Katherine Lamb Tait, depicting heroic saints of the Catholic Church. (Courtesy of Onslow County Museum.)

Five

School Days

Most of the earliest residents of Onslow County were not well educated; in fact, most were probably illiterate. Formal schools were rarely available, and children were generally educated by their parents or other literate relative. But even in colonial times, there was an awareness that education was necessary in the upbringing of a child. When orphans were brought before the justices for placement, their guardians were invariably told to not only teach a trade, but to also "read in the Bible and to write in a good legible hand." Onslow responded to the need for more complete education in 1783 with the chartering of two academies, in Swansboro and Richlands. As the population grew, the older academies were rechartered and newer ones were formed.

The North Carolina General Assembly established a statewide public school system in 1839; Onslow County divided the county into several superintendent-run school districts. By 1858, there were 20 official school districts. School was in session for at least five months, although this varied due to the shortage of schoolhouses. There were also small privately run schools dotted throughout the county by the middle of the 19th century, run by Northern-educated schoolmasters and schoolmarms such as Leonard Woodward at Richlands Academy and Delia Henry at Haws Run. The scourge of the Civil War temporarily halted formal educational pursuits, but as normalcy slowly returned, academies sprang up to fill the void. By 1886, six academies were in session. For African Americans, formal schooling commenced in 1868 with a missionary-run school located in Swansboro.

Walter M. Thompson became superintendent of schools in 1903 and did much to standardize school rules and requirements, such as school time schedules and record keeping. Richlands, always known for its dedication to education, opened the county's first high school in 1912. (The school also housed lower grades.) A countywide plan was established in 1925 to build additional high schools at Dixon, Tabernacle, and Swansboro to complement the ones in Richlands and Jacksonville. The African American school situation remained static, with few schools and teachers. The one bright spot was the emergence of Georgetown School in Jacksonville. The school focused on excellence, which was reflected in its accreditation by the Southern Association of Colleges and Secondary Schools.

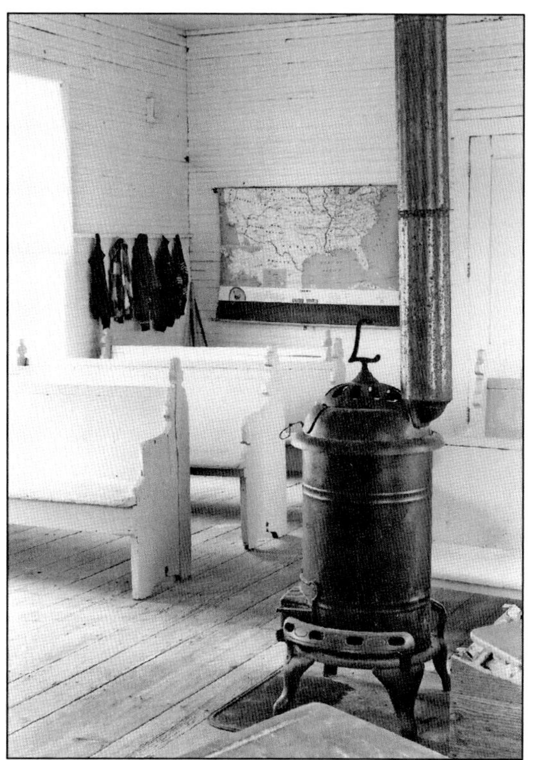

The land for the Adams Schoolhouse on Huffmantown Road in Richlands was given for the establishment of a school by William M. Barbee in the late 1880s. The restored interior, shown here, exemplifies the one-room schoolhouse of the era; Barbee, a carpenter, also made the pupils' wooden benches. (Courtesy of Onslow County Museum.)

The Richlands Graded School opened in about 1910, replacing Richlands Academy, and was heartily welcomed by area families eager for a good education for their children. The two-story structure, located on Academy Street, served all grades; the postcard view seen here shows faculty and students in about 1912. (Courtesy of Onslow County Museum.)

RICHLANDS GRADED SCHOOL, RICHLANDS, N. C.

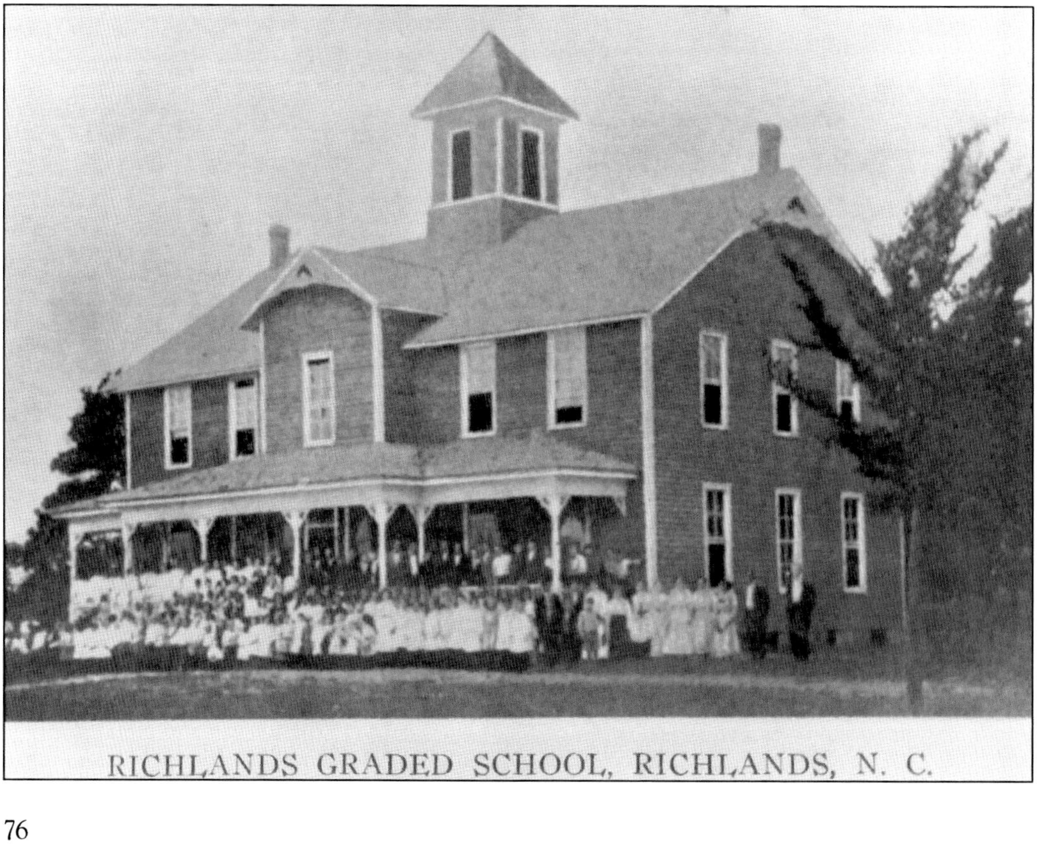

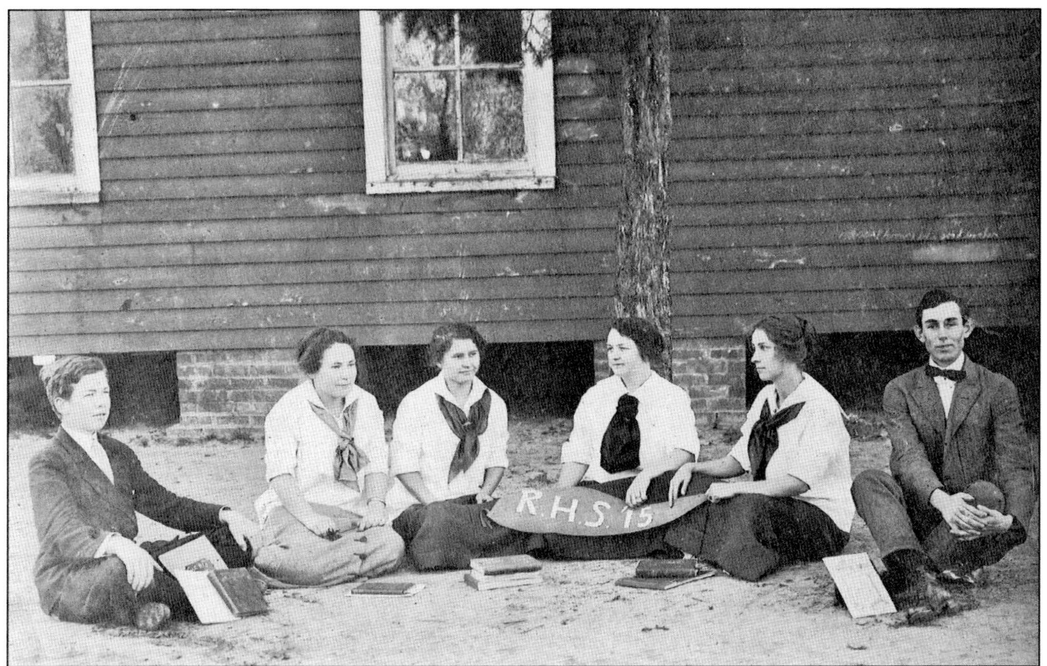

One of the early graduating classes is pictured here. Four young ladies, a young man, and their teacher proudly display a 1915 Richlands High School graduation banner. (Courtesy of Onslow County Museum.)

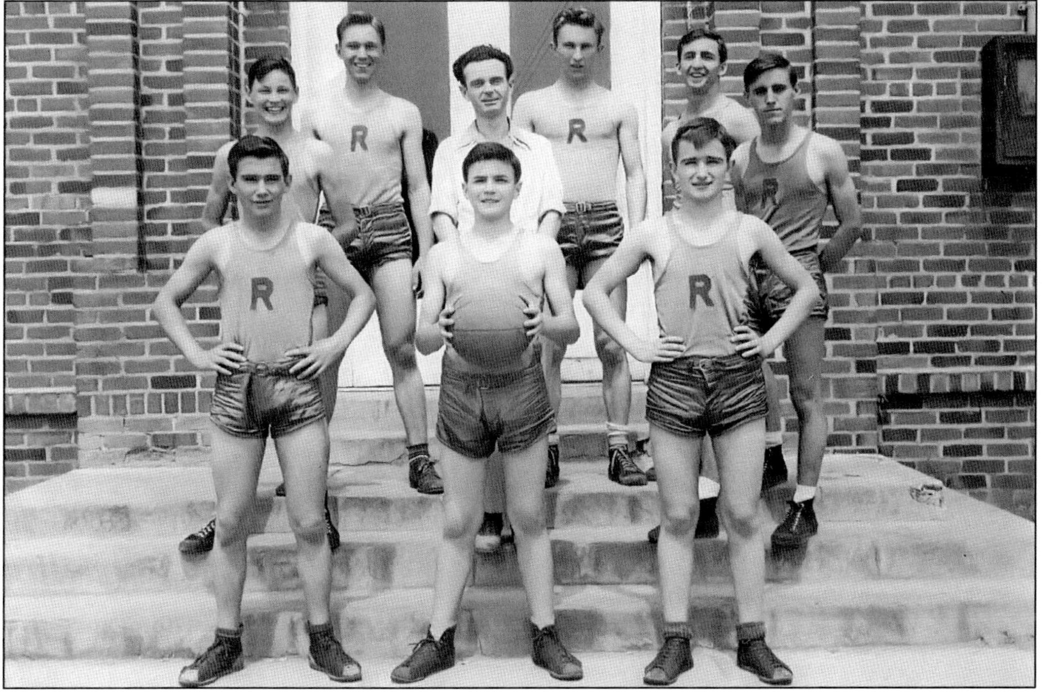

Basketball was a popular sport in high schools; it required little equipment, and the rules were simple. In 1947, the Richlands boys' basketball team and coach pose for a group picture on the steps of Richlands High School. (Courtesy of Onslow County Museum.)

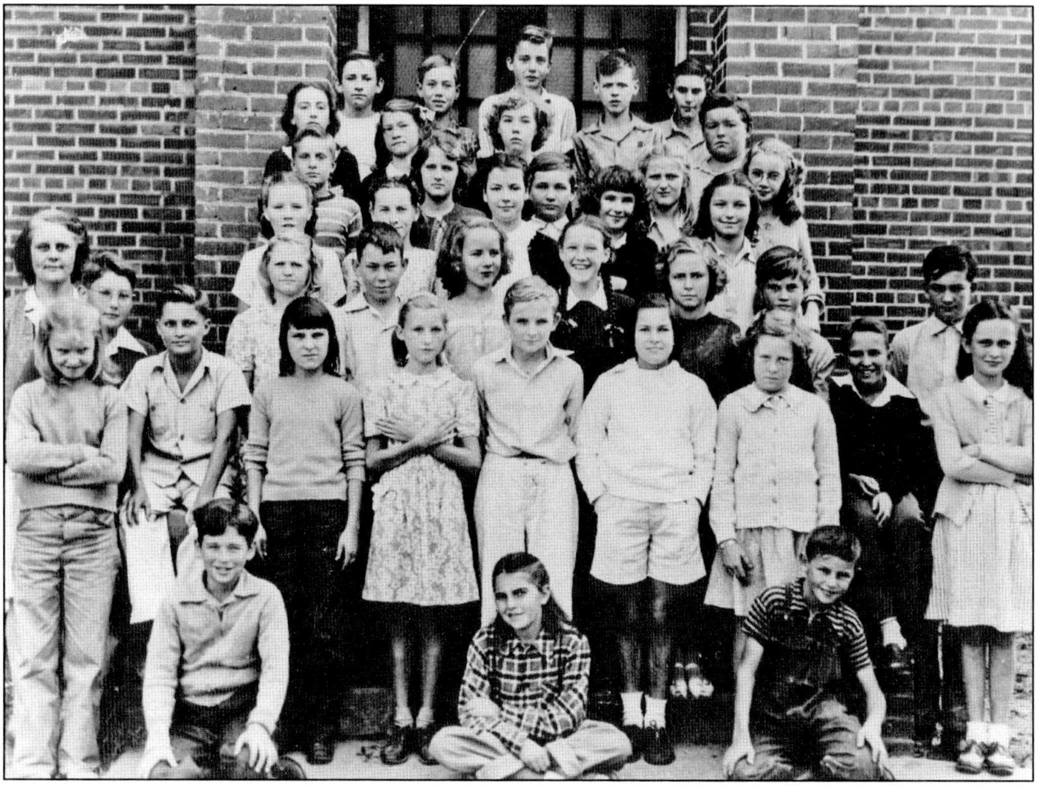

A group of elementary school children poses in front of the Richlands Elementary School probably in the late 1940s. Rural children were dressed better than their counterparts a decade before World War II. (Courtesy of Onslow County Museum.)

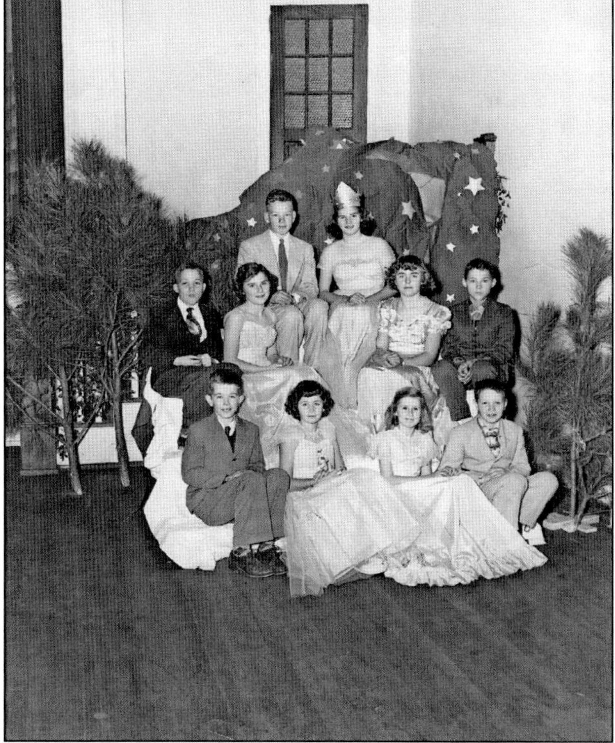

Kings and queens of each class were chosen annually in Richlands Elementary School. The lucky royalty pose for a picture in about 1953. The youngsters in the first row at left are Byron Ervin and Jo Bell. (Courtesy of Onslow County Museum.)

Richlands High School also elected a homecoming king and queen. Pictured here is Joyce Bell with her date in 1953. Bell later married US representative John P. Murtha Jr. (Courtesy of Onslow County Museum.)

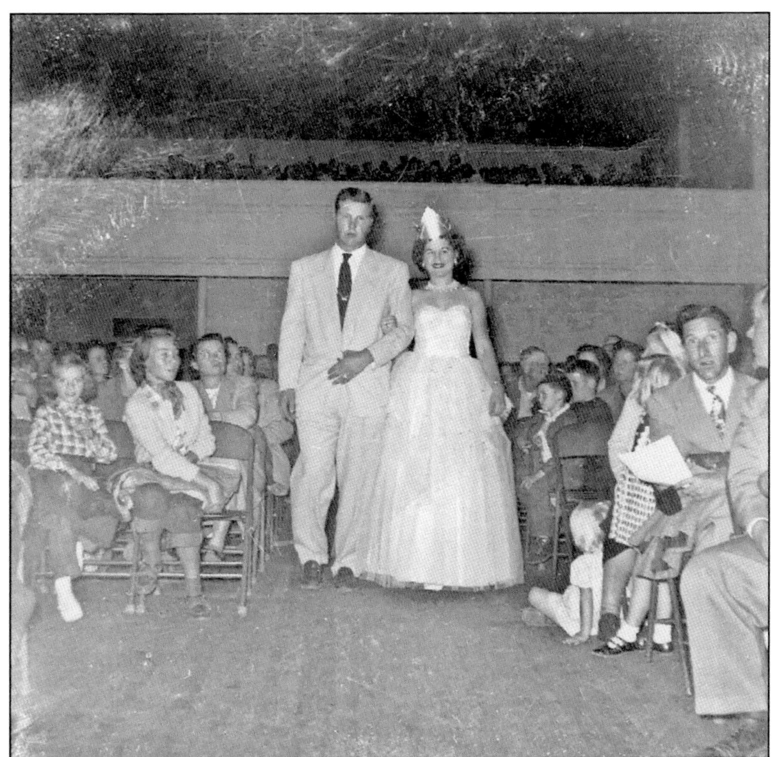

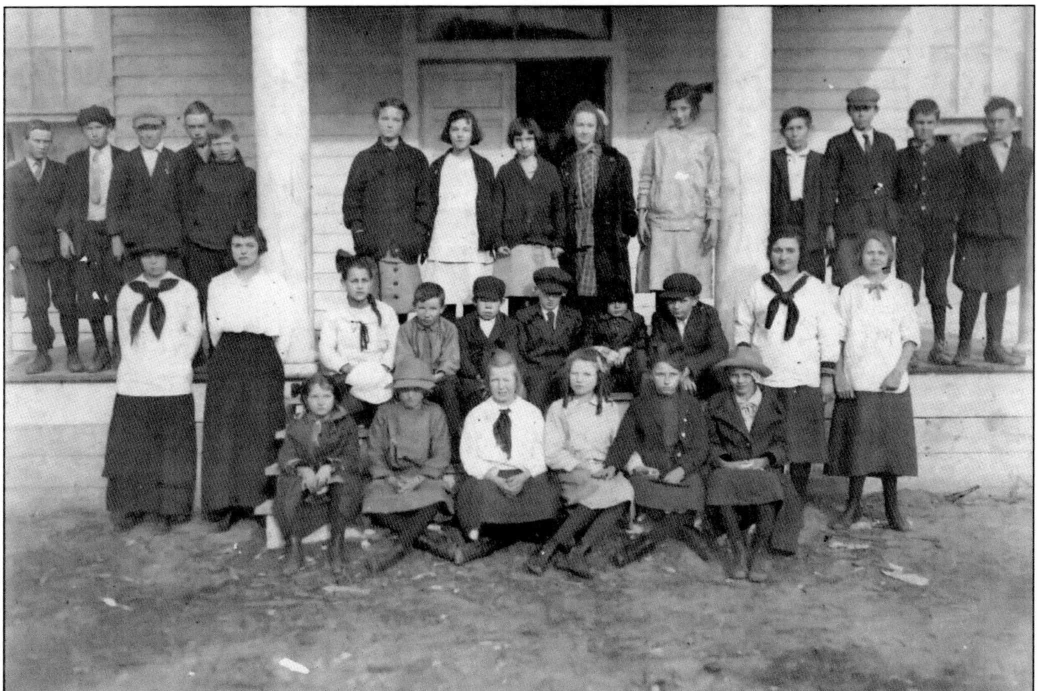

The Swansboro Graded School opened to great fanfare in 1911. Robert Lee Smith is believed to have been the principal carpenter. Here, a group of students poses on the front porch in about 1915. (Courtesy of State Archives of North Carolina.)

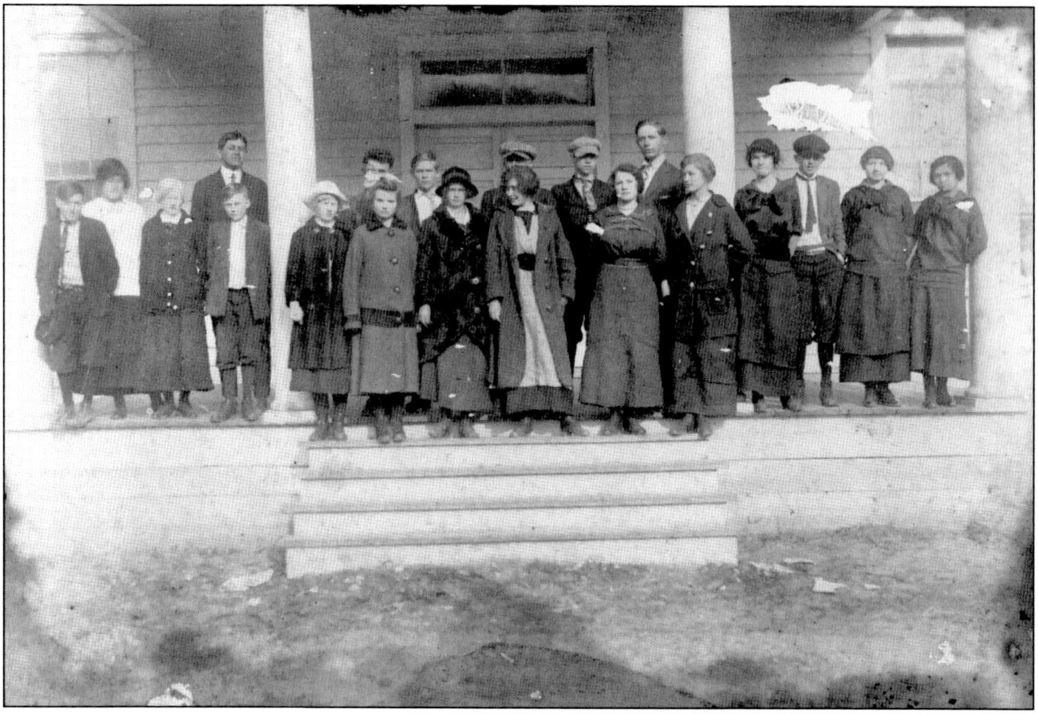

Another group of faculty and students is pictured here on the porch of the Swansboro Graded School in about 1920. (Courtesy of State Archives of North Carolina.)

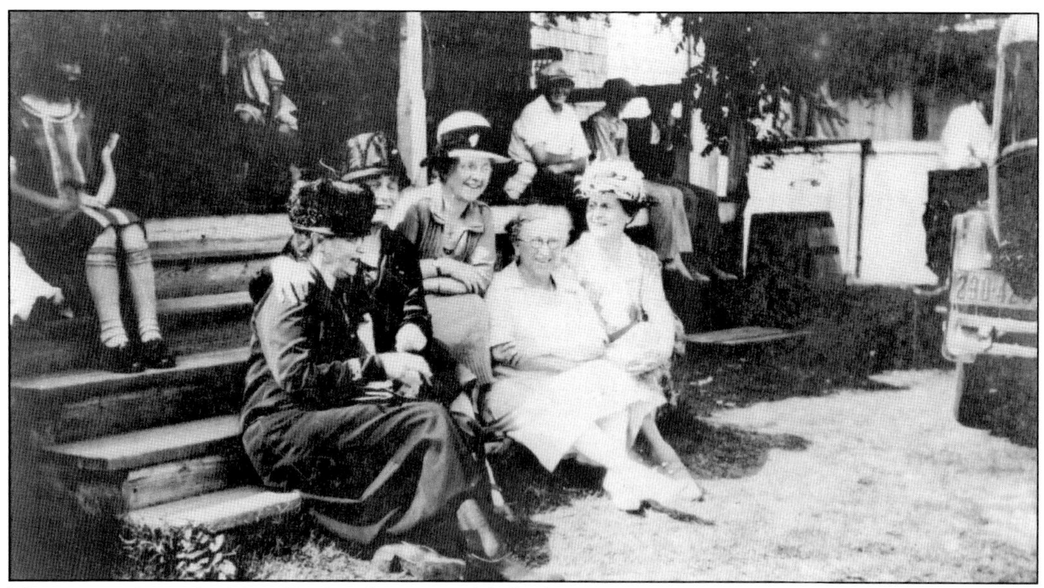

Unitarians from the New England area established a presence in Swansboro beginning in about 1902. The Reverend Margaret Barnard, pictured here (in the center, hatless) surrounded by her faculty members, was a driving force behind the Emmerton School. (Courtesy of State Archives of North Carolina.)

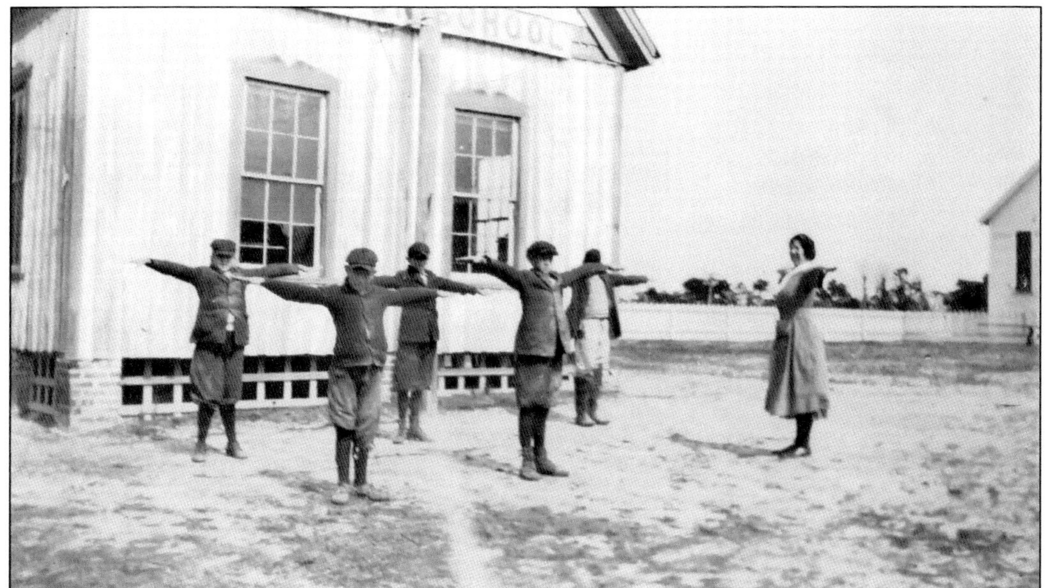

Students exercise with their teacher at the Emmerton School in about 1920. The Unitarians had made Swansboro one of their missionary efforts, pouring time, energy, and money into welfare and education. Although they appreciated the benefits, not many locals became Unitarian. (Courtesy of State Archives of North Carolina.)

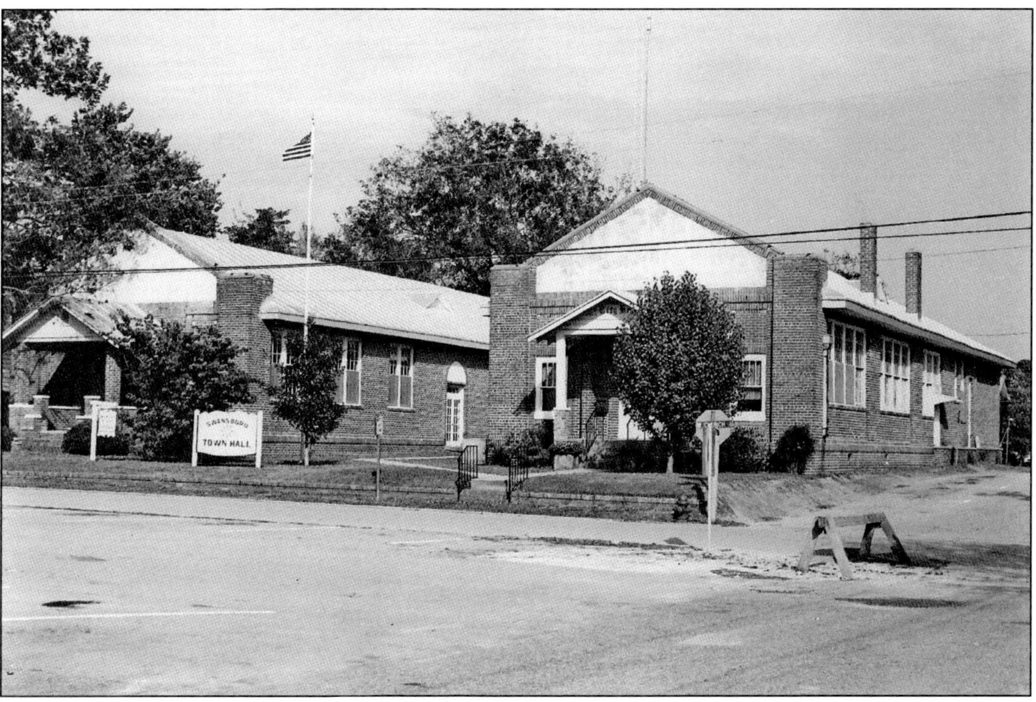

Forging ahead with their mission, the Unitarians and Reverend Barnard amassed enough funding to build a new Emmerton School in 1928. Shortly thereafter, Barnard returned to New England and the school declined. A fire in 1930 closed the school, and it was later reopened as the Methodist church until 1968, when it became the city hall. (Courtesy of Onslow County Museum.)

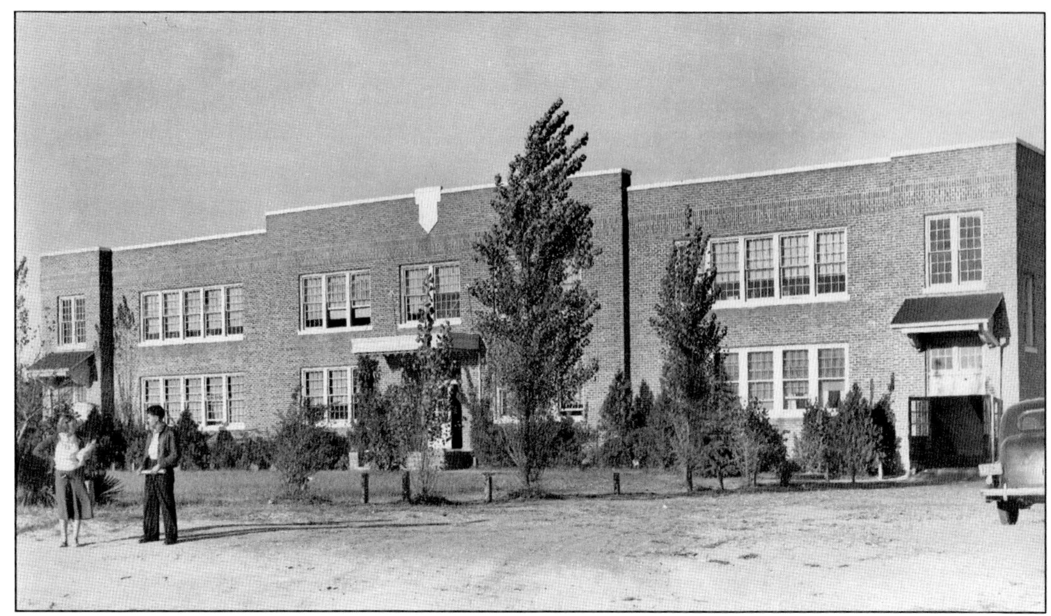

In 1930, a new brick school was built on Main Street Extension in Swansboro. This image was taken in the late 1930s. Many years later, when a new high school was erected and occupied, this building was adaptively remodeled for use as condominiums. (Courtesy of Onslow County Museum.)

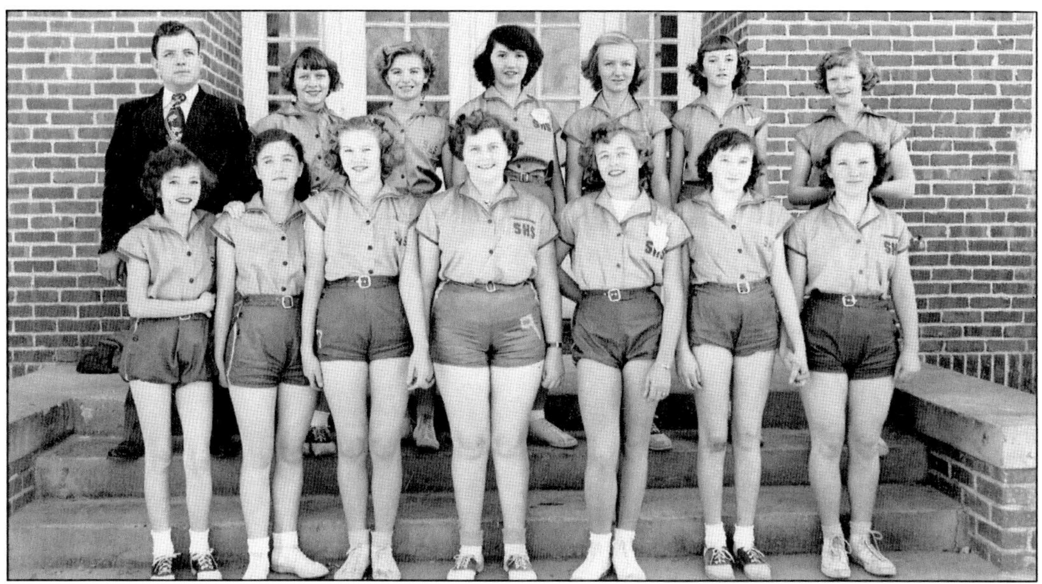

Thirteen members of the Swansboro High School girls' basketball team are pictured here with their coach in about 1952. Conchita "Connie" Riggs is in the first row, fifth from left, and Nelda Howell is directly behind her. (Courtesy of Onslow County Museum.)

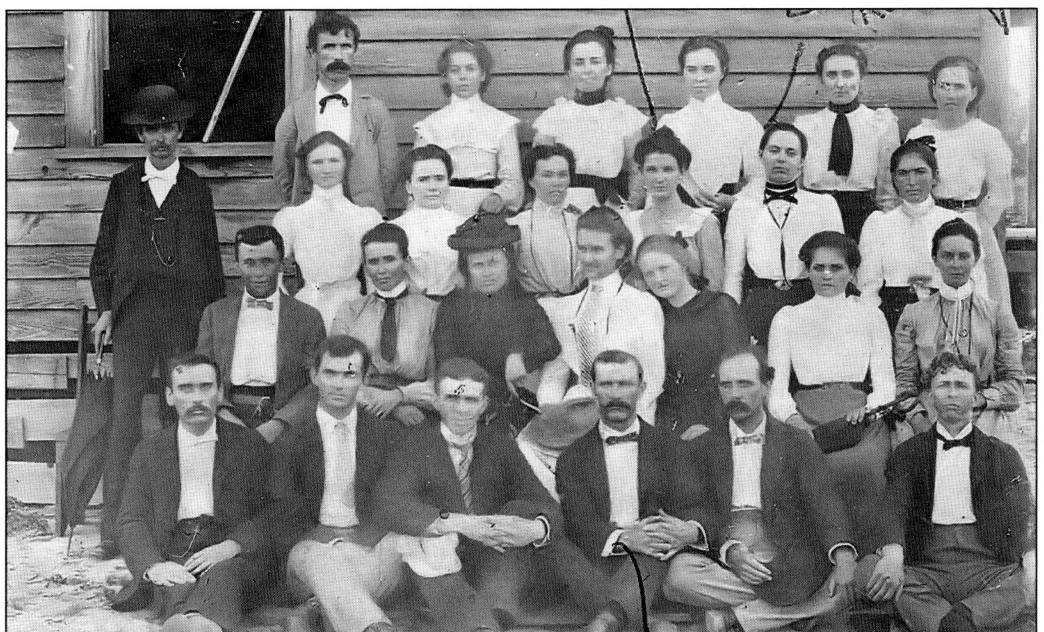

An assembly of Onslow County's teachers in about 1900 is seen here, possibly at one of the many one-room schoolhouses. Nicholas A. "Nick" Burton (1873–1962) is seated in the middle of the first row, fourth from left. His wife, Ella Gurganus, also a teacher, is in the third row. They married in 1903; their farm was on land that is now the N.A. Burton Park, home to businesses and to the Onslow County Administration Complex. (Courtesy of Onslow County Museum.)

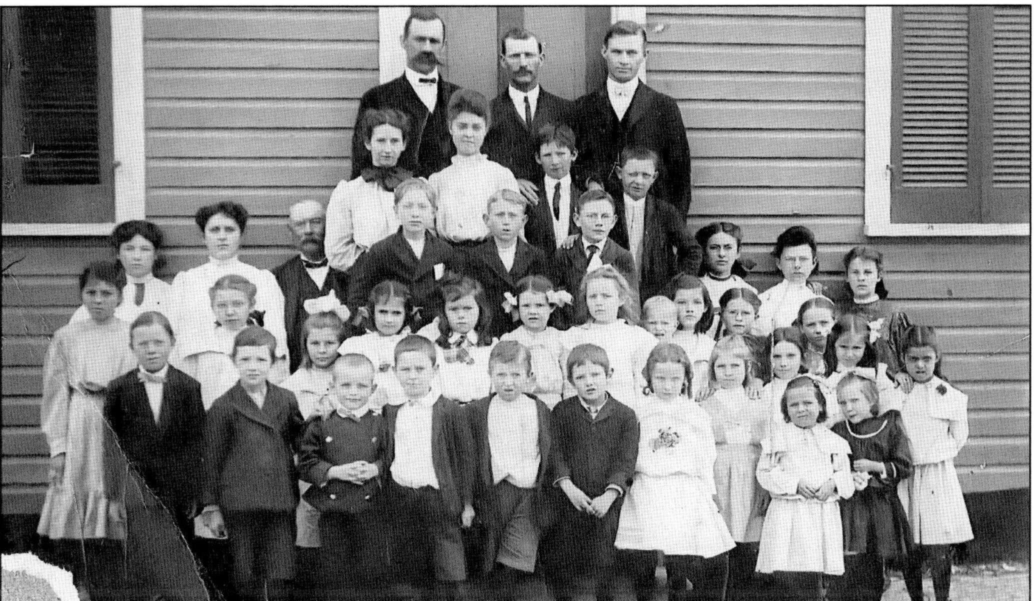

Students of all grades and their teachers pose on the steps of the old Jacksonville School, located in the downtown Jacksonville vicinity on what was commonly known as "schoolhouse lot," facing Third Street and bounded by Mill Avenue. Schoolmaster Nick A. Burton stands in the center of the fifth row. He taught at many different schools throughout the county from the 1890s to about 1905. (Courtesy of Onslow County Museum.)

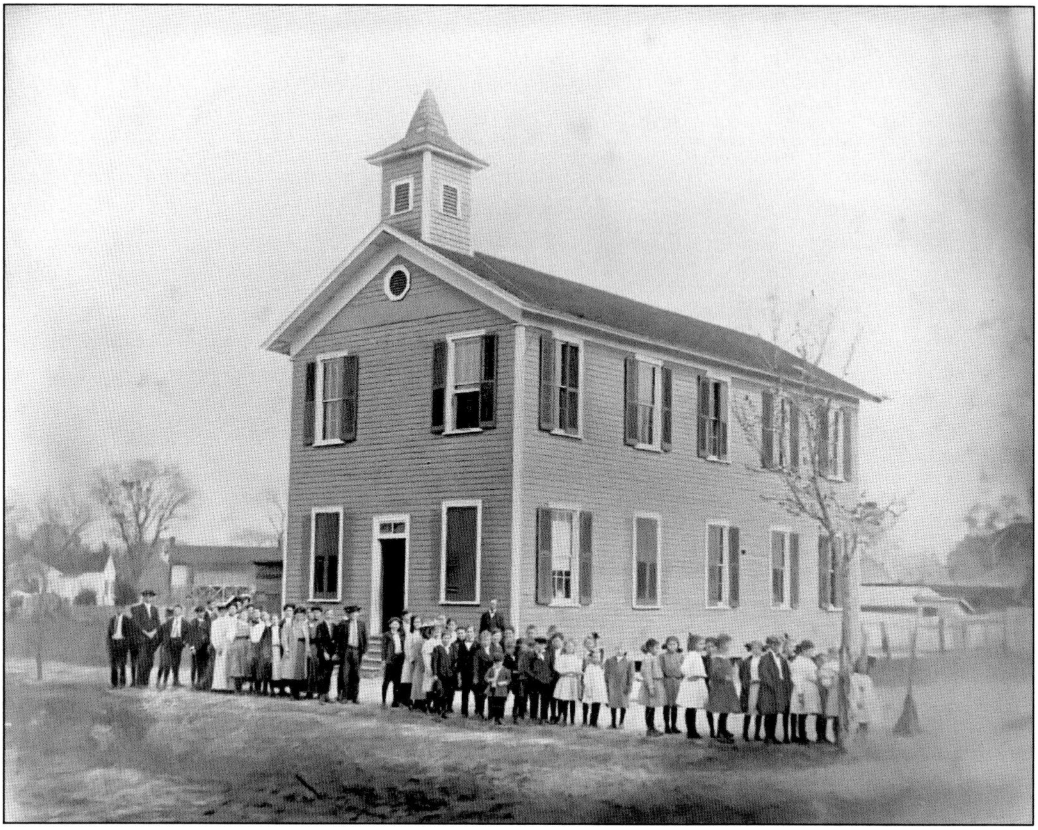

This is another view of the two-story wooden Jacksonville School in the old downtown area of Jacksonville. All students were assembled in front for this early 1900s photograph. The principal, H.M. Loy, stands behind the line of children. (Courtesy of Onslow County Museum.)

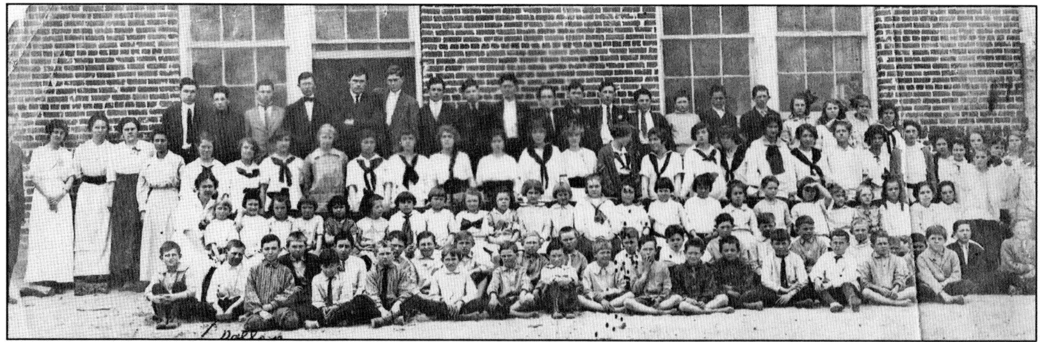

Students and faculty gather in front of the brick Jacksonville Graded School in about 1911. Dalton Burton, son of Nick and Ella Burton, is the little boy sitting in the front row, second from left. The school taught up to the eleventh grade, which was required to complete a high school diploma. (Courtesy of Onslow County Museum.)

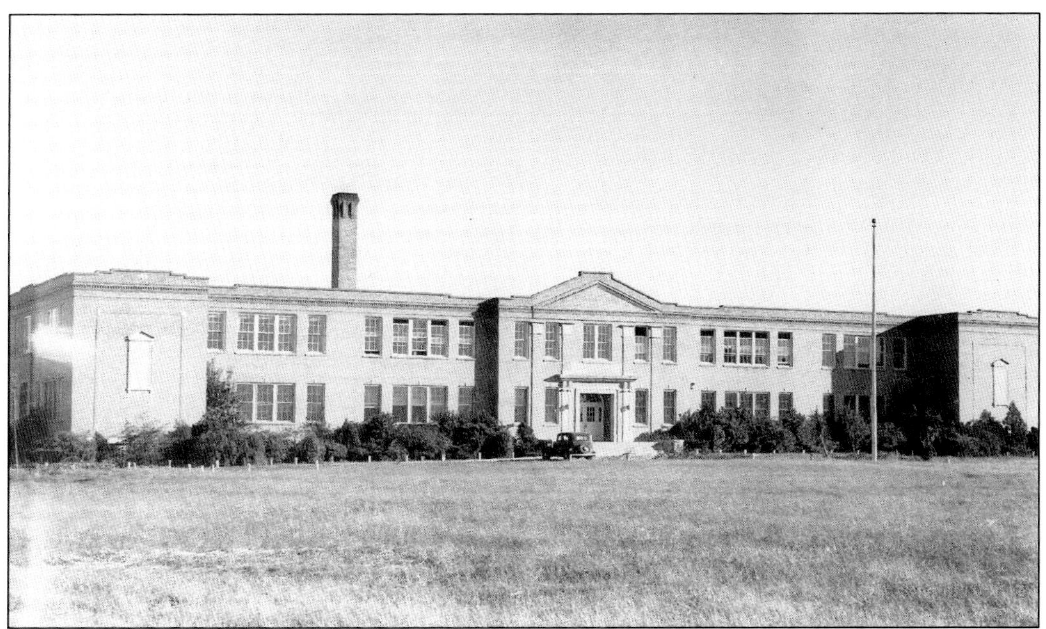

Jacksonville's high school was the second established in the county. This large brick school with classical elements was built in the late 1920s on New Bridge Street. In 1933, the state took over the operation of all schools, and for the first time, many students were required to attend school eight months a year. (Courtesy of Onslow County Museum.)

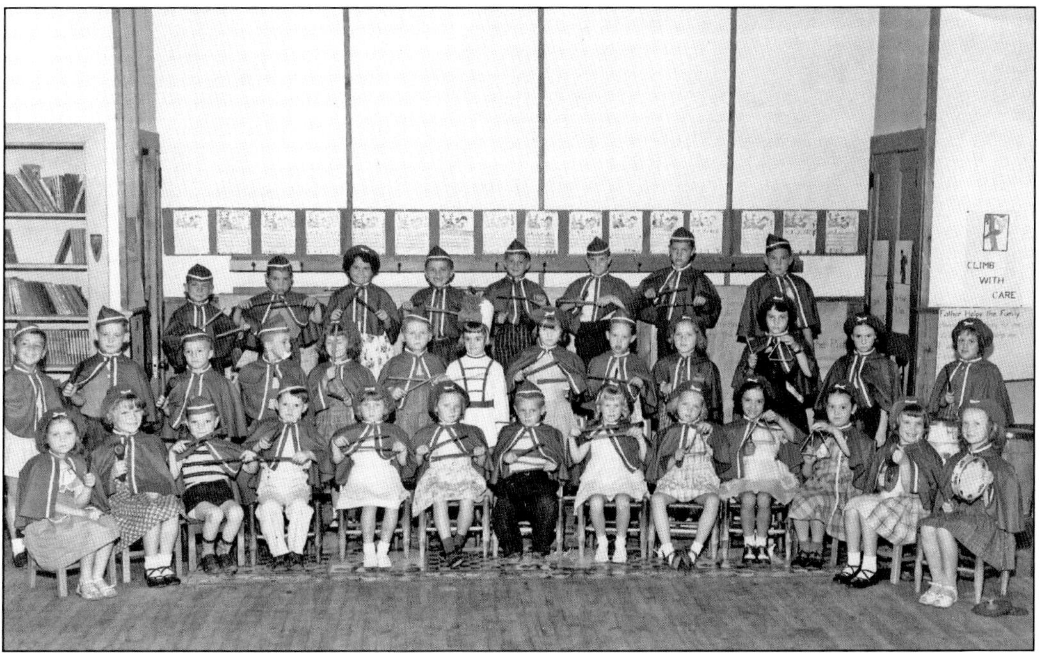

Rhythm bands in elementary schools were popular all over the nation in the 1940s and 1950s. The young Thompson Elementary music students in this 1950s image are outfitted with capes and caps for a performance with triangles, cymbals, tambourines, drums, and rhythm sticks. The school was named in 1954 for Walter M. Thompson, educator and longtime superintendent of schools. (Courtesy of Onslow County Museum.)

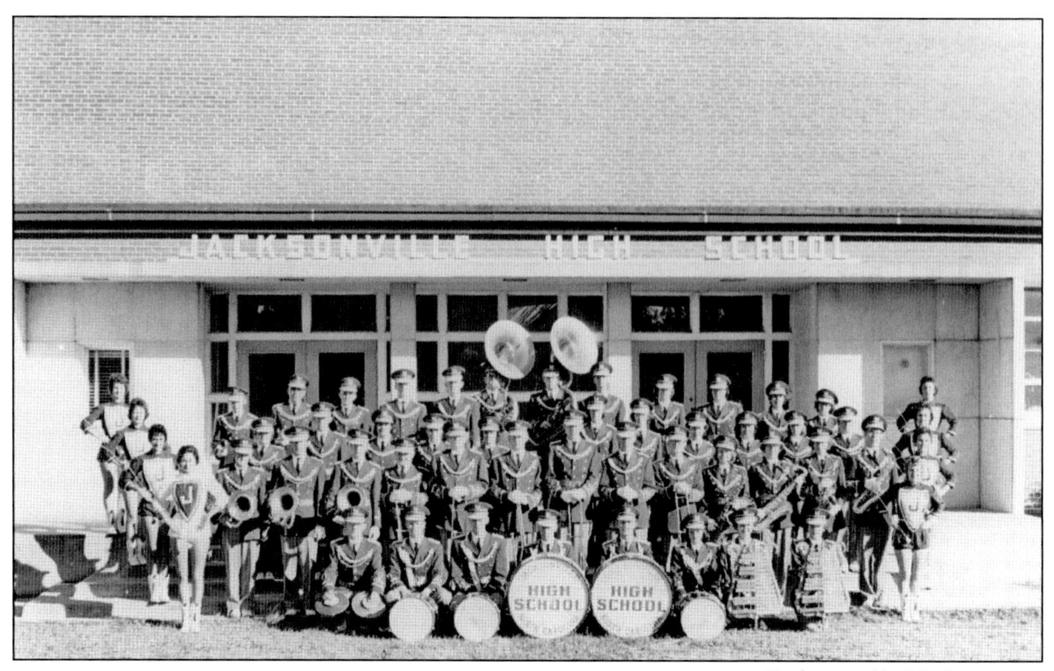

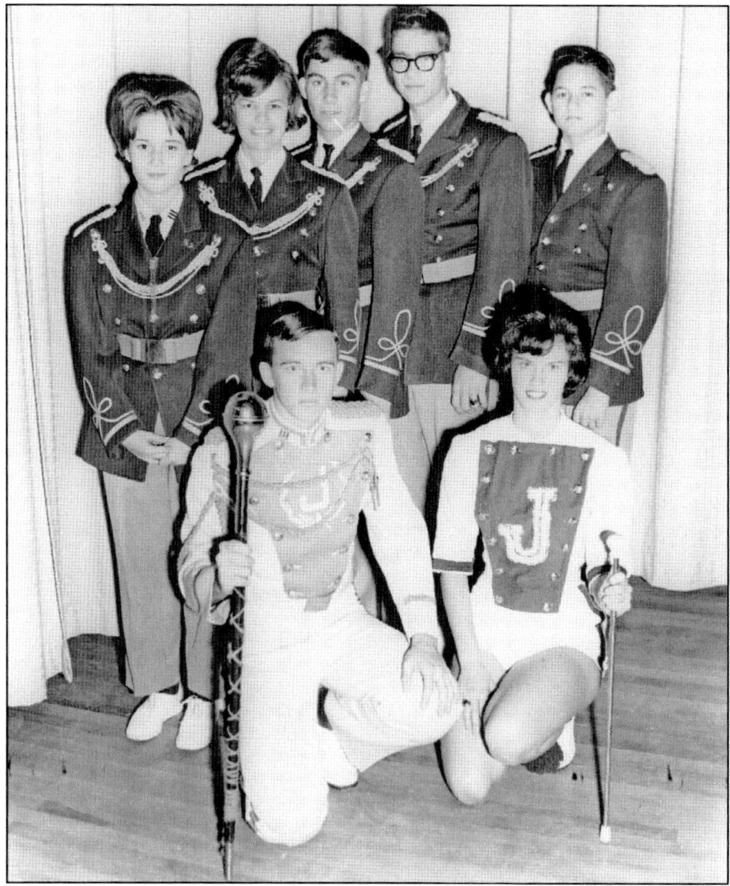

Jacksonville High School on Henderson Drive replaced the high school on New Bridge Street, which became a middle school. The school has always had an excellent band program; here, in the early 1960s, the band poses for a picture at the school. (Courtesy of Onslow County Museum.)

Posing here are Jacksonville High School band officers in 1964. Ron Singletary is the drum major kneeling in front. He later became superintendent of Onslow County Schools. (Courtesy of Onslow County Museum.)

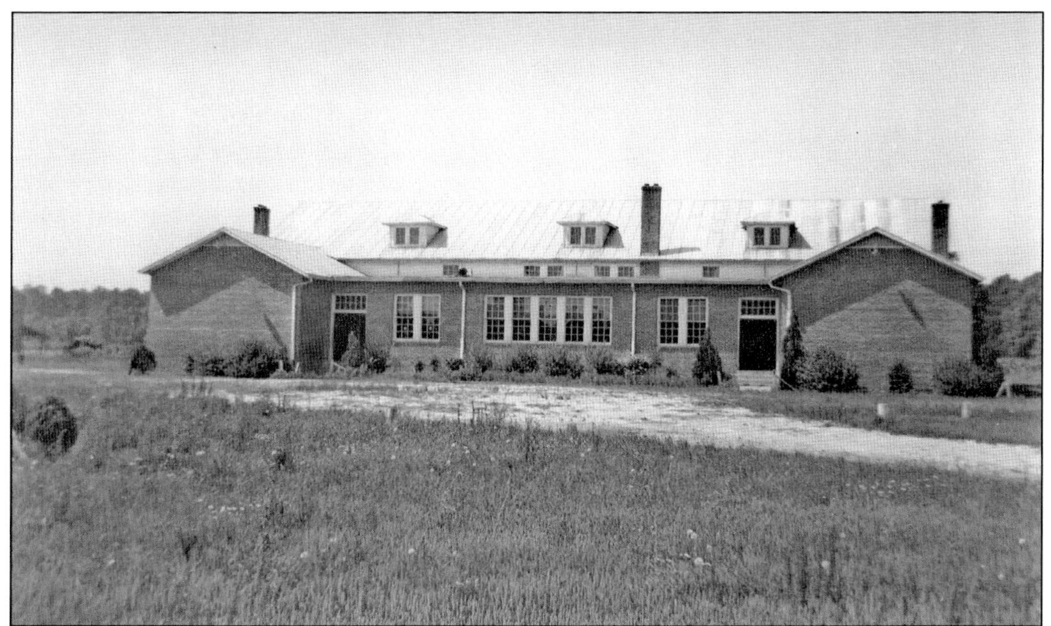

Georgetown School was located in the Georgetown area west of Jacksonville. During segregation, this was the only African American high school in Onslow County; it also housed elementary grades. Georgetown began as a private boarding school in 1908 but was taken over by Onslow County in 1919. Built in 1939 as a WPA project, the school had 12 classrooms, an auditorium/gymnasium, 2 restrooms, a principal's office, and storage rooms. Georgetown closed in 1966 due to desegregation. (Courtesy of Onslow County Museum.)

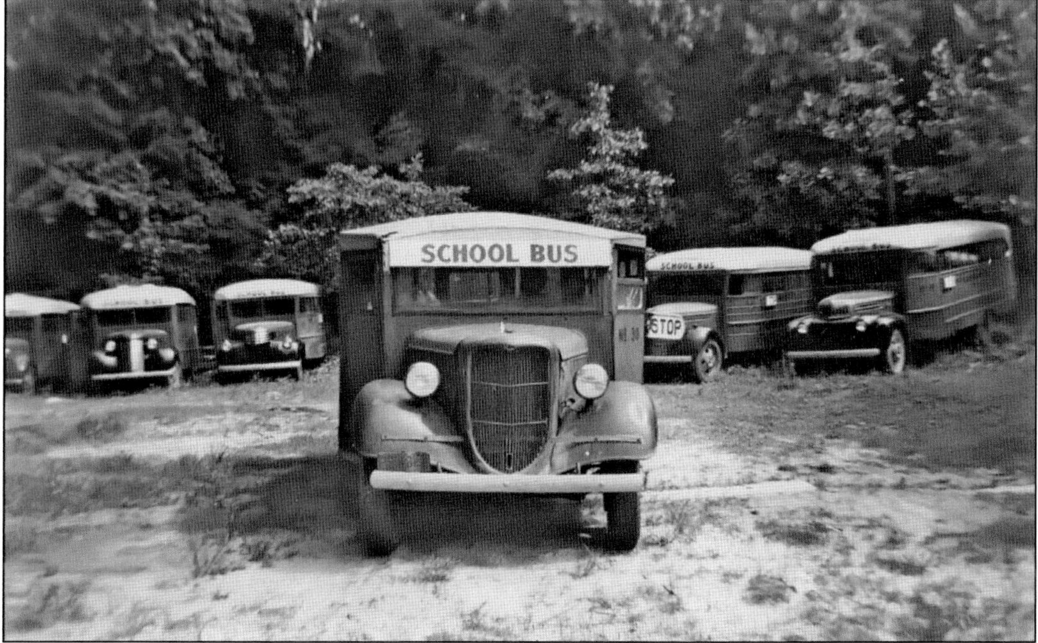

Georgetown School buses—or trucks, as they were often called—brought children to the school who otherwise would have had to walk long distances or not attend at all. (Courtesy of Onslow County Museum.)

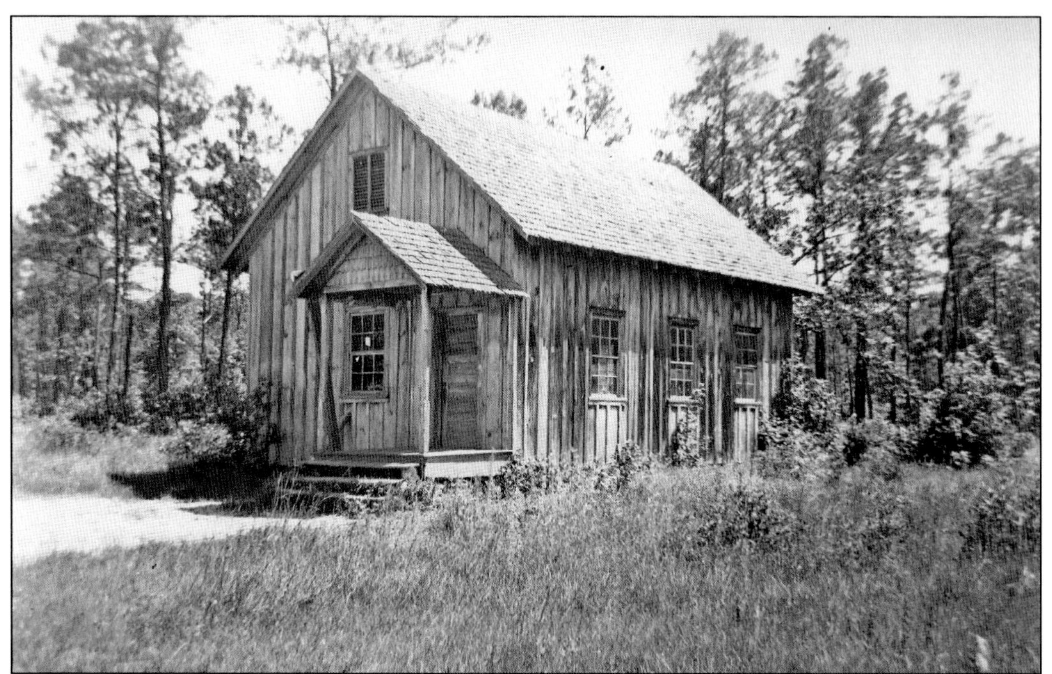
The frame-built Angola School for African American children was located in the southwest part of the county. (Courtesy of Onslow County Museum.)

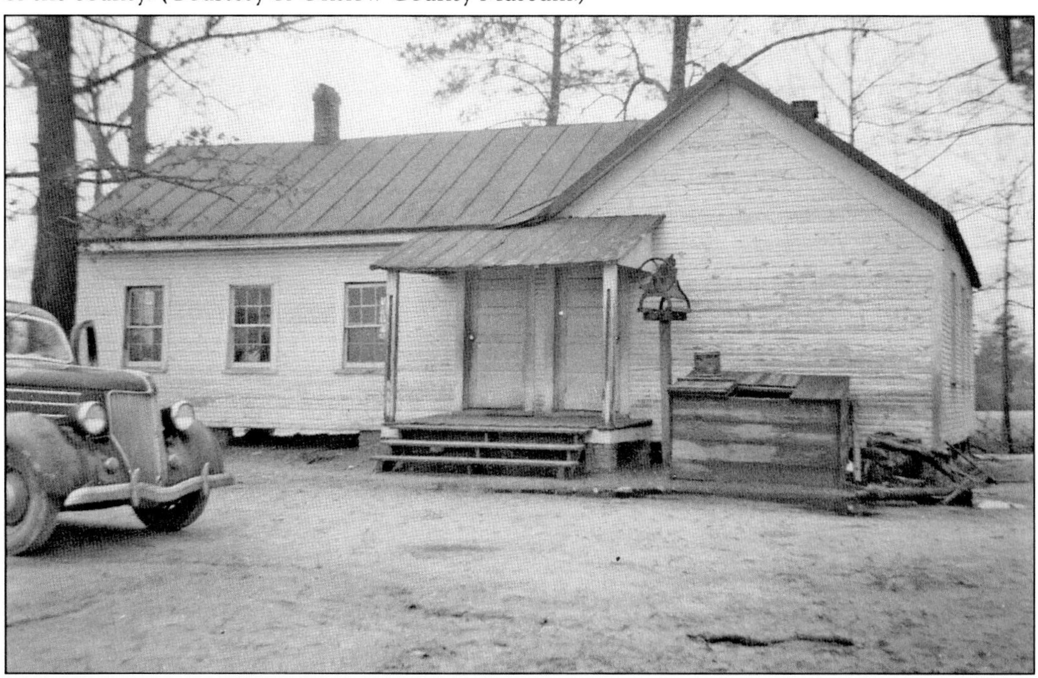
Located about five miles south of Richlands on Highway 24, Edney Chapel School is still standing on the grounds of Edney Chapel. Built between 1900 and 1905 for local African American children, the two-room schoolhouse was considered inadequate and in need of repair by 1947. The windows were protected by window shades bought by the teachers, who worked from homemade wooden tables. (Courtesy of Onslow County Museum.)

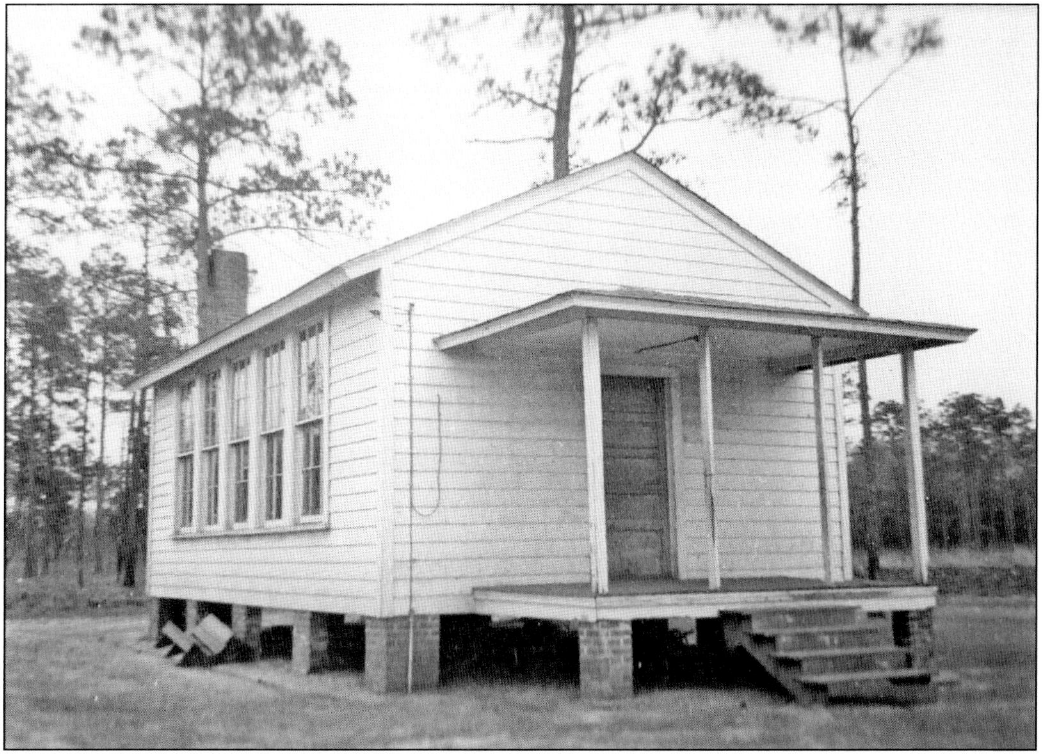

Kellumtown School was located about 8.5 miles southeast of Jacksonville on Highway 24. The 17-by-30-foot schoolroom was illuminated by a single lightbulb. Drinking water was obtained from an outdoor pump, and the children brought their own cups from home. (Courtesy of Onslow County Museum.)

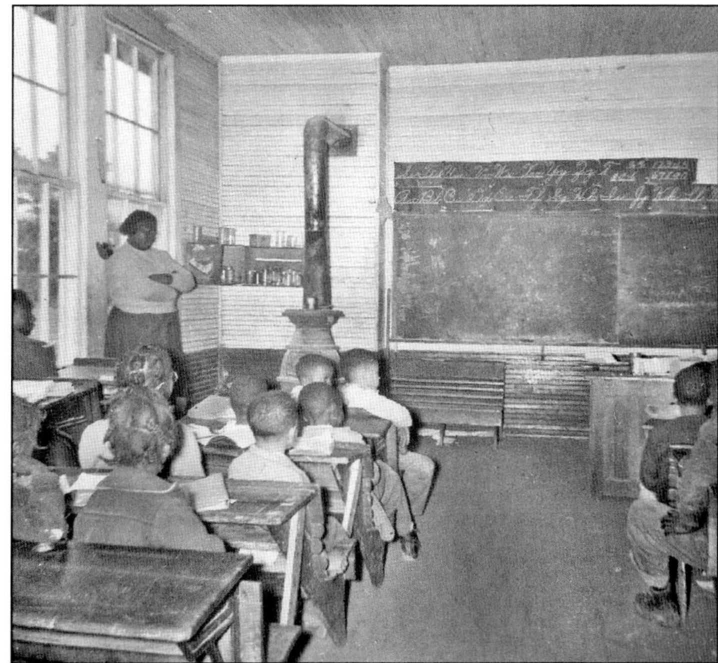

This image of the interior of the Kellumtown School was taken in 1948 by Edward N. Farnell, who took a series of photographs for illustrations in his master's thesis on black schooling in Onslow County. (Courtesy of Onslow County Museum.)

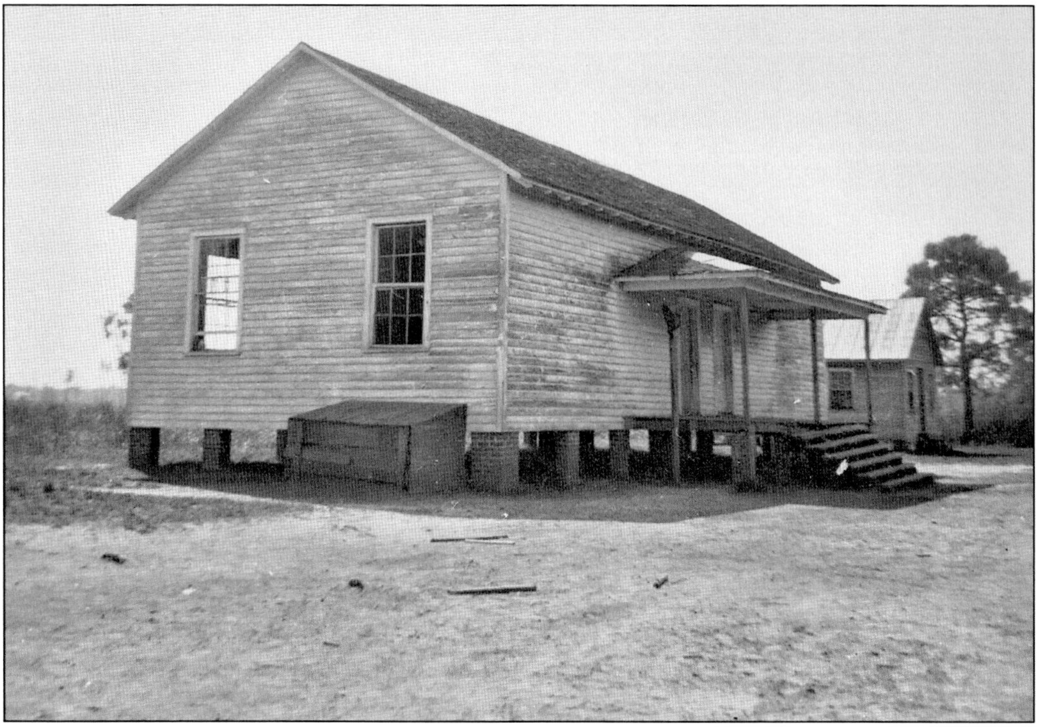

Belgrade School was an African American school located on the Belgrade-Swansboro Road. (Courtesy of Onslow County Museum.)

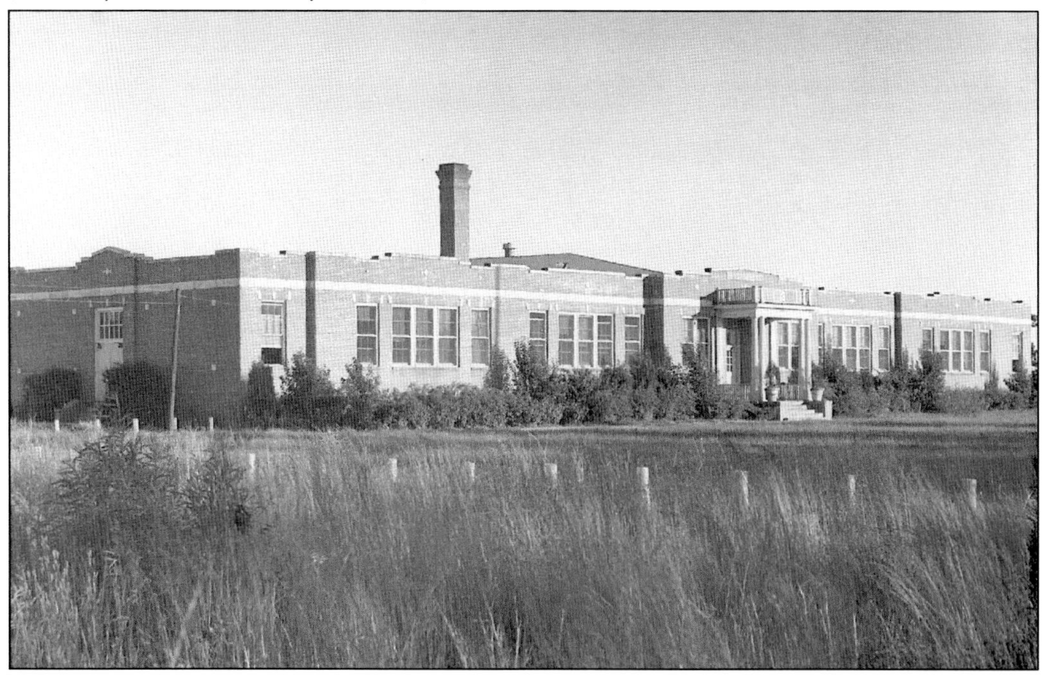

Tabernacle School was located on the Belgrade-Swansboro Road. It was built as a consolidated school in 1927 by Simon and Sons, out of Wilmington. It was closed in the 1990s and was later destroyed by a fire. (Courtesy of Onslow County Museum.)

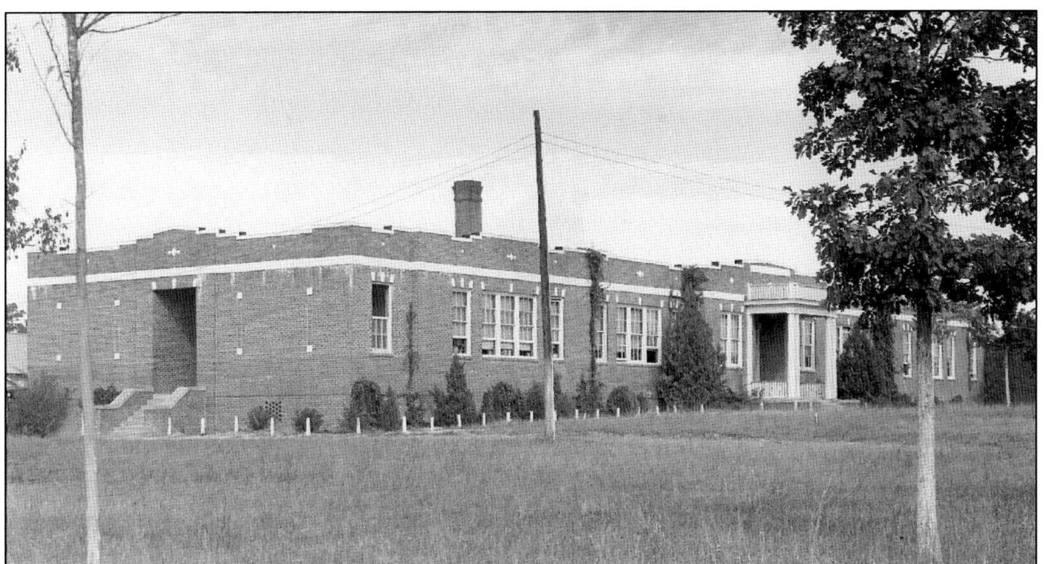

This image of Dixon School was taken in the late 1930s; the school was built a decade before as a part of a countywide plan to establish a high school in each township. Dixon was established on Highway 17 for the Stump Sound township in spite of opposition from some who wanted it built in Sneads Ferry. (Courtesy of Onslow County Museum.)

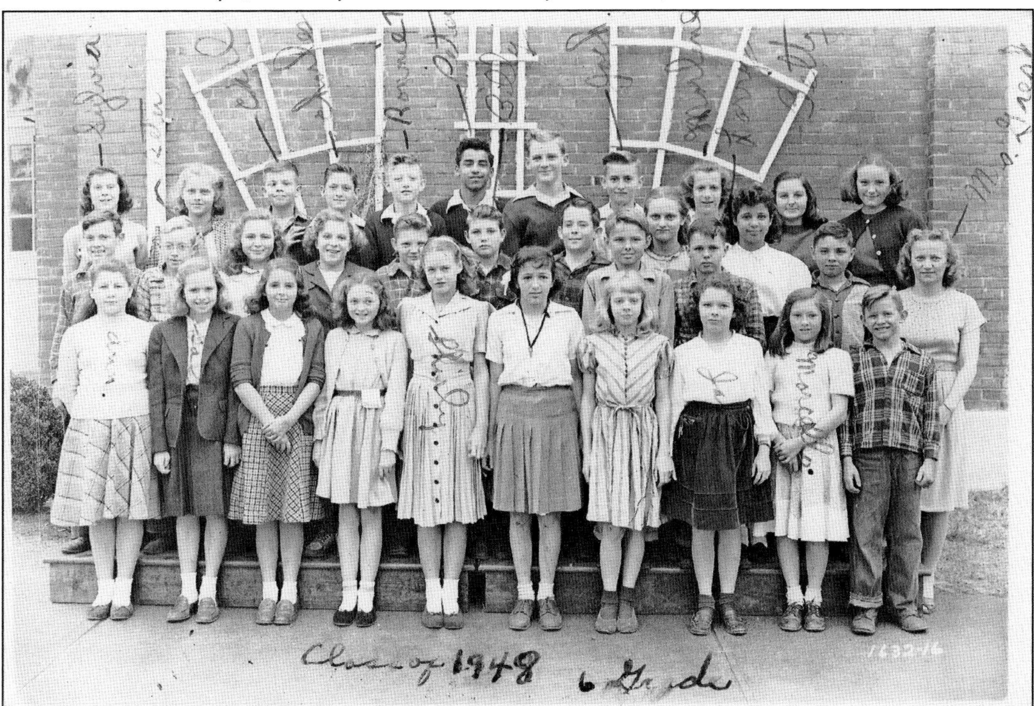

With the establishment of Camp Lejeune came the need for education for the children of families, both military and civilian, that lived on the base. The War Department set up a school on base, initially attended by all grades. Here, the sixth grade at Camp Lejeune School poses for a class picture in 1948. Robert Royster is in the third row, seventh from left. (Courtesy of Robert Royster.)

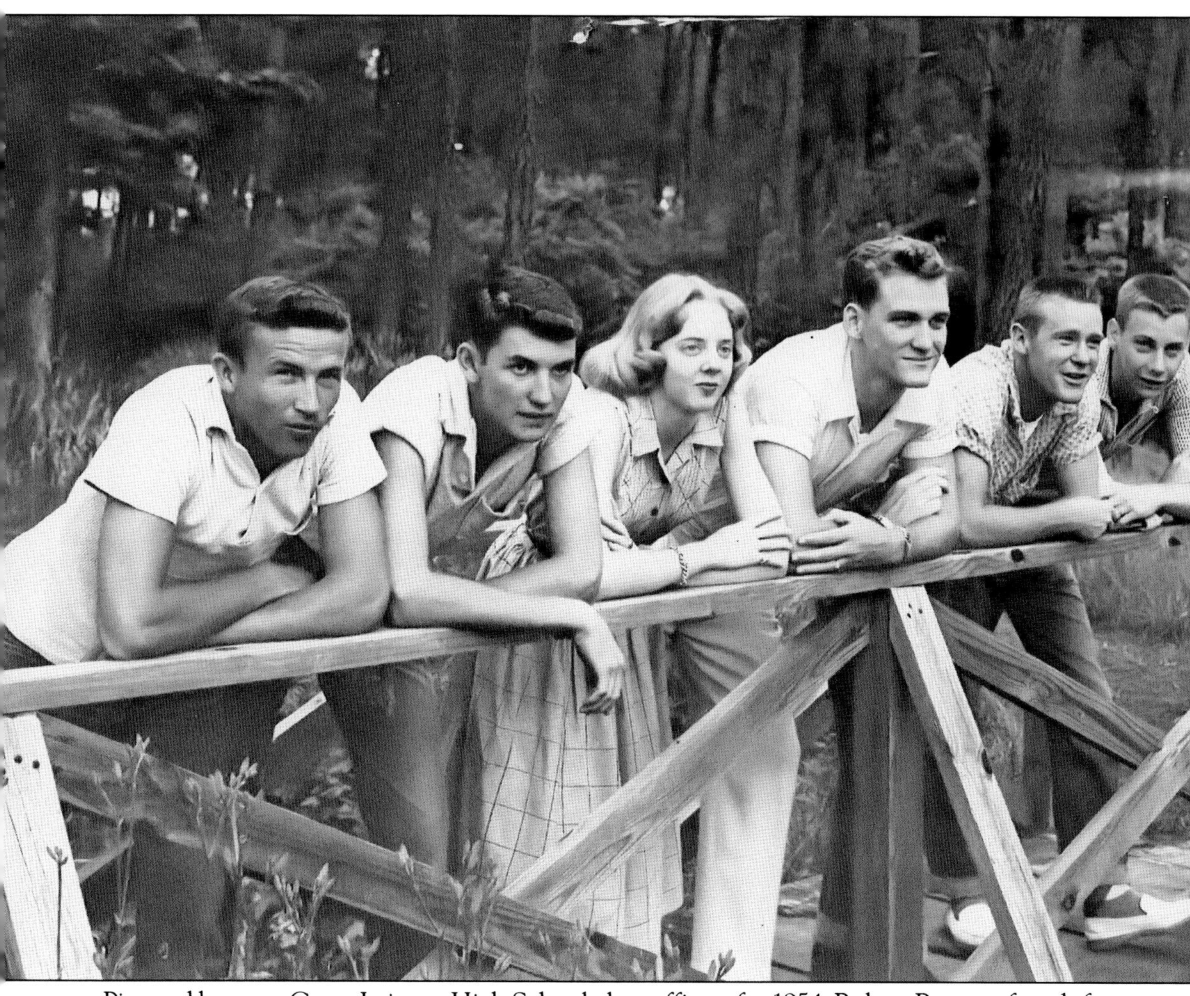

Pictured here are Camp Lejeune High School class officers for 1954. Robert Royster, fourth from left, attended Camp Lejeune schools until he graduated. (Courtesy of Robert Royster.)

Six

Pastimes and Traditions

From the beginnings of settlement to the 20th century, typical pastimes included hunting, fishing, and social gatherings, which usually included dancing, games, and eating. Horse racing was also a popular pursuit. In the rural atmosphere that was Onslow County, typical days were filled with hard, physical work. Leisure pursuits afforded respite from days filled with providing food and shelter for the family.

Banks parties (taking place on the banks of the rivers) and oyster roasts were widely held into the 20th century, and the celebration of Big August at Alum Spring became a well-loved tradition. Wagons—and later, cars—full of people and picnic baskets arrived in the morning for a full day of eating, dancing, socializing, and enjoying the cool mineral waters of the spring. In 1891, it was estimated that between 2,000 and 4,000 people attended the annual celebration, arriving from not only Onslow, but also from several surrounding counties.

Onslow's plentiful supply of fish and game made it the favored destination of sportsmen, both statewide and also hailing from other states. Lodges, clubs, and summerhouses were established by these men, and the fledgling tourism industry slowly grew.

One of the most interesting people to regularly visit Onslow was Herbert H. Brimley (1861–1946). Born in England, Brimley made his home in North Carolina at a young age and later became the curator and director of the North Carolina Museum of Natural History. He and his wife, Bettie, frequently stayed at the Onslow Rod and Gun Club. Brimley traveled throughout the state to gather specimens and take photographs for the museum's exhibits.

Dr. William Sharpe, a New York neurosurgeon, was another sportsman who fell in love with Onslow County. After spending several sporting seasons in Onslow, Sharpe decided to purchase his own retreat. His African American friend John Hurst discovered 4,600 acres on the mainland and Bear Island with a beautiful stretch of beach. Named the Hammocks, the property was managed by the Hursts, and the Sharpes enjoyed it for over 30 years. Sharpe willed the land to a black teachers' organization, which gave it to the state in 1961, and it became Hammocks Beach State Park.

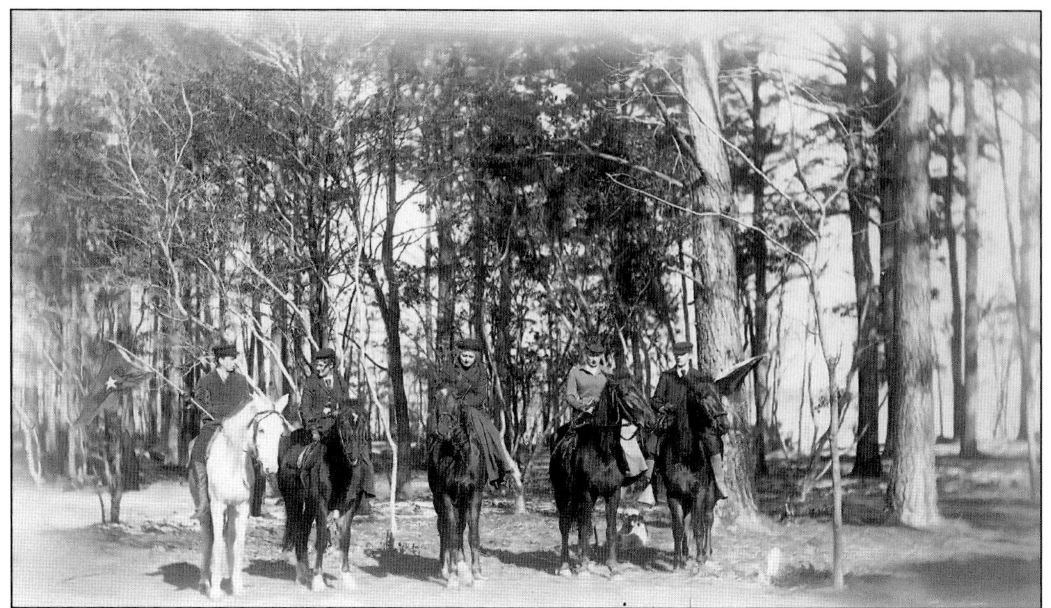

A part of Thomas A. McIntyre's ideal of a country estate was leisure pursuits. On February 1, 1894, possibly as a commemoration of the opening of the railroad to Jacksonville, Onslow Day was held at the Onslow Hall estate for guests and workers. Games and competitions were held around the racetrack, and colorful flags, such as the ones held by these equestrians, were carried. The three women in the middle are McIntyre's sisters. (Courtesy of Onslow County Museum.)

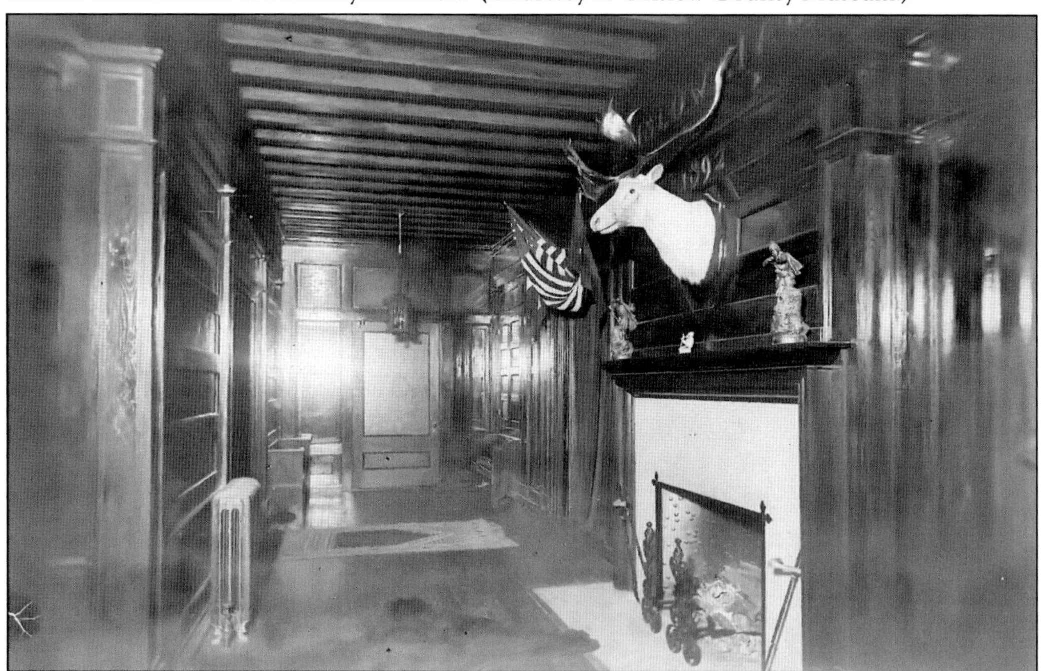

The wood-paneled hallway in McIntyre's mansion gave the impression of a stately hunting lodge, with the mounted moose head and bearskin rug. The house was decoratively paneled throughout in native woods and featured a studio on the third floor for McIntyre's photographic pursuits. (Courtesy of Onslow County Museum.)

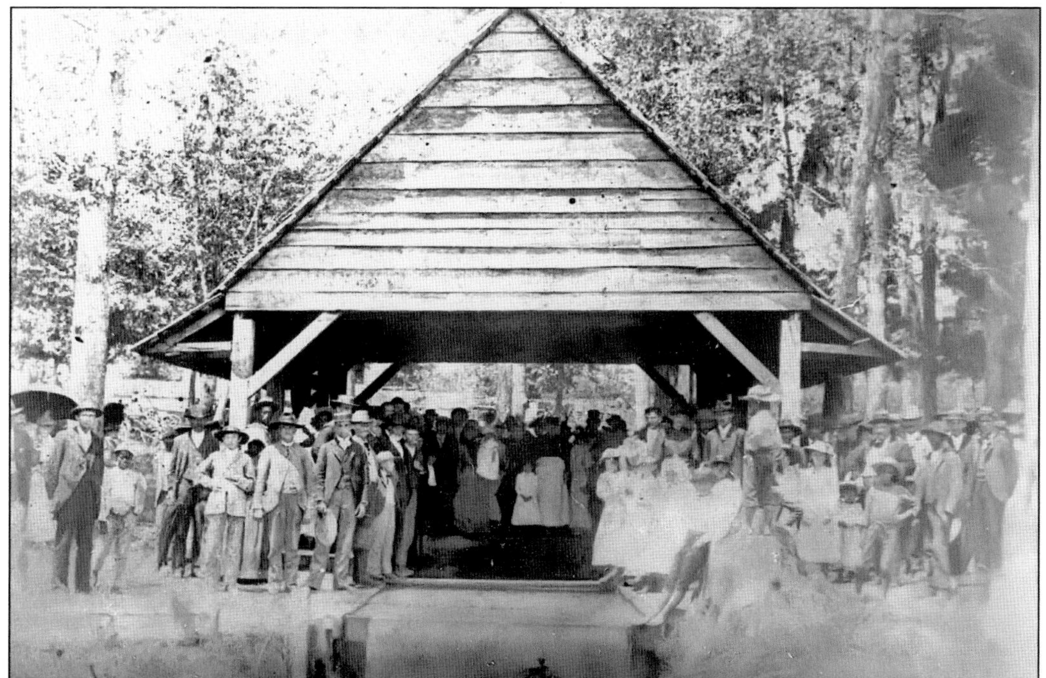

Alum Spring, in the Catherine Lake vicinity, was the location of a yearly celebration called Big August. These celebrations actually began as an annual picnic-themed Primitive Baptist Church meeting, but later, the event was attended by any and all at the mineral spring near Catherine Lake. The celebrants pose at the spring sometime in the late 1880s or early 1890s. (Courtesy of the Onslow County Museum.)

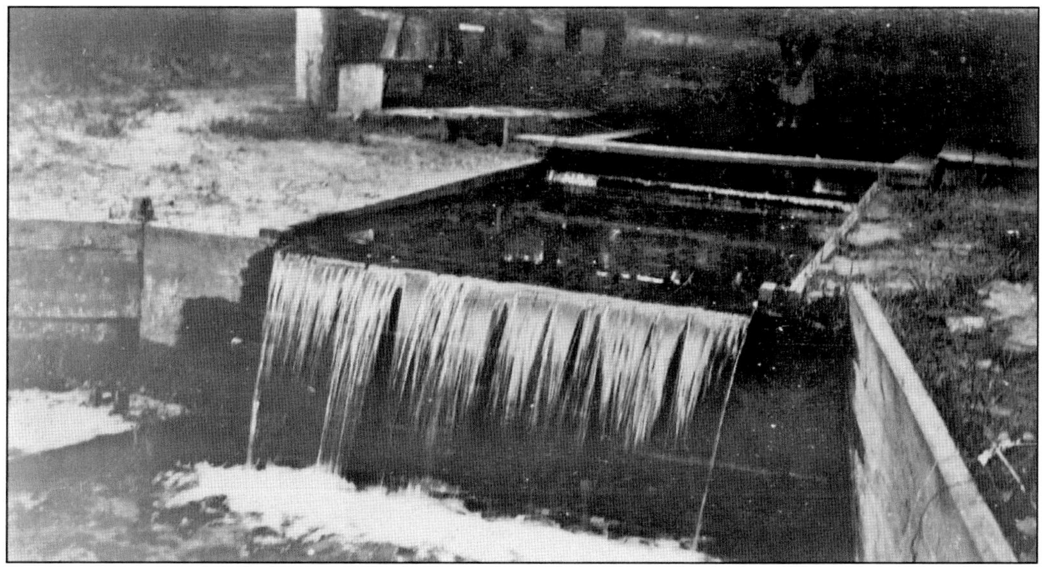

Whether used for bathing or drinking, the water at Alum Spring was said to be good for many ailments. Visitors also put watermelons in the spring to keep them cold. (Courtesy of State Archives of North Carolina.)

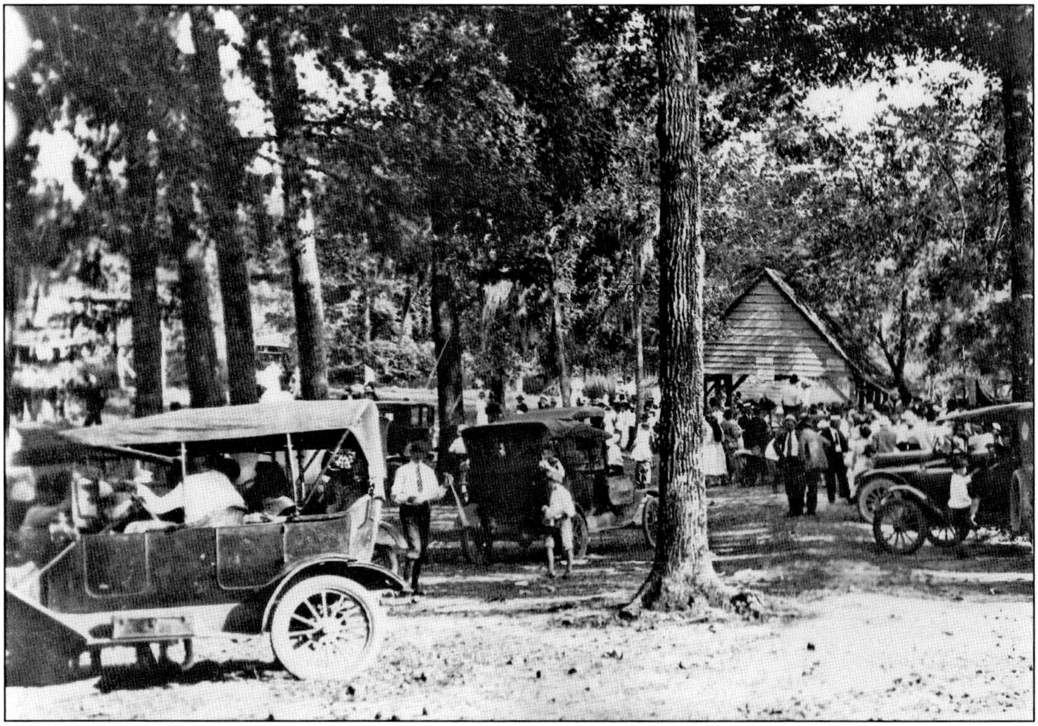

Alum Spring was often overwhelmed with picnic goers at Big August. The grounds were completely covered with buggies in the early days and, later, cars, as seen in this panoramic image taken in the late 1920s. (Courtesy of Onslow County Museum.)

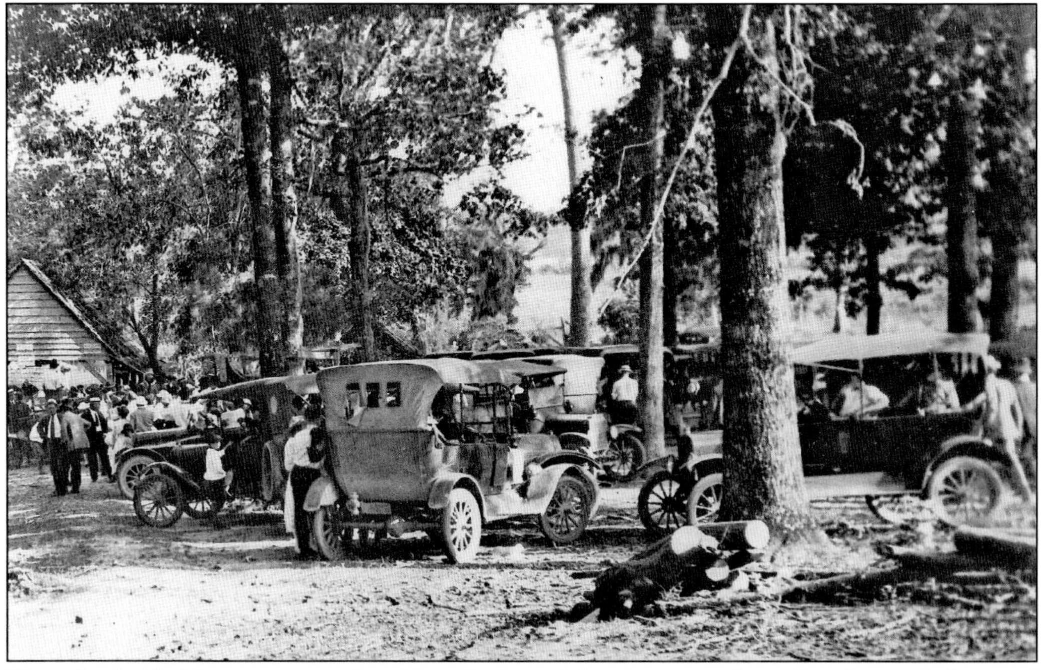

The other half of the panorama of an Alum Spring celebration is seen here. People crowded around the small dance pavilion for a chance to dance or sing. (Courtesy of Onslow County Museum.)

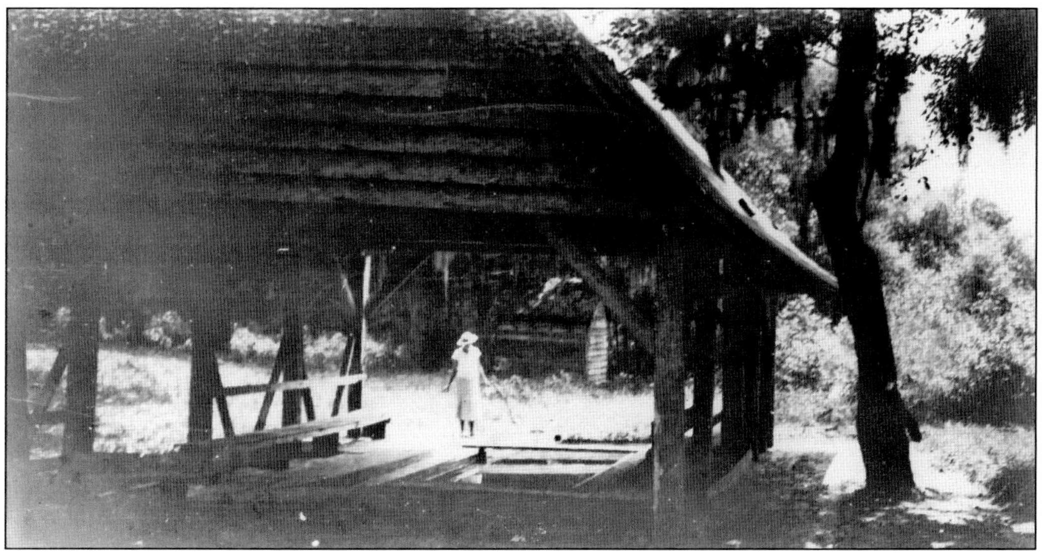

The spring and pavilion became a quiet place after the last Big August was held. Here, a woman gazes at the mineral spring and aging pavilion in the late 1930s in this image. (Courtesy of State Archives of North Carolina.)

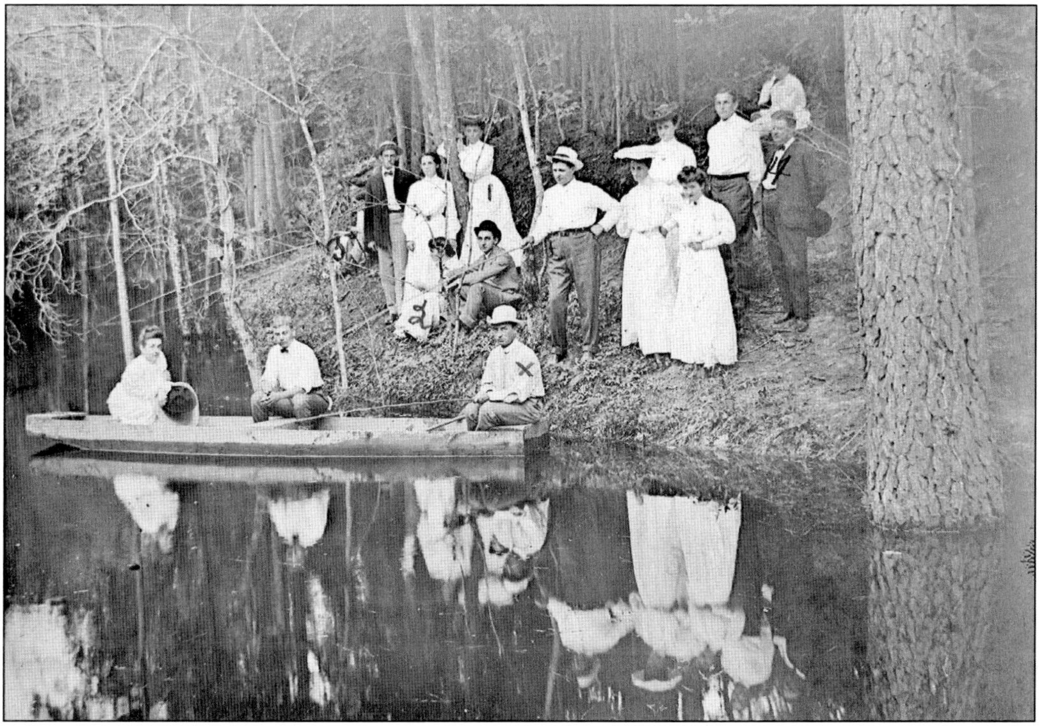

In Jacksonville, picnicking near the New River was a common pastime, especially for young people. In this late-19th-century image, a group of eight women and eight men considers canoeing on the river. (Courtesy of Onslow County Museum.)

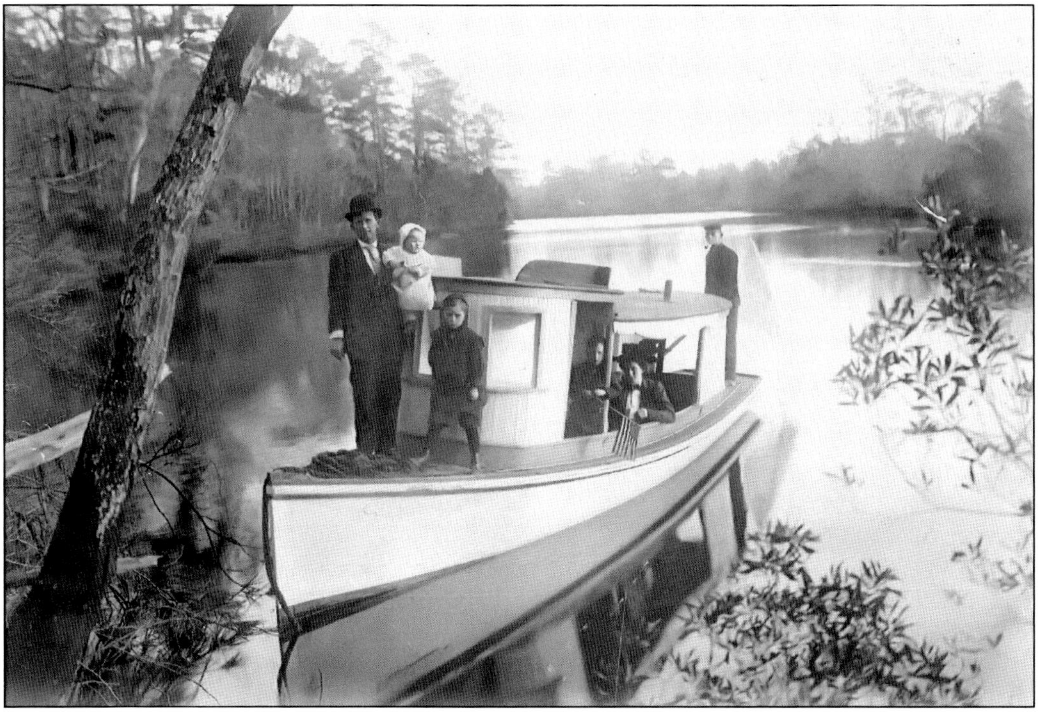

Families enjoyed taking short cruises down the river as well. The Ketchum family is shown here in the early 20th century on a small pleasure boat on the New River. One of the little boys is holding an American flag. (Courtesy of Onslow County Museum.)

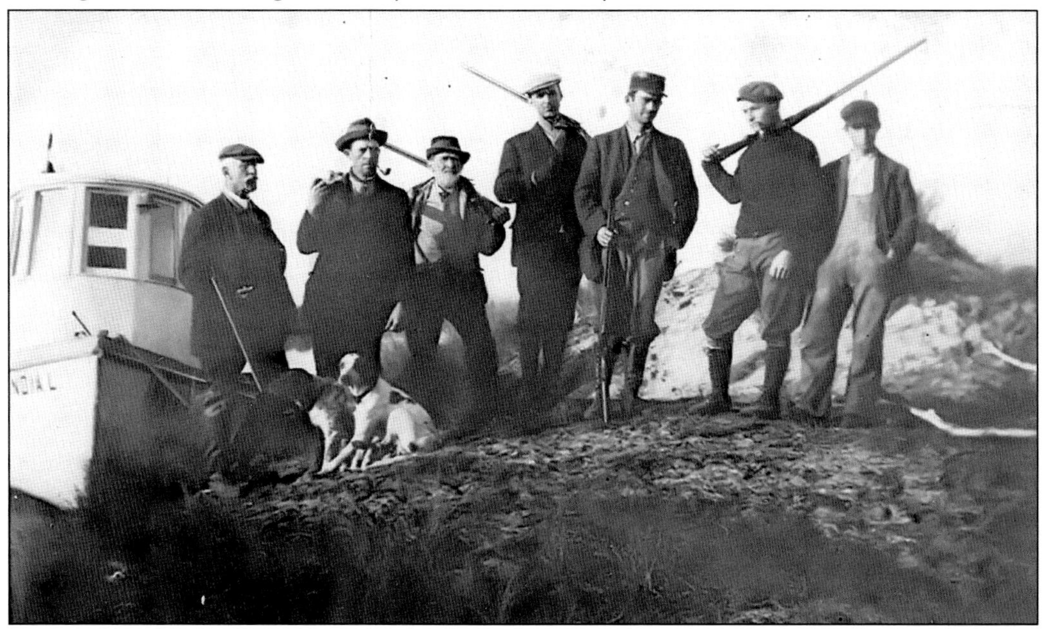

Hunting was probably one of the most common and well-liked pastimes throughout the 19th and early 20th centuries. In this image, a group of hunters poses near a boat as the men commence their hunting trip. Dr. Richard W. Ward is third from the left, and the hunters on the right are probably visiting sportsmen. (Courtesy of Onslow County Museum.)

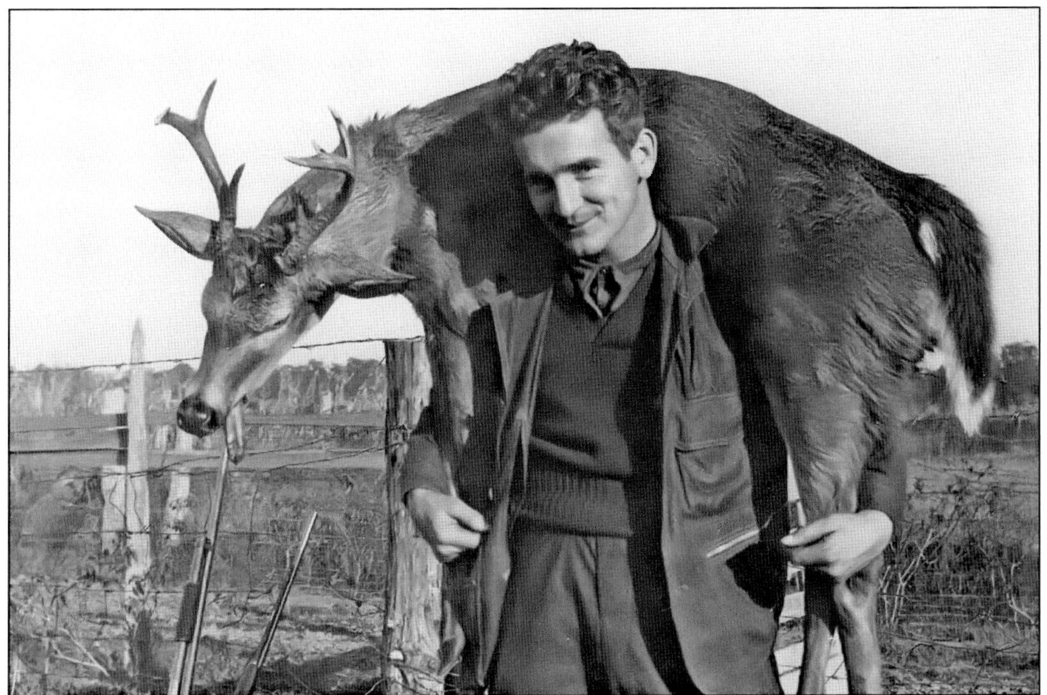

Deer were one of the most commonly hunted animals. This proud hunter brings in a whitetail deer in the late 1930s. Note the guns propped against the fence on the left. (Courtesy of Onslow County Museum.)

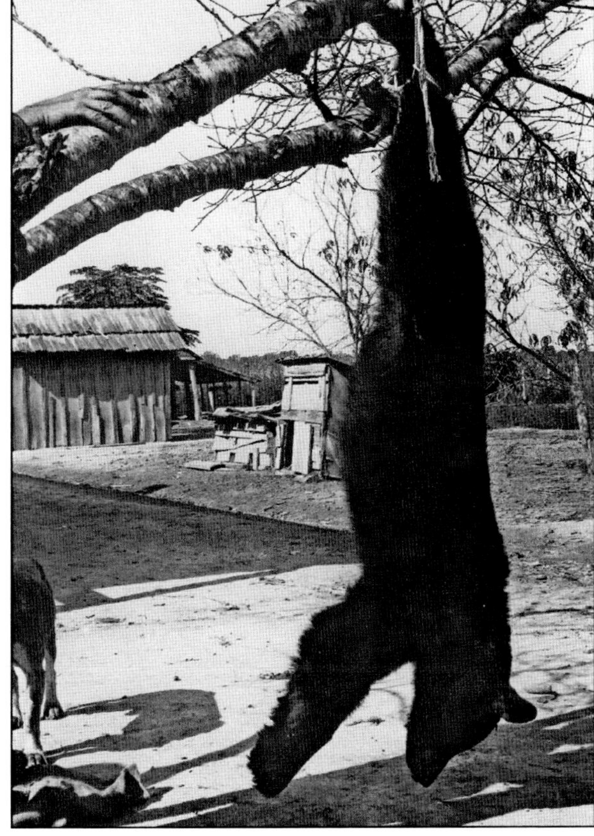

Along with turkey and deer, bear was a common target for hunters, as was this large black bear. Bounties were placed on bears in the 1890s because of their high numbers. (Courtesy of Onslow County Museum.)

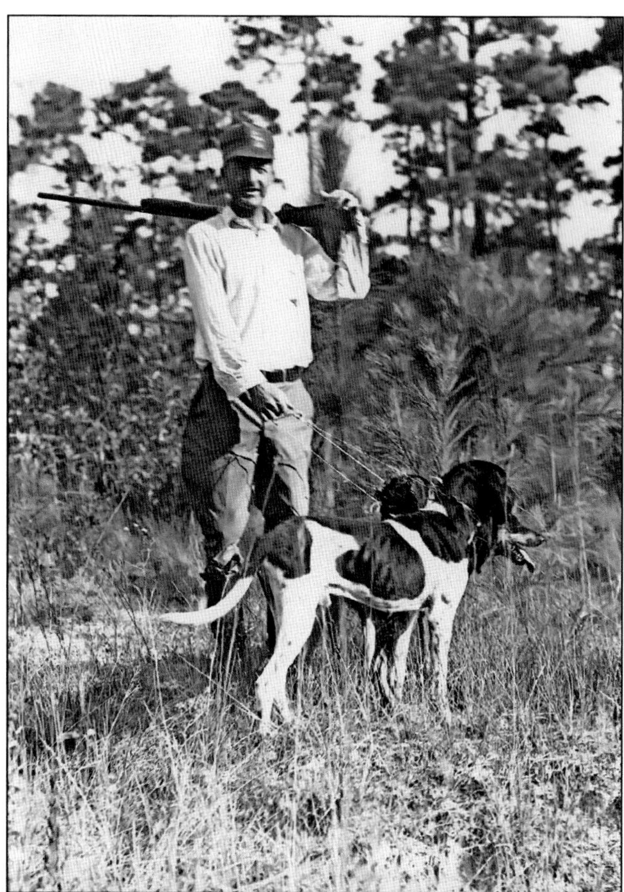

William N. Henderson is pictured with his hunting dogs in about 1939. Born at Mile Hammock Bay, he later became the resident gamekeeper for Camp Lejeune. (Courtesy of Onslow County Museum.)

Weil Hunting Lodge was one of the two main lodges built on the New River for out-of-town sportsmen. The Shingle Style Weil Lodge was located between French Creek and Duck Creek, and stood until the coming of the Marine base. (Courtesy of Onslow County Museum.)

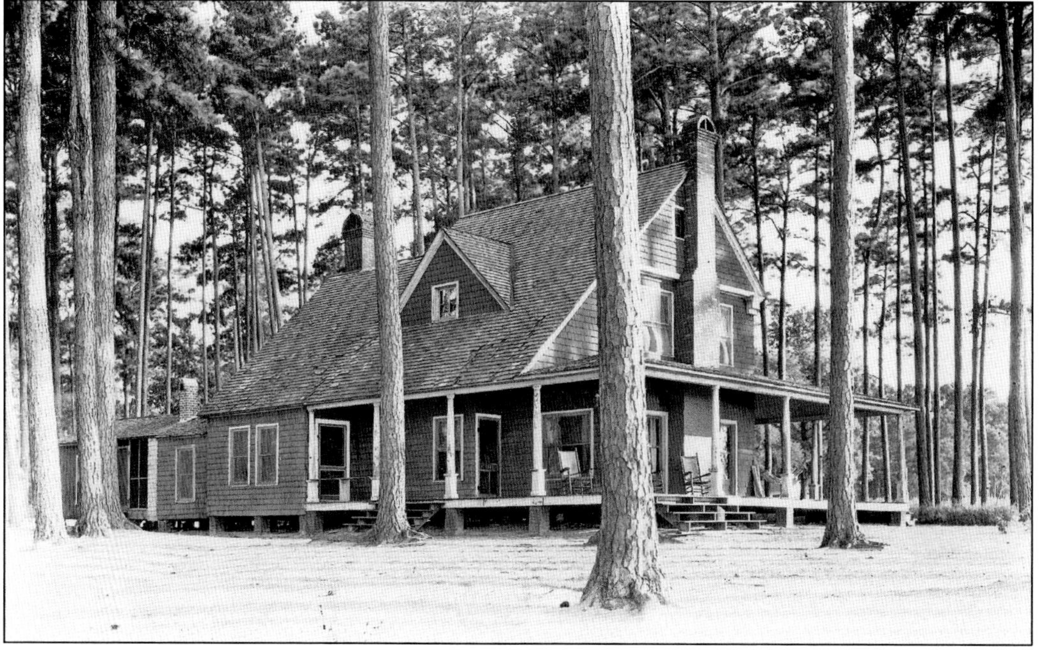

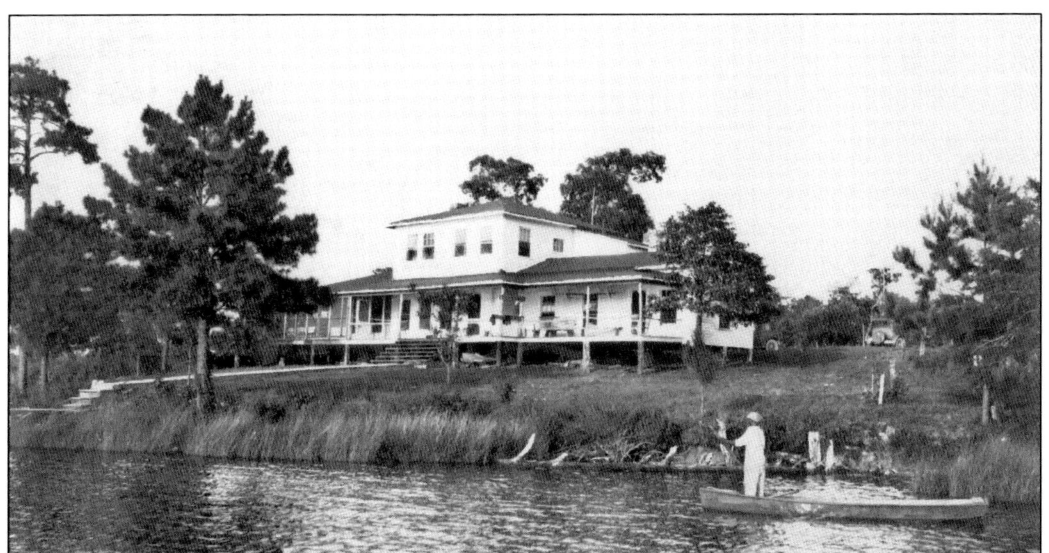

The other sizable lodge was known as the Onslow Hunt Club or the Onslow Rod and Gun Club. The large frame building was used by locals and out-of-town visitors alike. This peaceful scene was probably taken in the late 1920s by Herbert H. Brimley. (Courtesy of State Archives of North Carolina.)

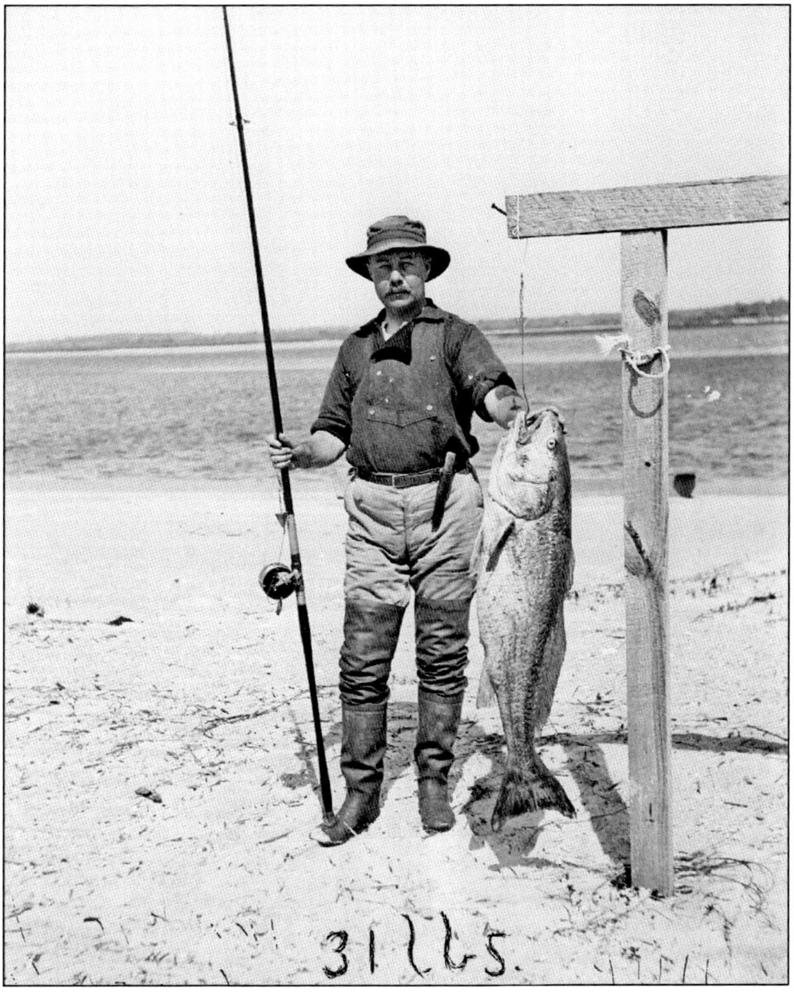

Herbert H. Brimley poses in this late-1920s shot with an impressive catch—31 pounds, as written on the bottom of the image. The bountiful nature of Onslow's waterways was known throughout the state. (Courtesy of State Archives of North Carolina.)

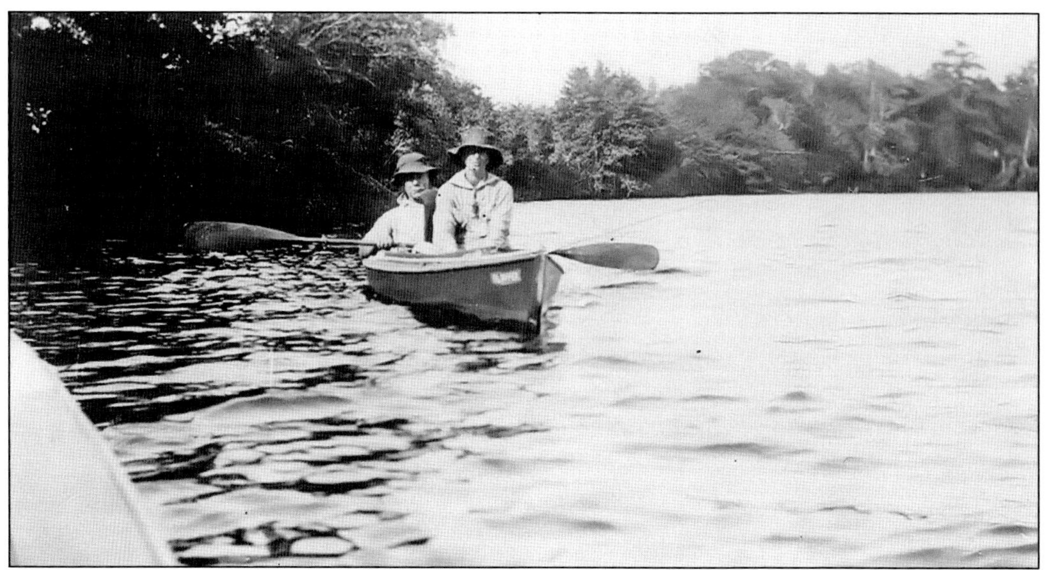

Herbert Brimley and his wife, Bettie, were frequent visitors to the Onslow Rod and Gun Club. Canoeing was an efficient and pleasurable way to navigate the New River. (Courtesy of Onslow County Museum.)

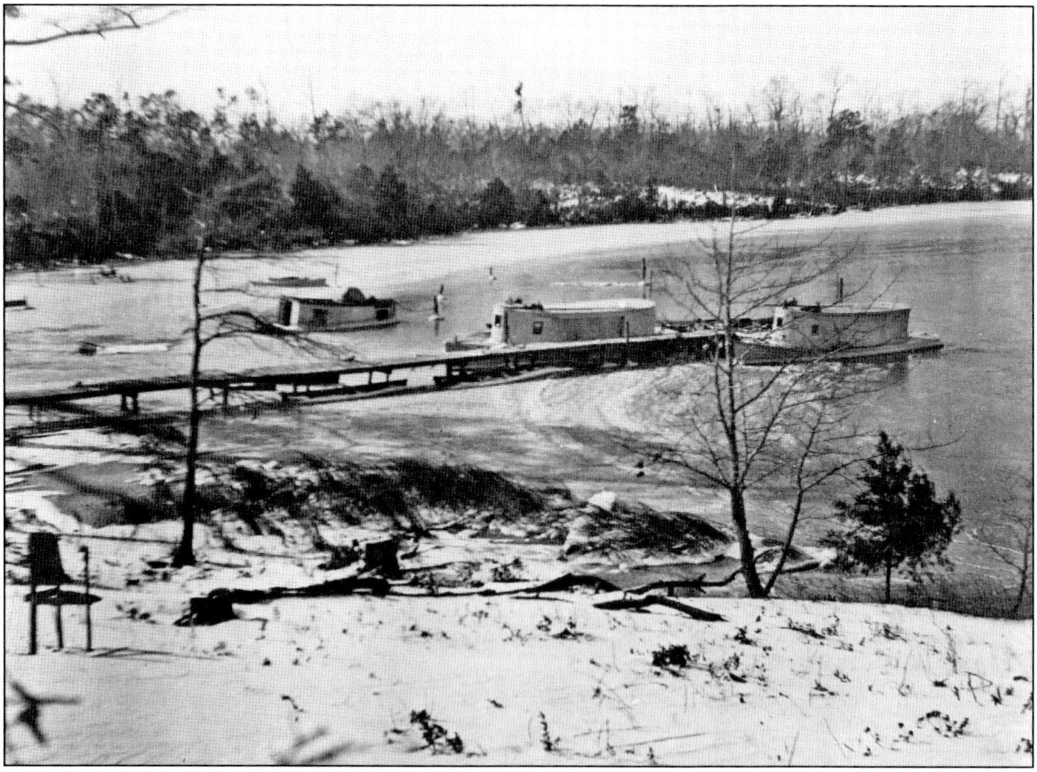

This view from the Onslow Rod and Gun Club in the frozen winter of 1918–1919 shows the intensity of the cold. The river was completely frozen over, stranding the boats in the ice for several days. (Courtesy of State Archives of North Carolina.)

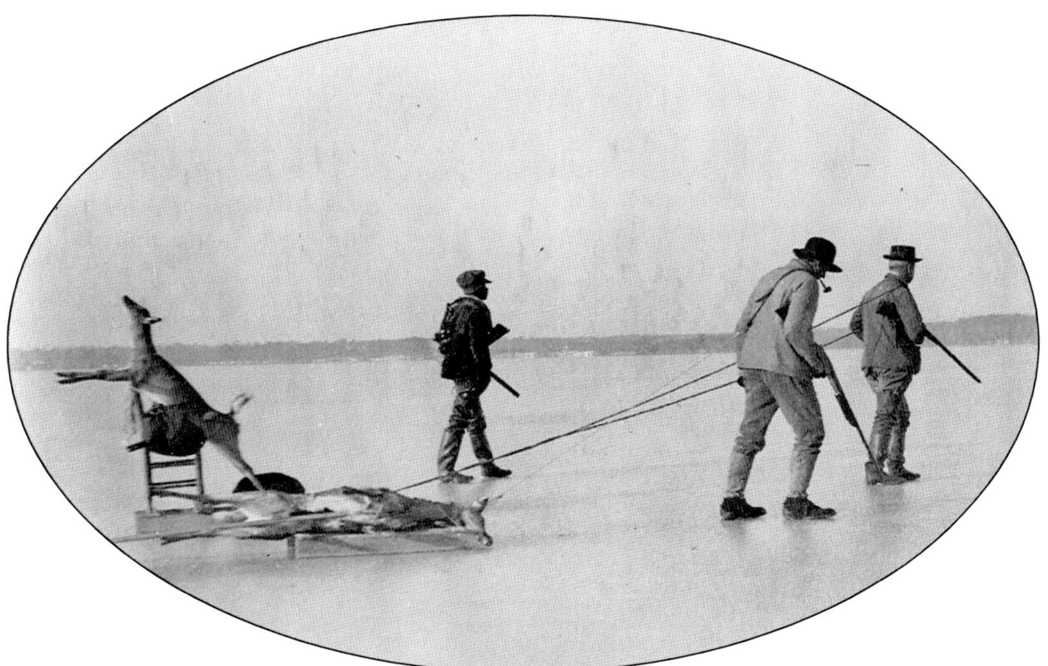

Three huntsmen walk confidently across the frozen New River in January 1919 with a rigged sled to hold deer. (Courtesy of Onslow County Museum.)

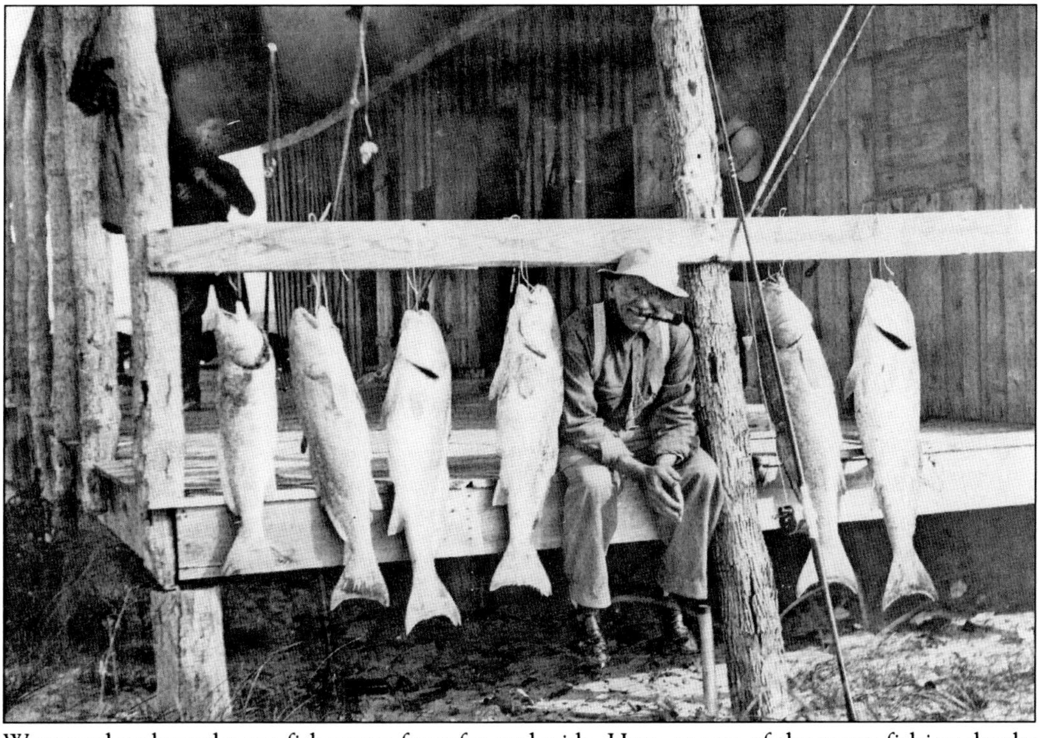

Warmer days brought out fishermen from far and wide. Here, at one of the many fishing shacks found on the New River in the 1920s, is a lucky angler with a large catch. (Courtesy of State Archives of North Carolina.)

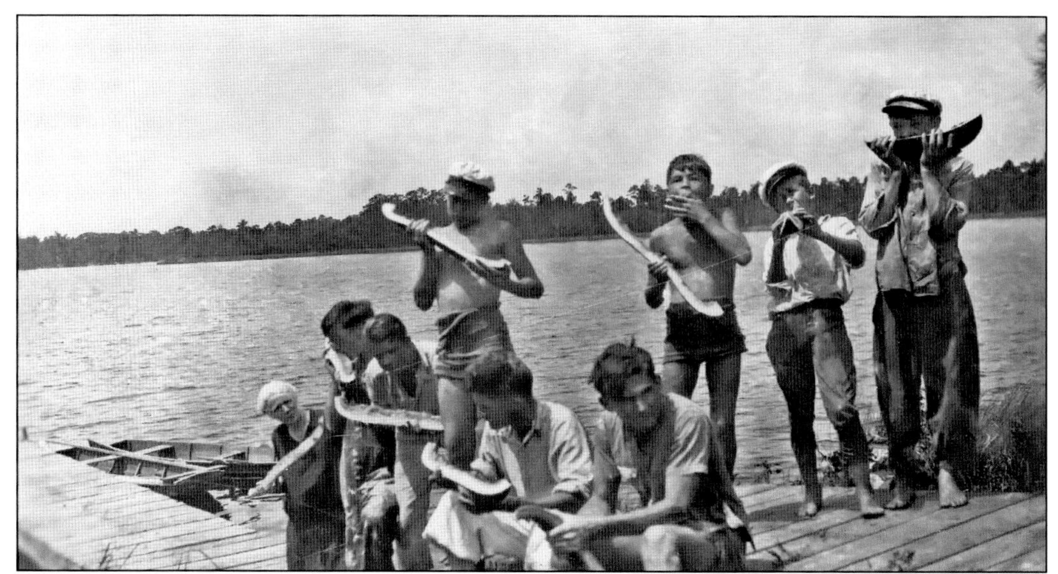

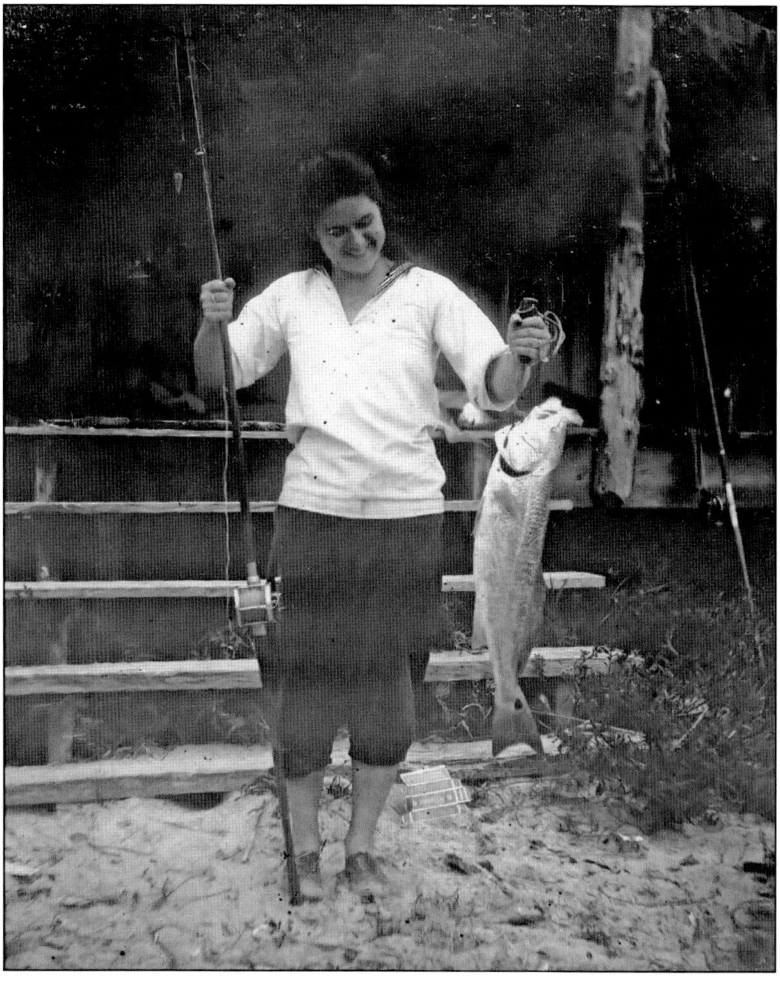

Boy Scouts made use of the Onslow Rod and Gun Club upon occasion for hunting or fishing excursions. Here, a troop eats cold watermelon on the pier in front of the club in the late 1920s. (Courtesy of State Archives of North Carolina.)

Fishing was not only for men and boys. This young lady shows off her catch near the porch of the Onslow Rod and Gun Club in the late 1920s. (Courtesy of State Archives of North Carolina.)

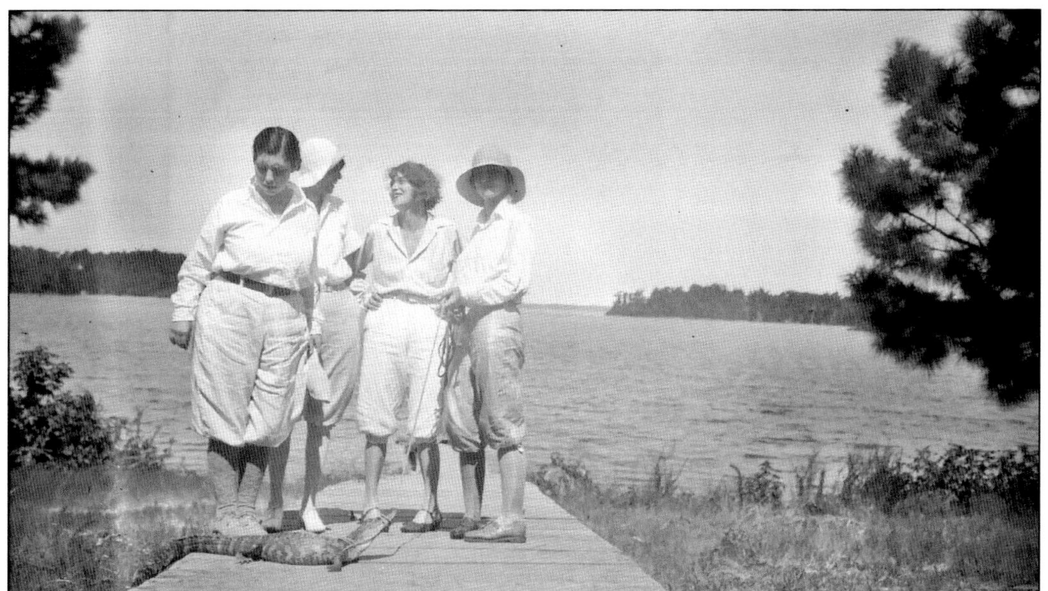

Vacation time at the Onslow Rod and Gun Club sometimes included families and old friends. Except for the concerned woman on the left, this group of ladies seems at ease with the small alligator one of the women is keeping on a leash. (Courtesy of State Archives of North Carolina.)

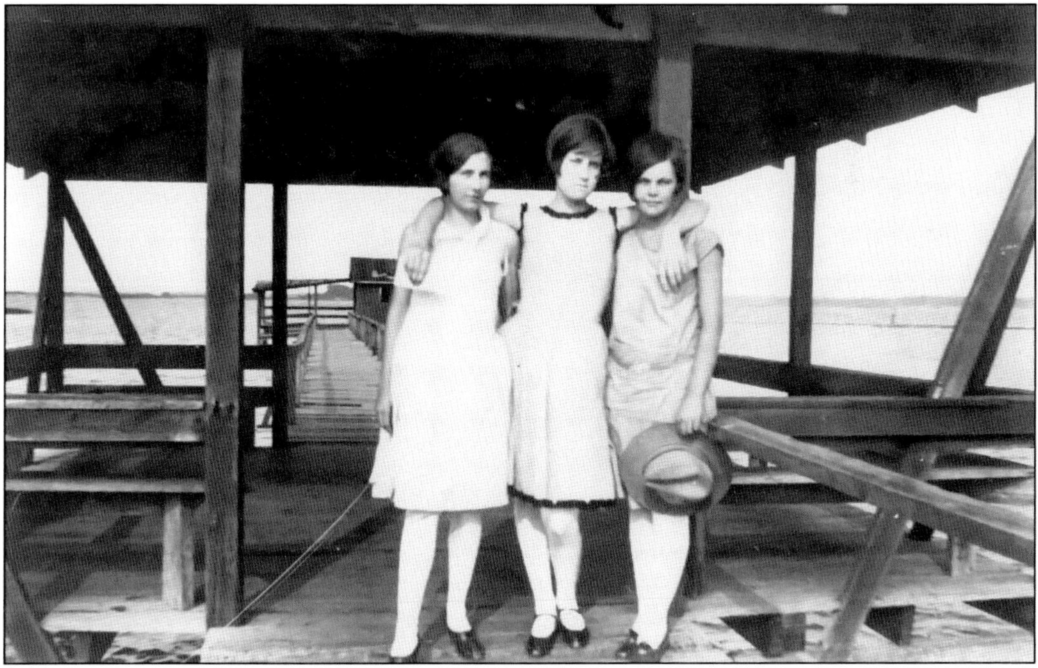

The Tarrymore Hotel in Swansboro was a social hub into the 1930s. Posing near the bathhouse are, from left to right, Travis Woodhull Ward, Aleta Webb Kellum, and Helen Canady Wade. (Courtesy of State Archives of North Carolina.)

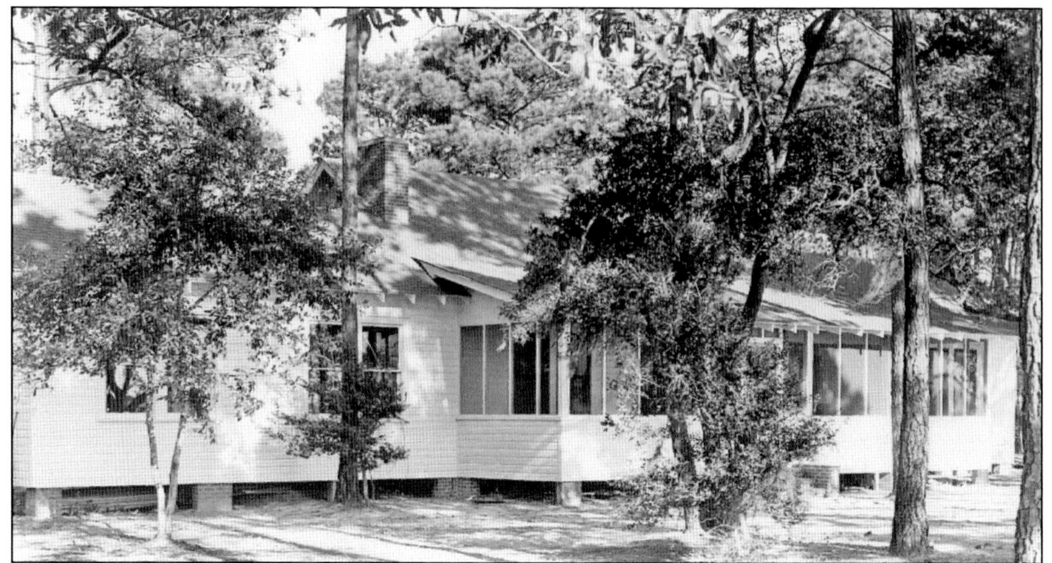

This was the summerhouse of Dr. C.I. Carlson near Marines. There were several summer homes owned by nonresidents before World War II. This home was eventually swallowed up by the base, but it served as a temporary officers' club for a short time in the early 1940s. (Courtesy of Onslow County Museum.)

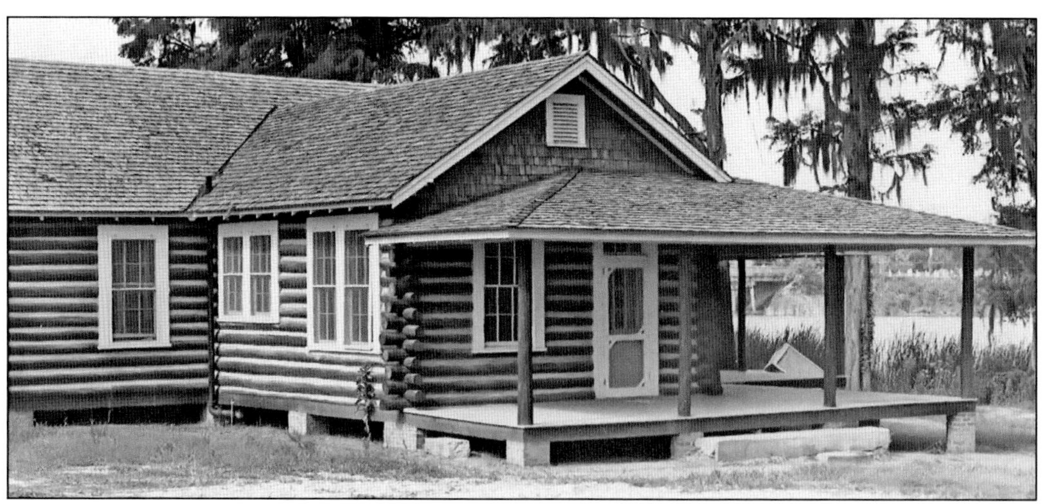

The WPA built this community center in Jacksonville in the 1930s on the New River near the Pelletier House. Known as Pine Lodge, the center was frequently used for meetings and dances and was temporarily used as the USO while the Tallman Street facility was being completed in the early 1940s. (Courtesy of Onslow County Museum.)

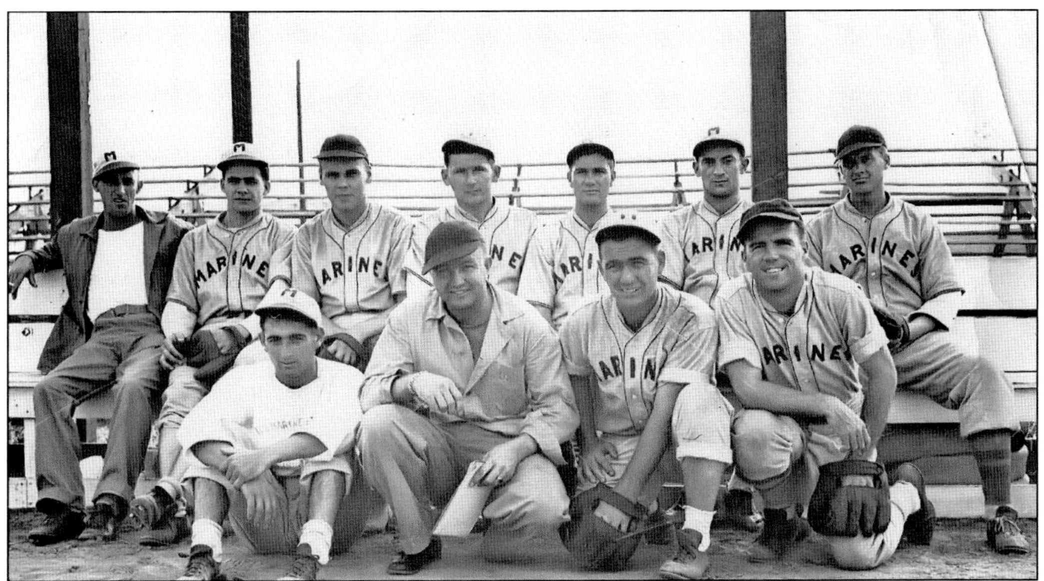

Baseball champs of 1949 pose proudly for a photograph. The Marines had a number of baseball leagues and teams. (Courtesy of Onslow County Museum.)

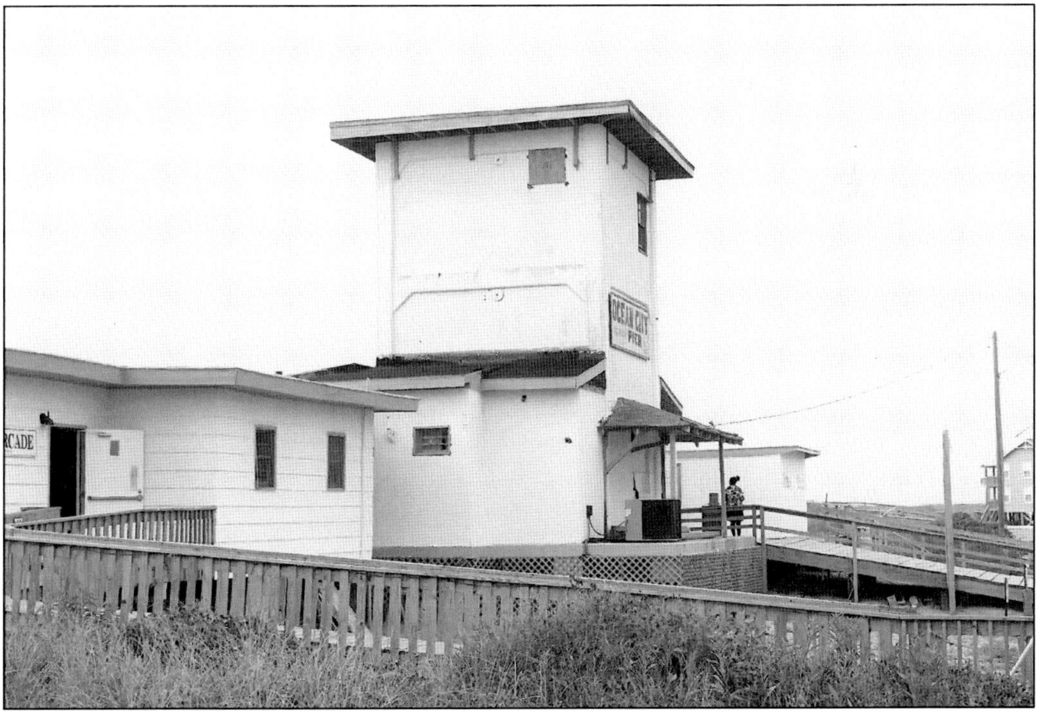

Ocean City Beach was established in 1949 and soon became a popular choice for African Americans wishing to own beachfront property. (Courtesy of Onslow County Museum.)

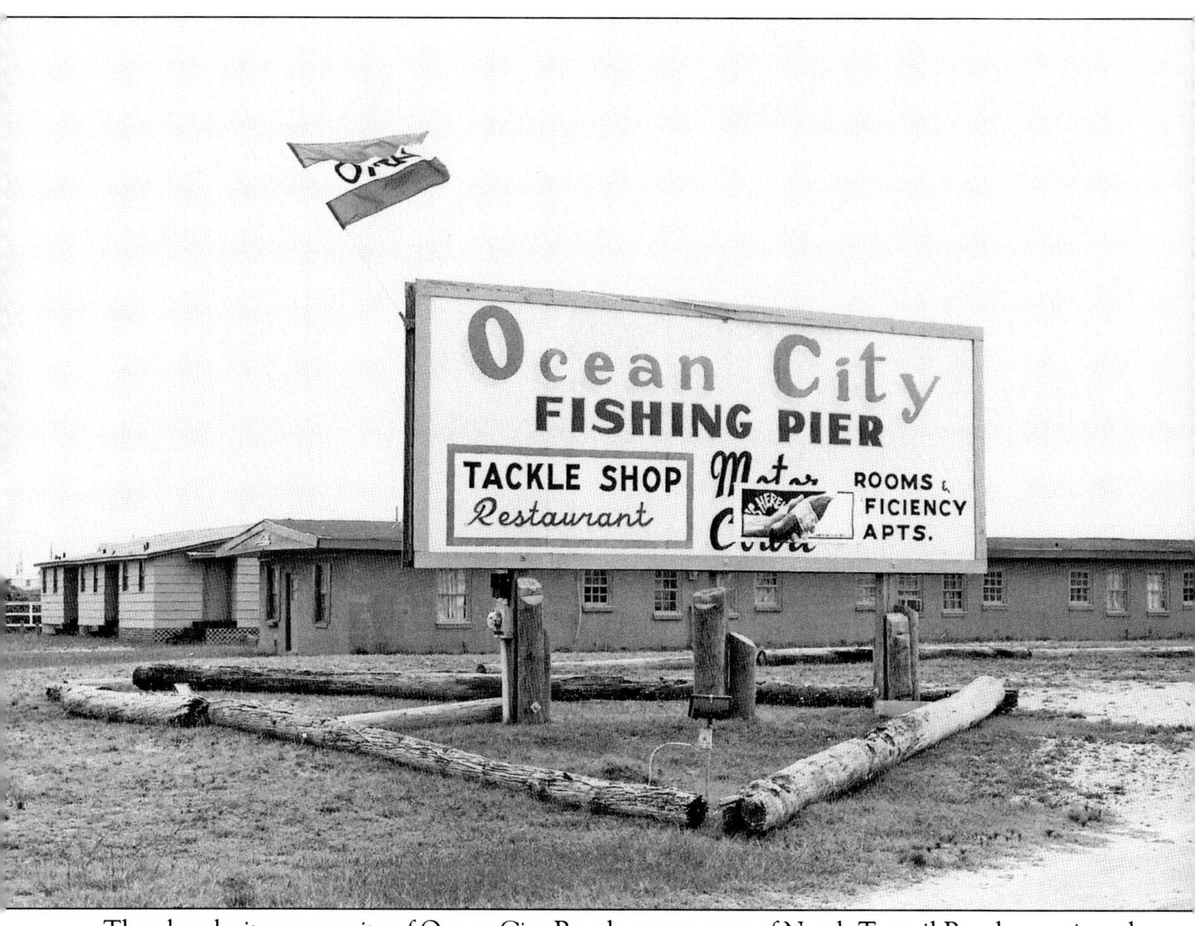

The close-knit community of Ocean City Beach, now a part of North Topsail Beach, continued to grow in spite of numerous storms, such as Hurricane Hazel in 1954. (Courtesy of Onslow County Museum.)

Seven

The Military Presence

The winds of war in the late 1930s changed the slow-paced lifestyle of Onslow County forever. In the United States, there was a movement toward expanding and improving the military forces in preparation for any outside threat. Onslow County became an important site for military training operations.

Land encompassing 46,483 acres in the southern part of Onslow and into Pender, including Holly Ridge and Topsail Island, was leased by the government for the establishment of an Army base that would train soldiers in antiaircraft artillery. Construction began in December 1940, and the first troops arrived in April 1941. Thousands of carpenters and laborers streamed into the area seeking employment; more than 17,000 civilian workers were employed by May 1941. After the war, Camp Davis was briefly used as a ramjet missile testing area by the US Navy until operations were ceased in 1948.

Shortly after Camp Davis construction began, what became Camp Lejeune began taking shape. Onslow's waterways, access to the ocean, and rural nature made it an ideal location for an amphibious training base. The government purchased the land; at least 700 families were affected by the transactions. Many of the residents descended from families that had settled the area in the colonial era. Over 111,000 acres were acquired, and ground was broken in April 1941. The massive influx of hopeful workers, sometimes with their families in tow, taxed the resources of the small town of Jacksonville, which had a population of only 873 in 1940.

Construction proceeded rapidly and escalated with Japan's bombing of Pearl Harbor on December 7, 1941. Originally known as Marine Barracks, New River, the base was officially named Camp Lejeune in honor of Lt. Gen. John A. Lejeune. Camp Lejeune was also the site of war dog training, Marine Corps Women's Reserve Schools, and the first training for African American Marines at Montford Point.

Originally known as Peterfield Point, New River Air Station, located across the New River from Camp Lejeune, was in use during the latter part of World War II, closed, and then reopened for the Korean War. In 1972, it was officially designated McCutcheon Field in honor of Gen. Keith B. McCutcheon.

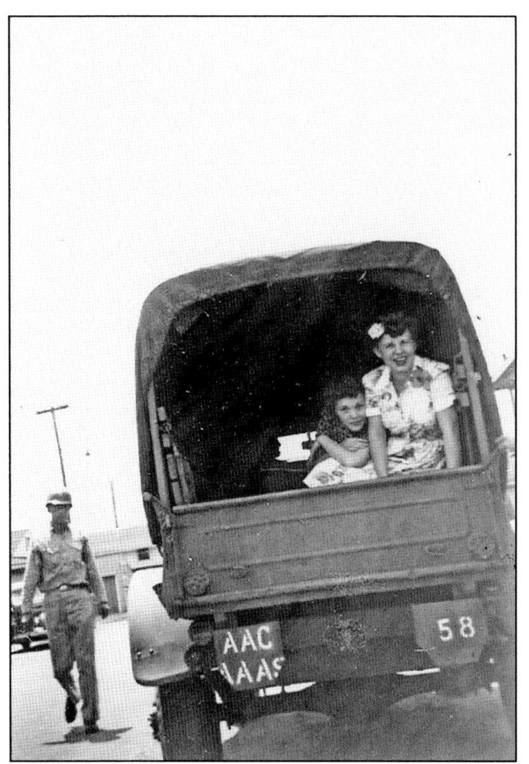

Camp Davis brought an influx of workers, both male and female, from around the country. Rachel Burcham was one of the many young women who found employment as secretaries, telephone operators, and other occupations. Burcham, in the flowered dress, and another woman sometimes hitched rides on military vehicles. (Courtesy of Onslow County Museum.)

Social opportunities abounded at Camp Davis. On February 26, 1944, the 14th TOW Target Squad held an officers' party. The knotty pine–paneled room was festively decorated with crepe paper streamers and a small band entertained the attendees, many of whom were headed for overseas assignments. (Courtesy of Onslow County Museum.)

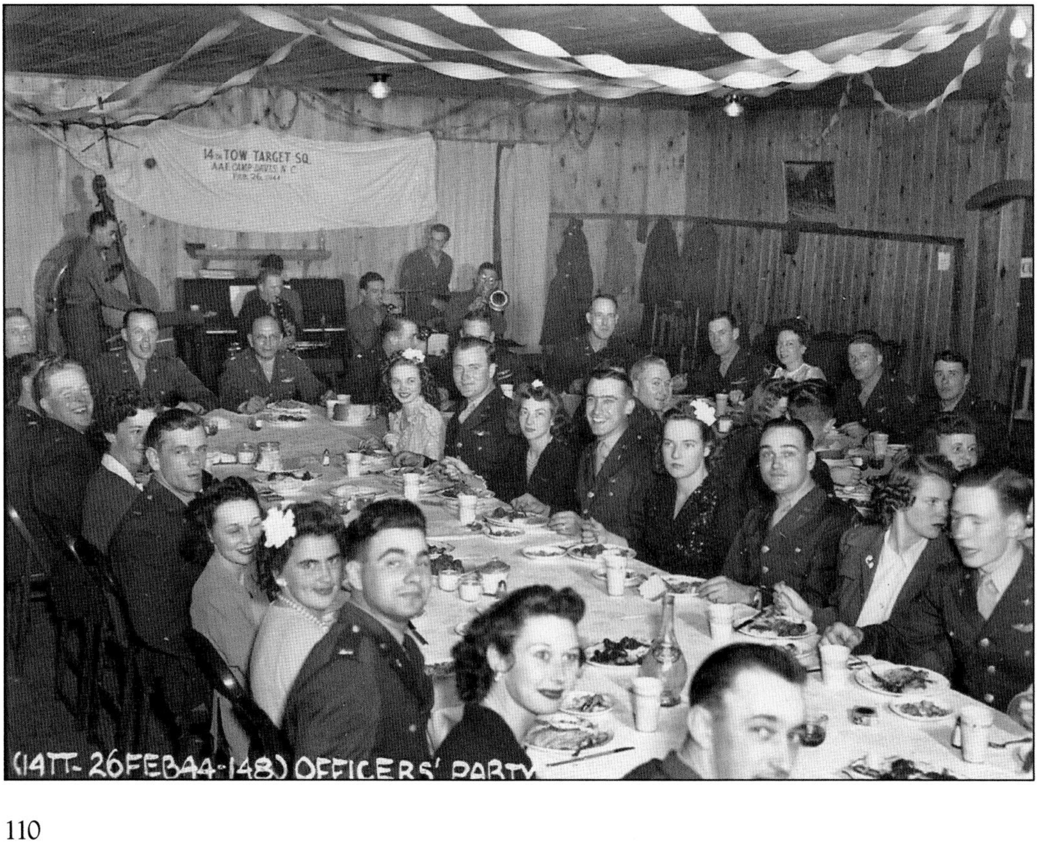

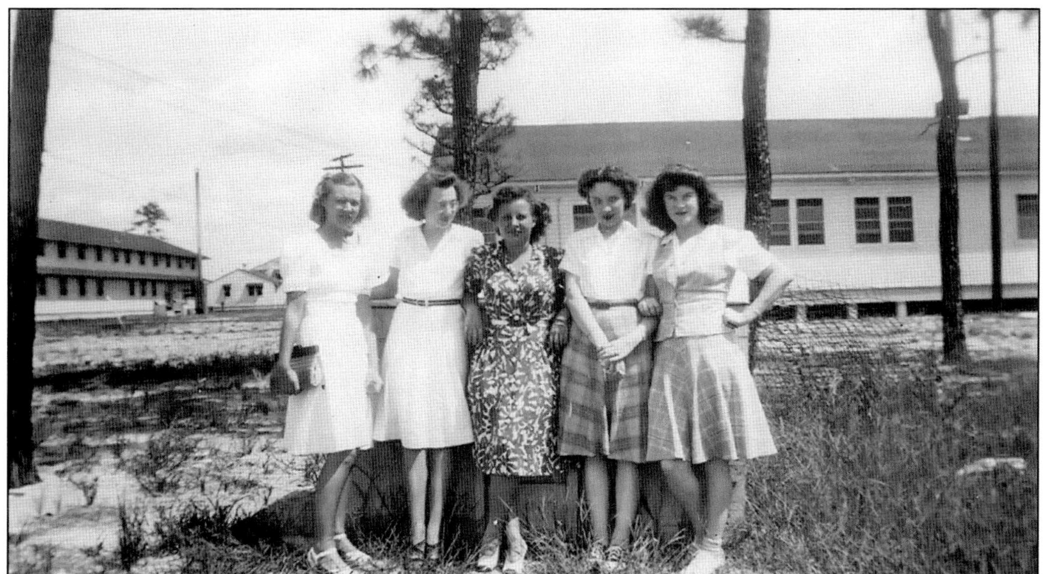

There were a number of job opportunities available for young women when most men were enlisting in the armed forces. Rachel Burcham is in the middle of this group of friends she made while working at Camp Davis in 1943. (Courtesy of Onslow County Museum.)

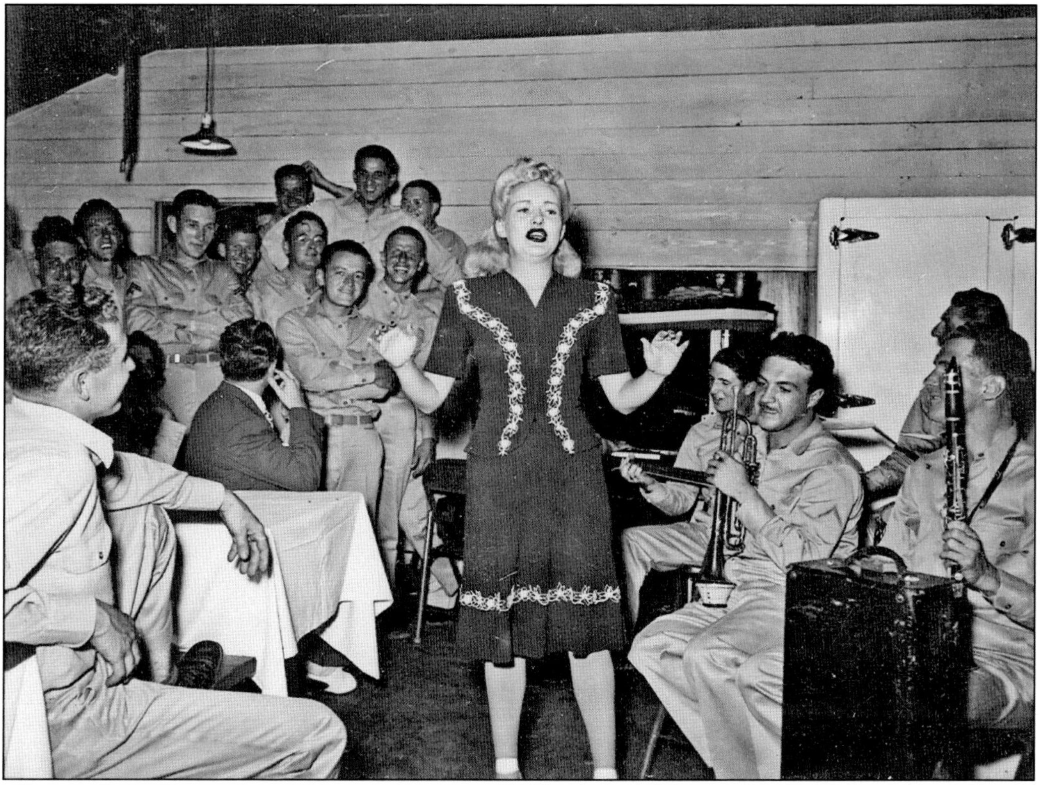

Several famous entertainers visited Camp Lejeune or Camp Davis during World War II. Betty Grable's visit in 1943 included both bases; this image was taken at Camp Davis, where she impressed the troops with her talent and beauty. (Courtesy of Onslow County Museum.)

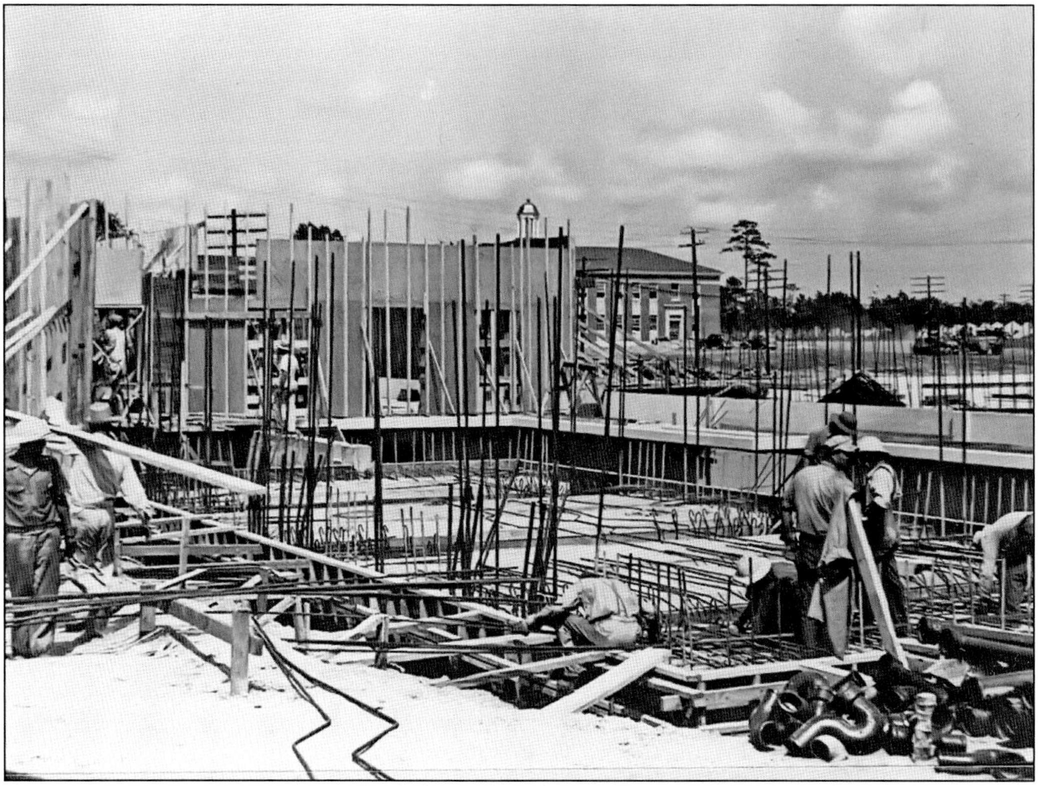

Camp Lejeune's construction was divided into four phases. Phase one, from April 1941 to September 1942, encompassed the main areas of the base, including the Tent Camp, which later became Camp Geiger, and the main hospital. (Courtesy of Onslow County Museum.)

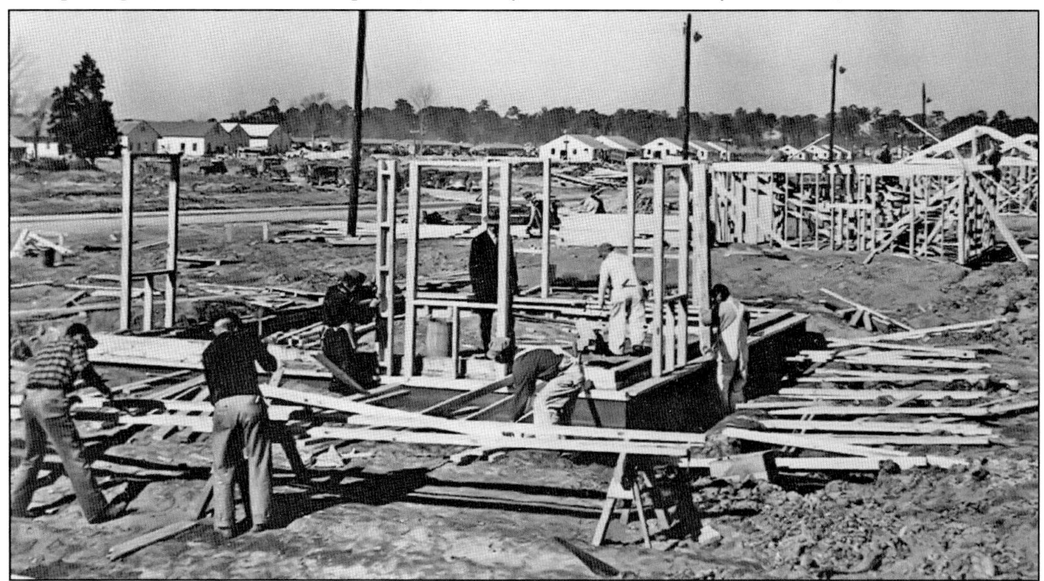

Construction on a 415-acre tract of land that became Camp Lejeune's Midway Park housing began in October 1941. Both enlisted Marines and civilian workers were housed there. (Courtesy of Onslow County Museum.)

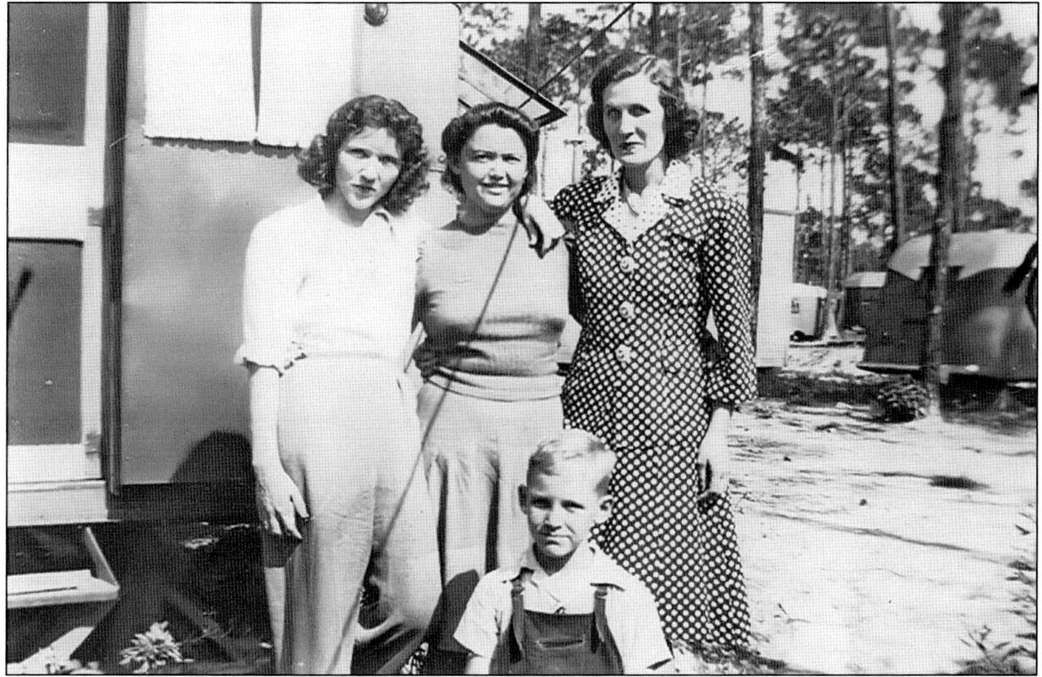

Because of the tremendous housing shortage, the government eventually provided trailers for the workers' families. Civilian worker Sam Royster's family lived in Village A in the Midway Park Trailer Park in 1942 until housing was available. Standing at far right is Doris Royster, and her son Robert is the little boy. (Courtesy of Robert Royster.)

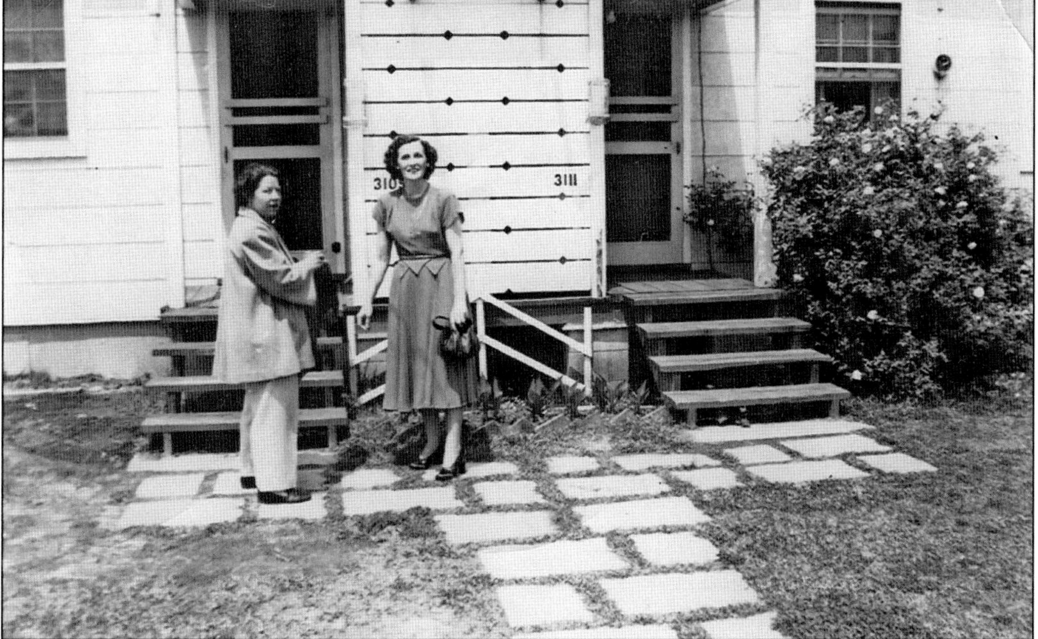

After the housing was finished, the Royster family moved into 3111 Lee Avenue in Midway Park. In this snapshot, Doris Royster stands on the right in front of her quarters. (Courtesy of Robert Royster.)

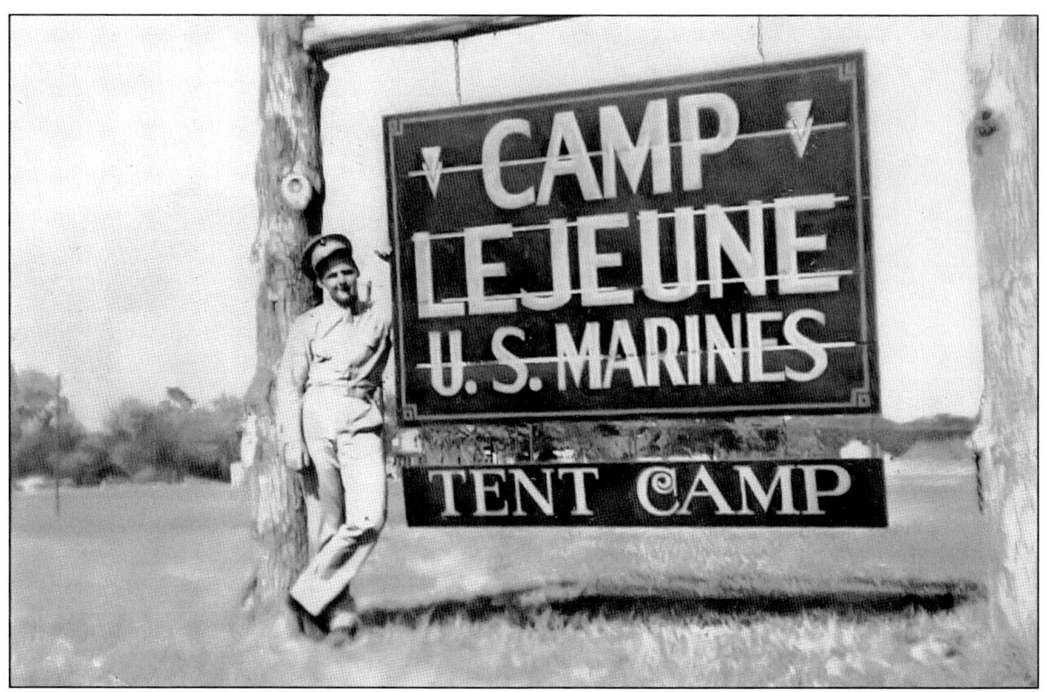

Initially, most of the Marines in training were housed at what was called Tent Camp, because of the hundreds of canvas tents hastily set up for the tide of enlistees. This young Marine poses next to the original Tent Camp sign in 1942. (Courtesy of Onslow County Museum.)

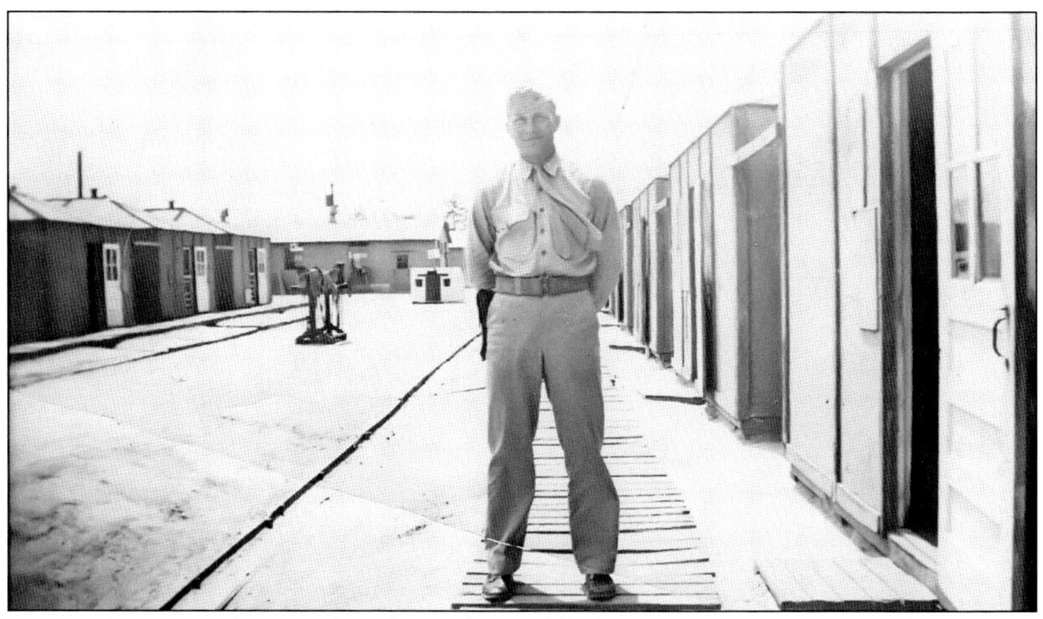

A young Lieutenant Day stands in front of one of the huts in Tent Camp No. 2, which was an extension to the original Tent Camp. Because of the shortage of canvas and wood, these huts were made of Homasote, housing 12 to 14 men. Note the swab rack in the center. Each hut had an oil-fueled stove. (Courtesy of Onslow County Museum.)

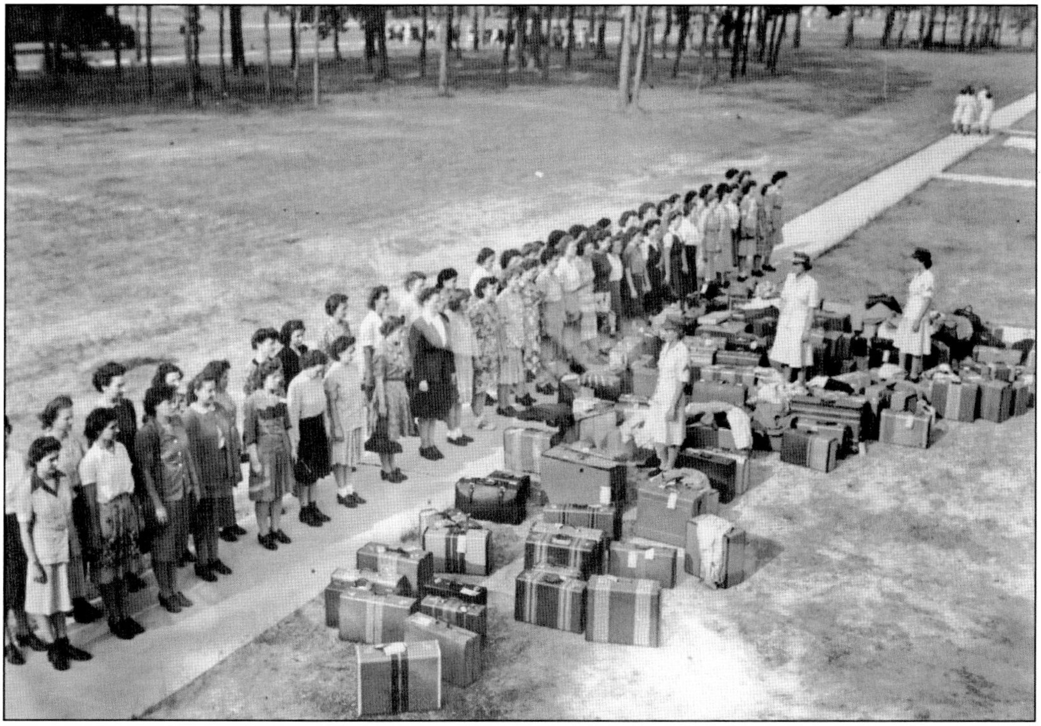

The Marine Corps Women's Reserve (MCWR) was headquartered on Camp Lejeune beginning in the summer of 1943. In this image, one of the first groups of woman Marine recruits arrives at Camp Lejeune to begin training to "free a Marine to fight." (Courtesy of Marine Corps Archives and Special Collections.)

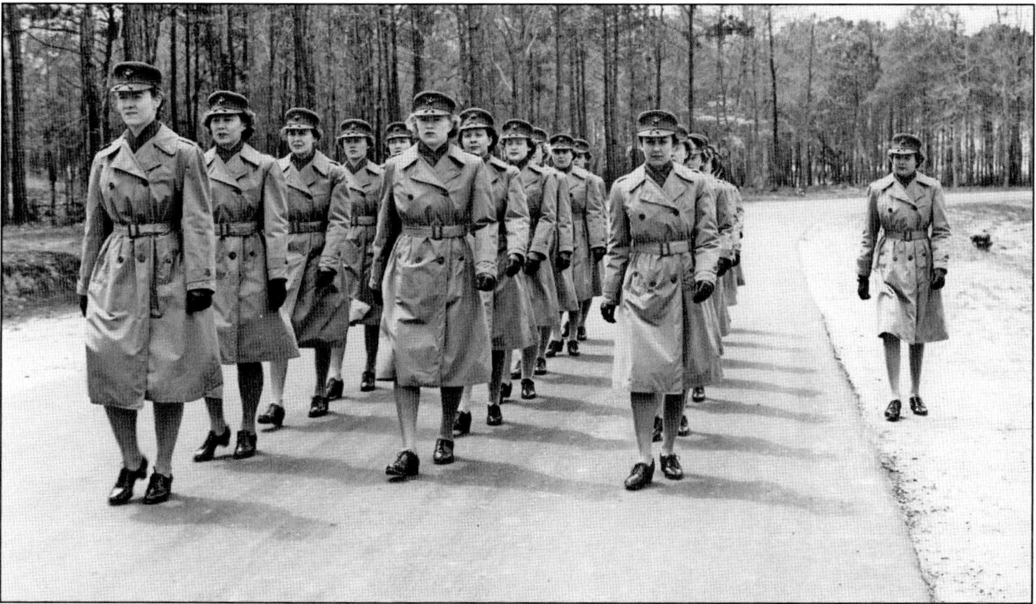

Led by 2nd Lt. Caroline Helmuth, the 13th reserve officers training class at MCWR Schools, Camp Lejeune, marches along on an obviously cold day in 1944. Women Marines eventually filled over 200 military occupations. (Courtesy of Marine Corps Archives and Special Collections.)

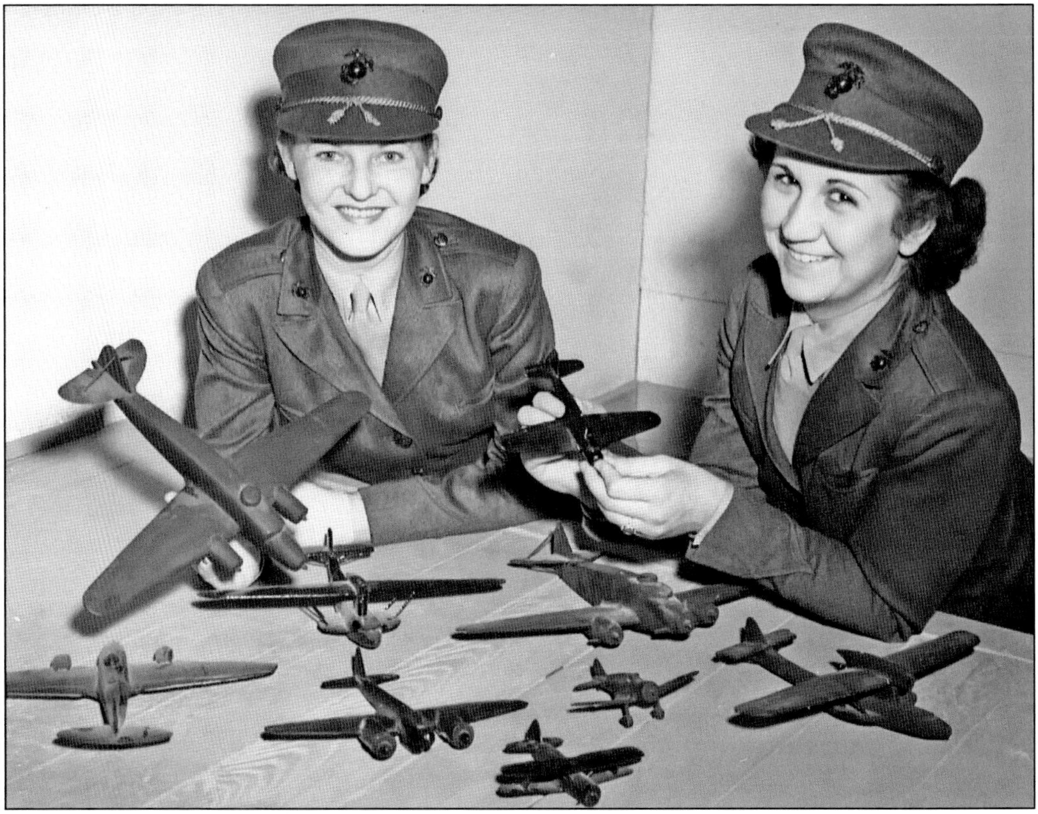

Woman Marines were also involved in aviation-related occupations. In January 1944, Pvt. Ethel Mae Wilbur (left) and Pvt. June Bongiovanni study aircraft characteristics in an aircraft identification course at Camp Lejeune. (Courtesy of Marine Corps Archives and Special Collections.)

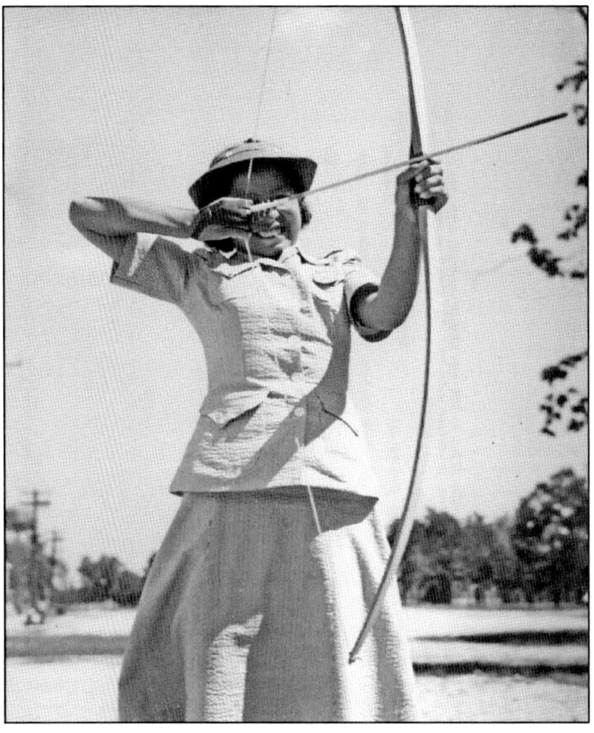

In July 1943, Pvt. Minnie Spotted Wolf, a Blackfoot Indian from Montana, was the first Native American woman to enlist in the Marine Corps Women's Reserve. This image was taken in October 1943, at Camp Lejeune, where she was trained. (Courtesy of Marine Corps Archives and Special Collections.)

When at leisure, some woman Marines (WM) took advantage of recreation equipment; these WMs have chosen to take a sailboat out on the tranquil New River in about 1944. From left to right are Pvt. Doris Irwin, Pvt. Audrey Ewry, Pvt. Marguerite Hopper, and Pvt. Elinore Bertrand. Note the misspelling of Camp Lejeune on their T-shirts. (Courtesy of Marine Corps Archives and Special Collections.)

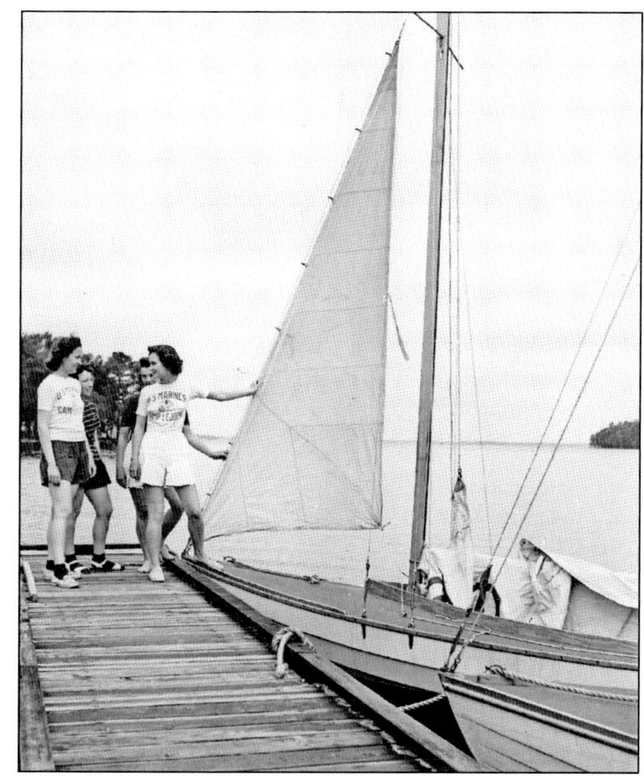

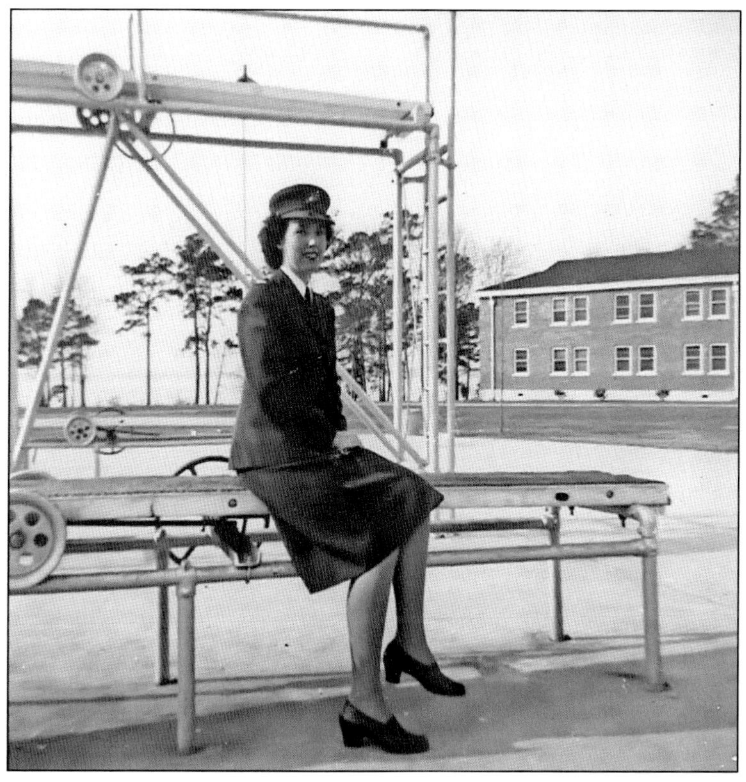

Lt. Rilda Stuart poses in her green service uniform at Camp Lejeune in about 1944. By the end of World War II, these women had won over the skeptics who were unsure about the ability of women to serve in the Marine Corps. (Courtesy of Onslow County Museum.)

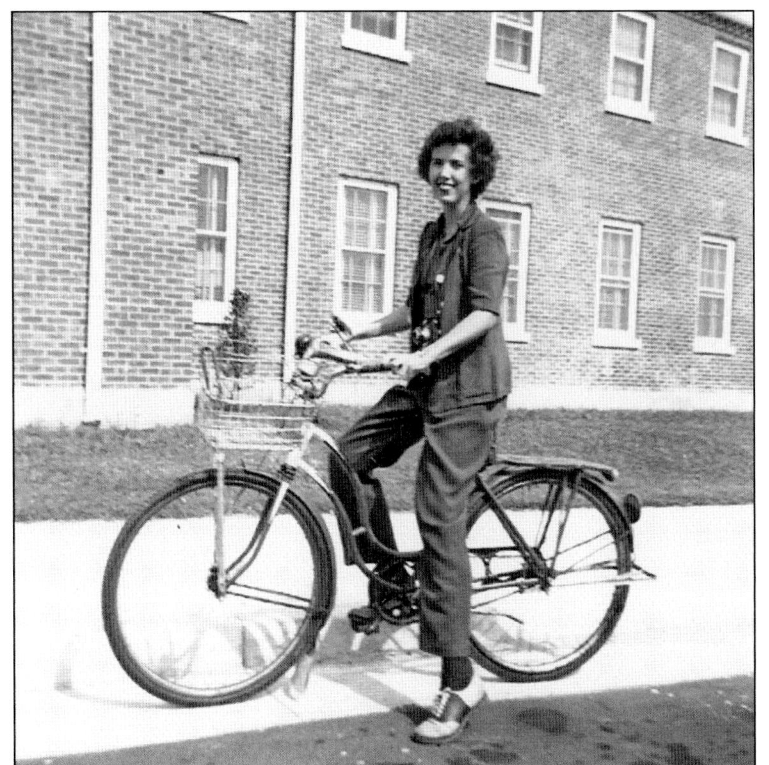

Lt. Rilda Stuart pauses while riding a bicycle aboard Camp Lejeune in about 1944, probably near her barracks. The MCWR barracks were located on Virginia Dare Drive, Molly Pitcher Road, and Lucy Brewer Avenue. (Courtesy of Onslow County Museum.)

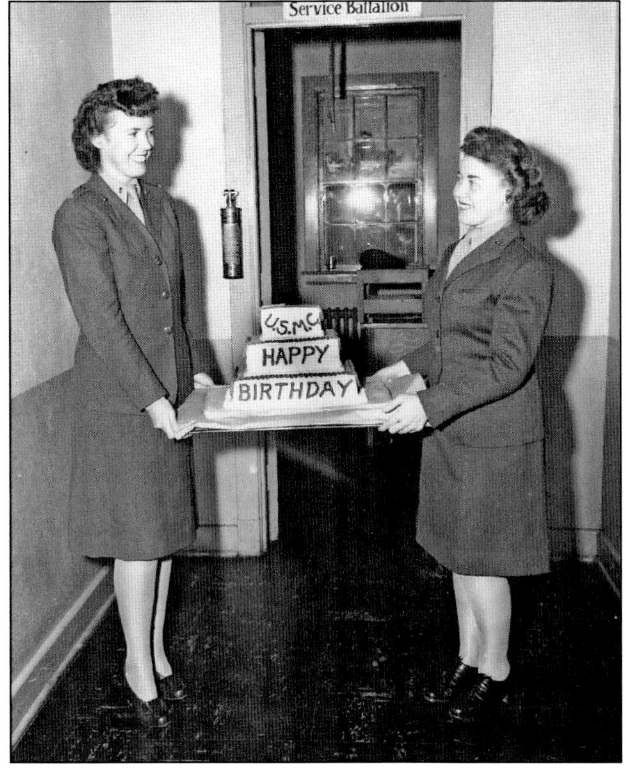

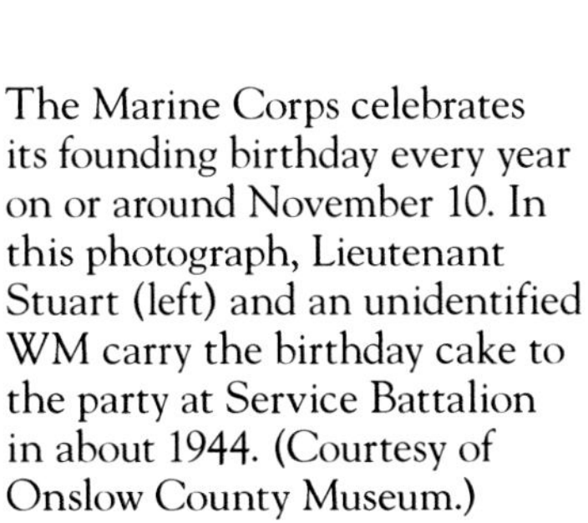

The Marine Corps celebrates its founding birthday every year on or around November 10. In this photograph, Lieutenant Stuart (left) and an unidentified WM carry the birthday cake to the party at Service Battalion in about 1944. (Courtesy of Onslow County Museum.)

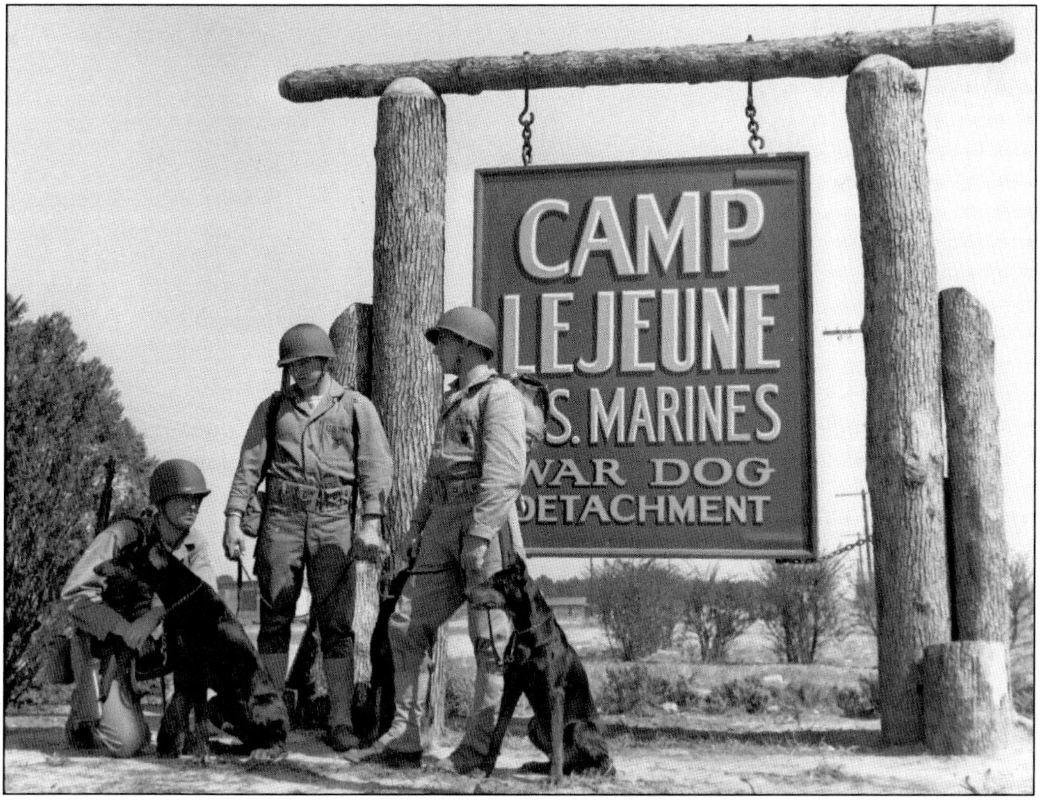

The Camp Lejeune War Dog Training Center was established at Camp Knox, a former CCC (Civilian Conservation Corps) camp, on July 7, 1943. The mission in the Pacific was ongoing, and it was thought that sentry, scout, and messenger dogs would be ideal in those surroundings. (Courtesy of Marine Corps Archives and Special Collections.)

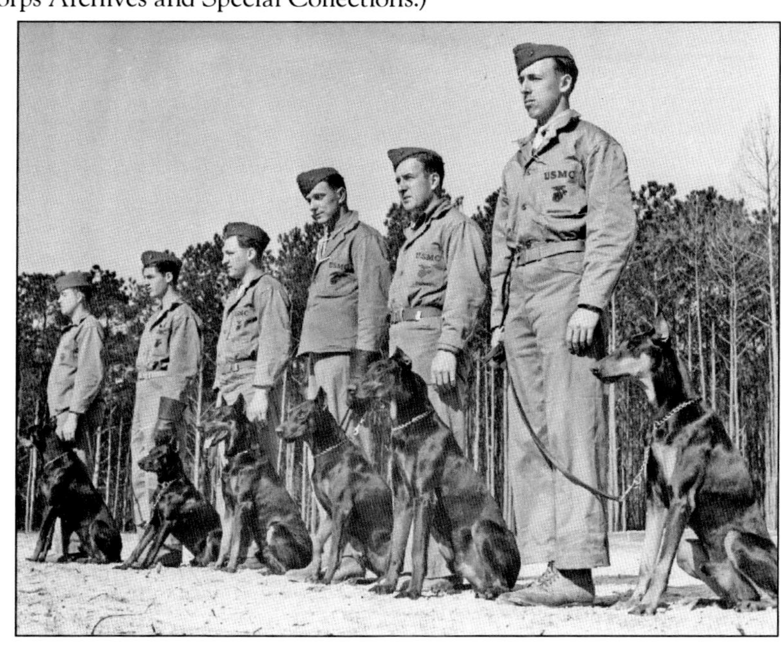

"Devil Dogs" and their handlers were put through training in close order drill to establish discipline and trust between handler and dog. Obedience training lasted about six weeks; the dogs were taught to respond to both voice and hand commands. (Courtesy of Marine Corps Archives and Special Collections.)

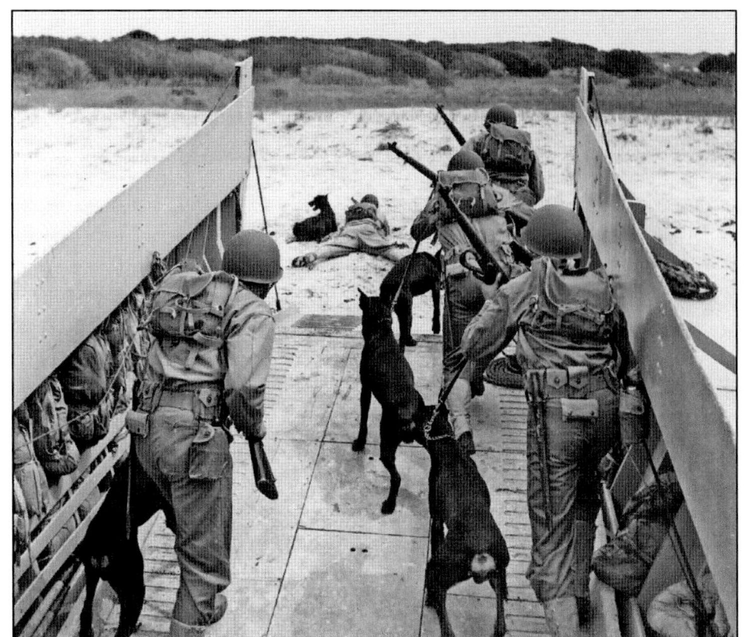

Camp Lejeune's war dogs practice a beach landing with their Marine handlers, probably at Onslow Beach, in May 1944. The entire training program lasted 14 weeks. (Courtesy of Marine Corps Archives and Special Collections.)

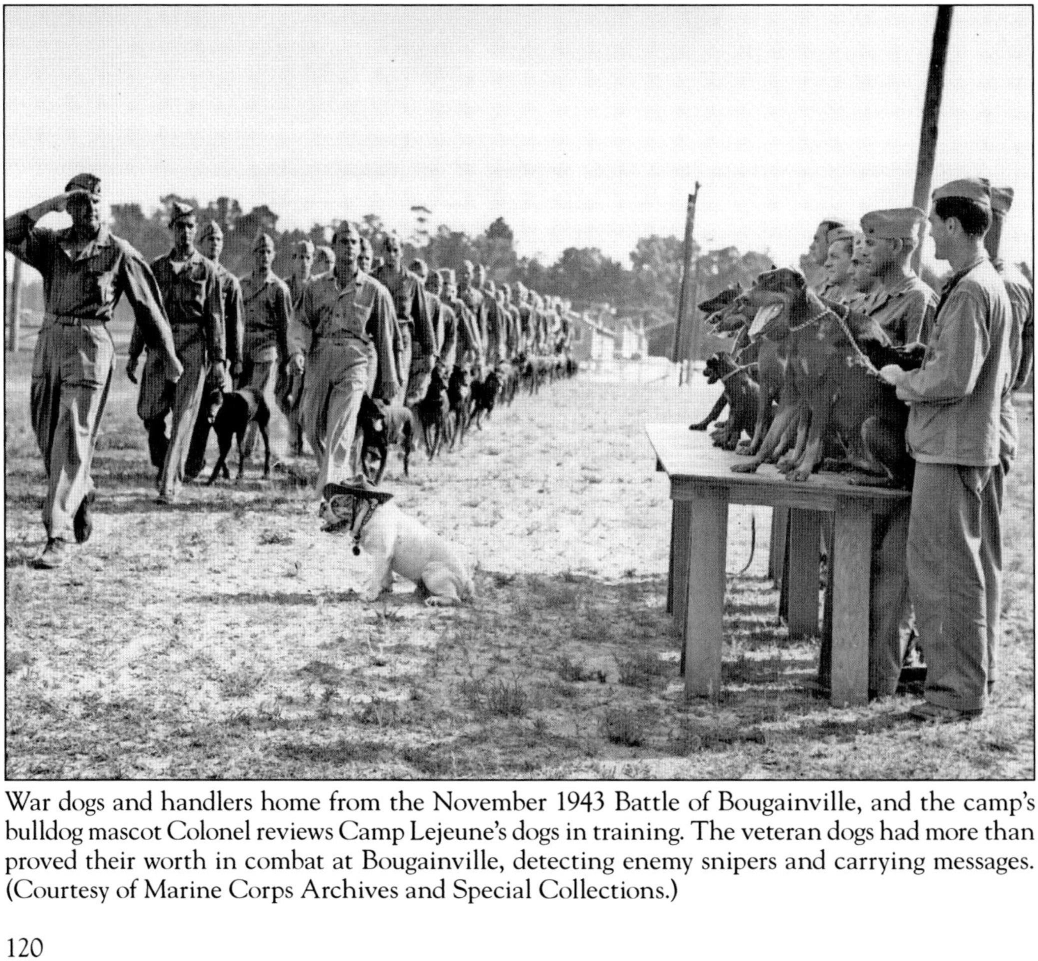

War dogs and handlers home from the November 1943 Battle of Bougainville, and the camp's bulldog mascot Colonel reviews Camp Lejeune's dogs in training. The veteran dogs had more than proved their worth in combat at Bougainville, detecting enemy snipers and carrying messages. (Courtesy of Marine Corps Archives and Special Collections.)

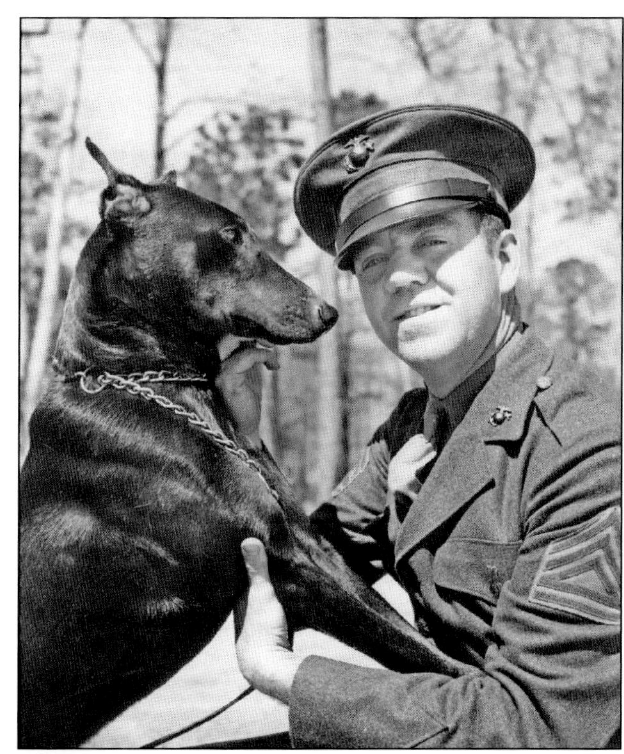

Tech Sgt. Thomas Gately, a dog trainer in civilian life, was one of the dog trainers at the War Dog Center on Camp Lejeune. Here, he is shown with a Doberman pinscher he was training; Marines favored Dobermans because it was believed that their short coats were better suited to tropical climates. (Courtesy of Marine Corps Archives and Special Collections.)

The Marine Corps preferred Doberman pinschers, such as this one, but also trained a few German shepherds, Labrador retrievers, and boxers. Approximately 450 graduated from the school; 39 were killed in action, mostly on Guam. After the end of the war, the need for the dogs diminished, and the center was deactivated on August 15, 1946. (Author's collection.)

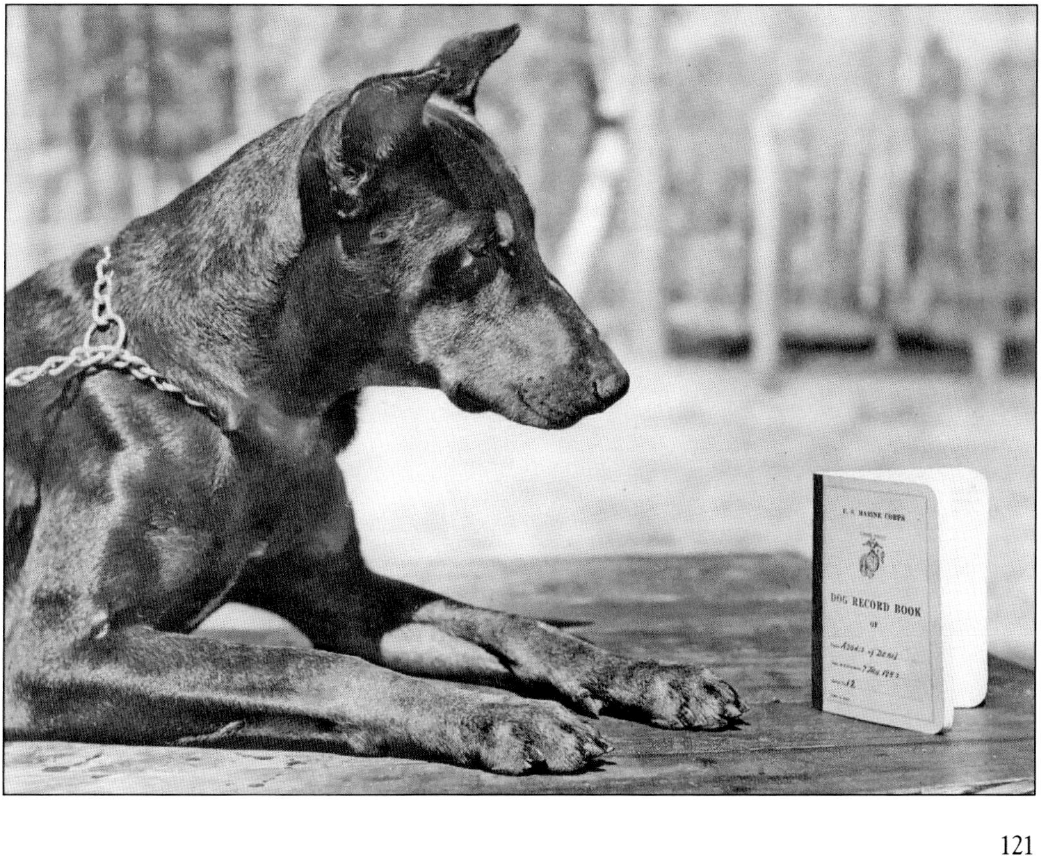

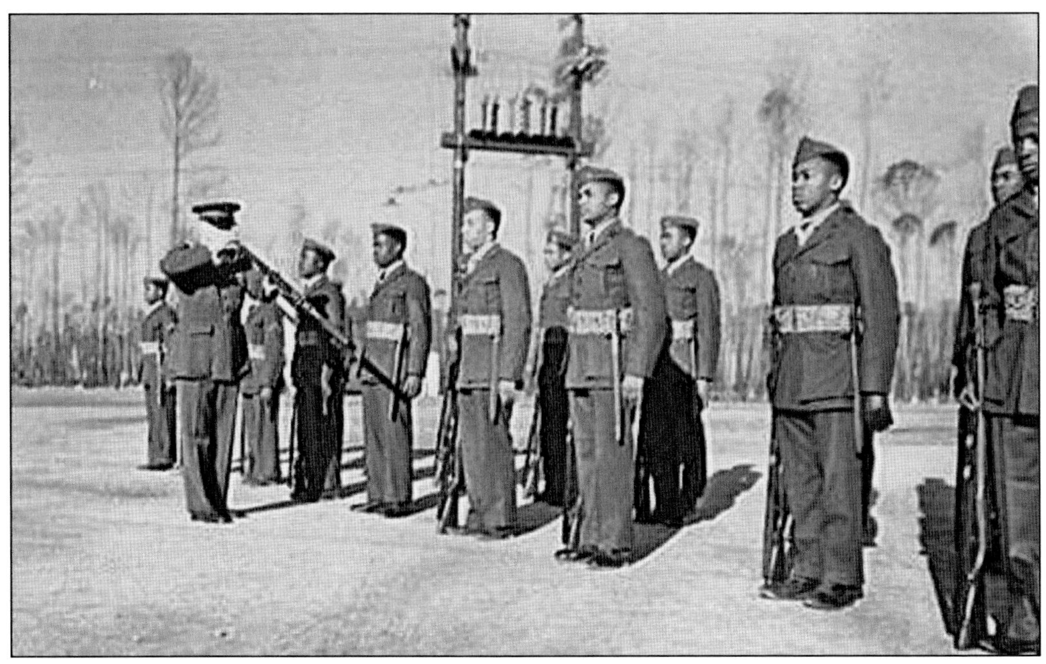

The first training site for African American Marines was established at Montford Point in 1942. These young men came from all walks of life, but all were determined to succeed. In this image, Col. Samuel Woods, commanding officer, inspects the troops. (Courtesy of Onslow County Museum.)

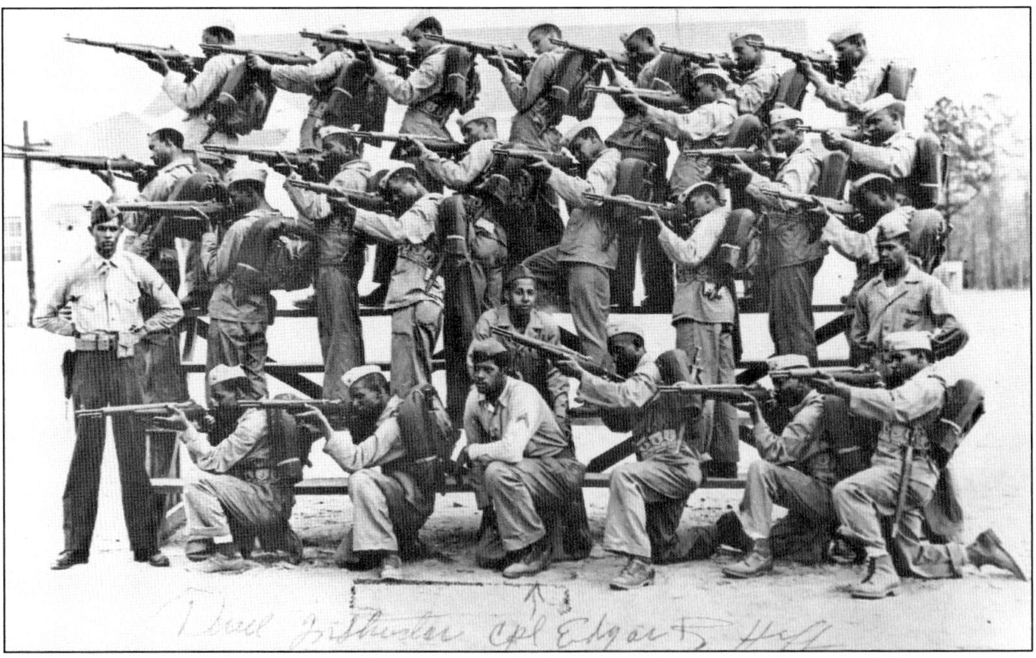

More than 20,000 men graduated from Montford Point. Edgar R. Huff, one of the two most legendary drill instructors, is pictured here, first row, third from left, with one of his many platoons. He said that he wanted to join the Marines because it was the "toughest outfit going." (Courtesy of Onslow County Museum.)

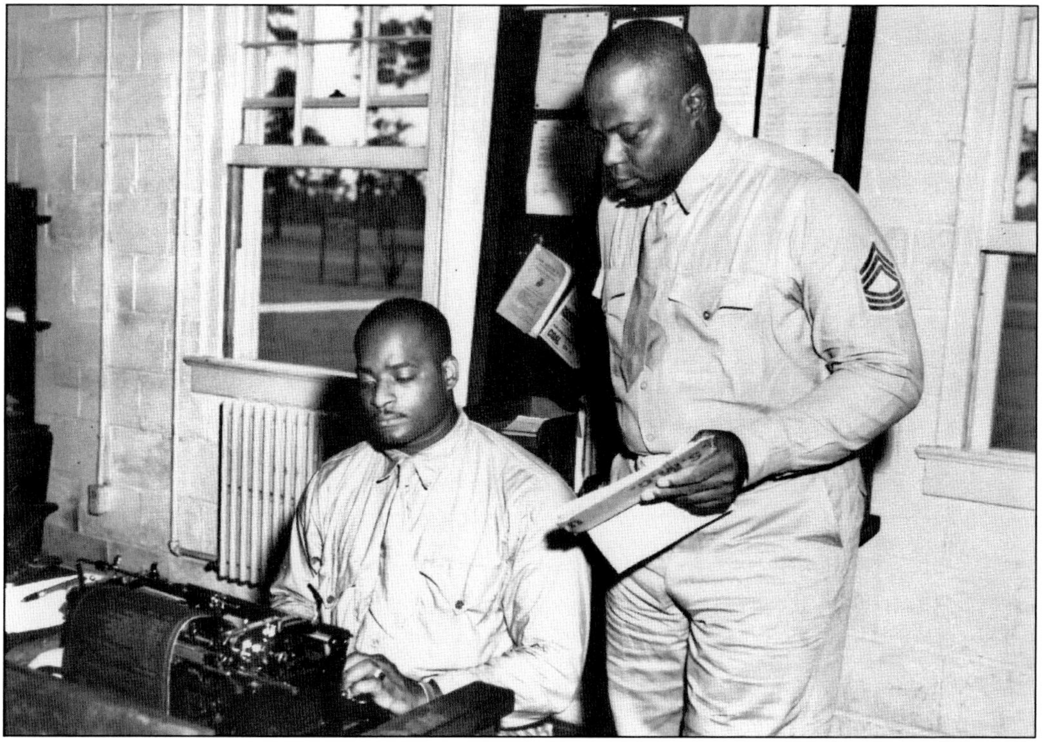

Sgt. Maj. Gilbert H. Johnson (right) had served his country in both the US Army and US Navy before transferring to the Marine Corps. Trained as a drill instructor, he was nicknamed "Hashmark" because of the service stripes on his sleeve. Two years after his death in 1972, Montford Point was renamed Camp Gilbert H. Johnson, in his honor. (Courtesy of Onslow County Museum.)

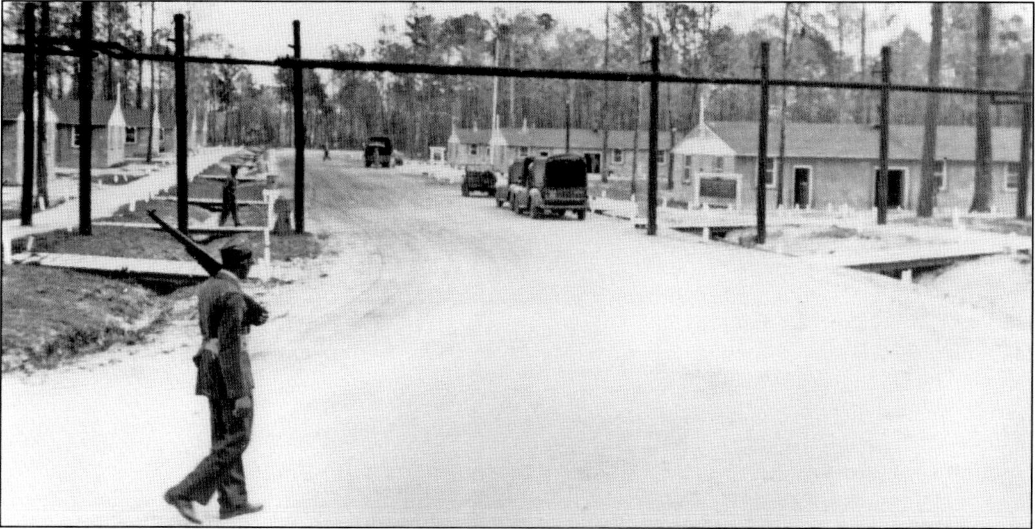

The 51st and 52nd Defense Battalions were trained at Montford Point. The African American Marines were trained in separate units from the white Marines; initially, the command structure was primarily white, which gradually changed as more men were trained. During World War II, the camp had huts, an administration building, a chapel, warehouses, a library, a theater, and a beer hall. Here, a Montford Point Marine patrols the 500 area. (Courtesy of the Onslow County Museum.)

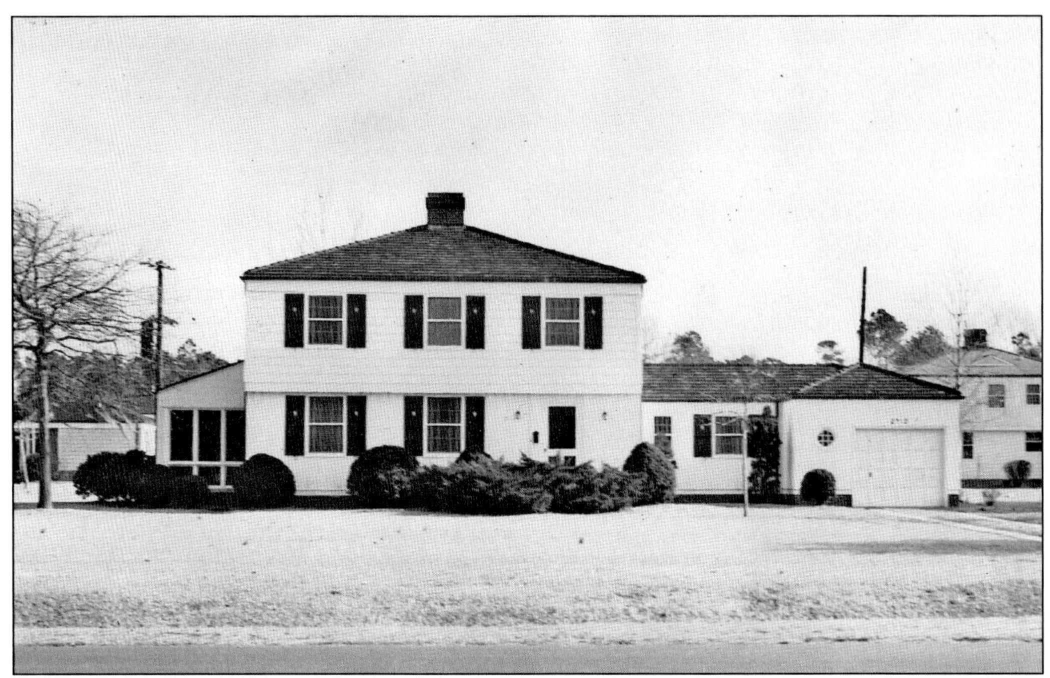

In spite of the haste in constructing Camp Lejeune, its design and planning were thoughtfully carried out. Housing on Camp Lejeune was placed in what were considered the most advantageous locations. Much of the officers' housing, as seen here in the 1950s, was built near the cool breeze of the New River. (Courtesy of the Onslow County Museum.)

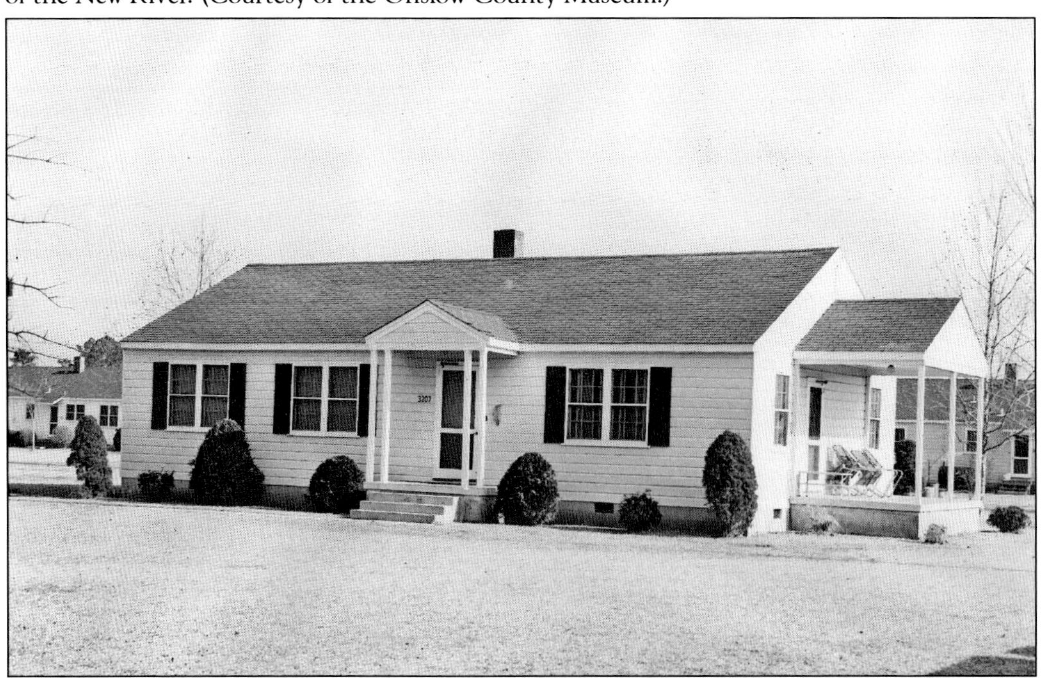

The houses were very well built. This modest home is an example of junior officer quarters on Camp Lejeune in the 1950s. Many of these houses are still in use, a tribute to the construction workers and carpenters of the 1940s. (Courtesy of Onslow County Museum.)

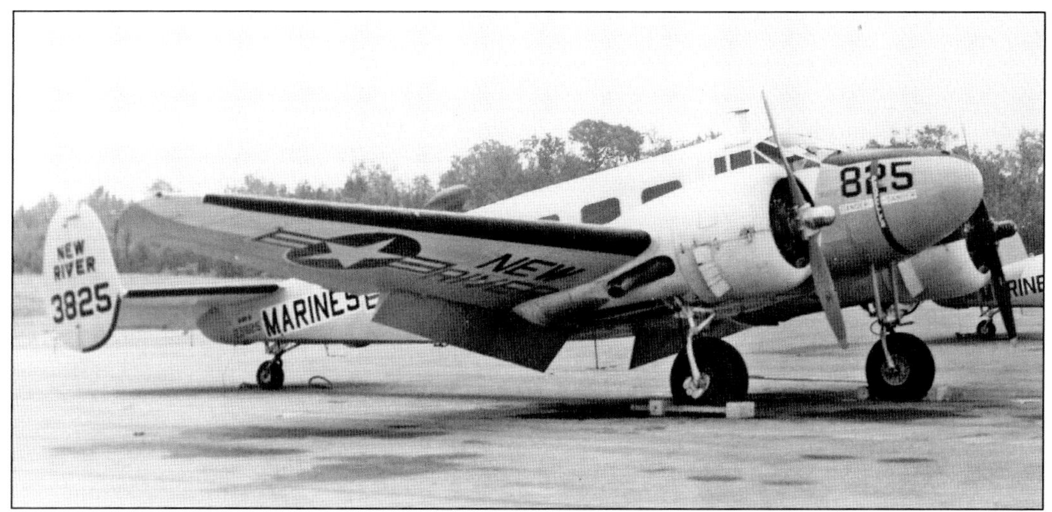

First known as Peterfield Point, the area acquired by the government in 1941 for aviation support later became known as Marine Corps Air Station (MCAS), New River, and officially became McCutcheon Field in 1972, named for helicopter pioneer Gen. Keith McCutcheon. One of the aircraft utilized at the air station in the 1950s was this Beechcraft C-45 Utility/Trainer. (Courtesy of Onslow County Museum.)

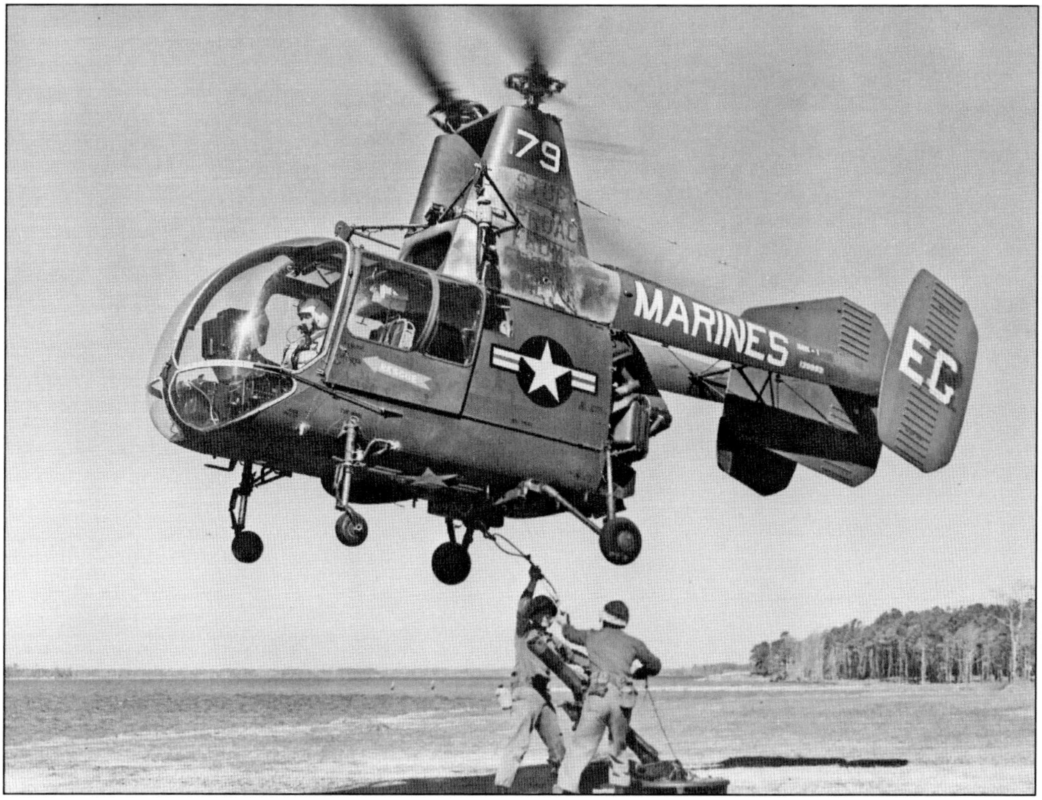

MCAS New River is home to Marine Aircraft Groups 26 and 29. Its most famous occupant is probably the V-22 Osprey, a multi-mission tilt-rotor aircraft. In the 1950s, Marines trained at New River with helicopters such as this Kaman H-43B Huskie. (Courtesy of Onslow County Museum.)

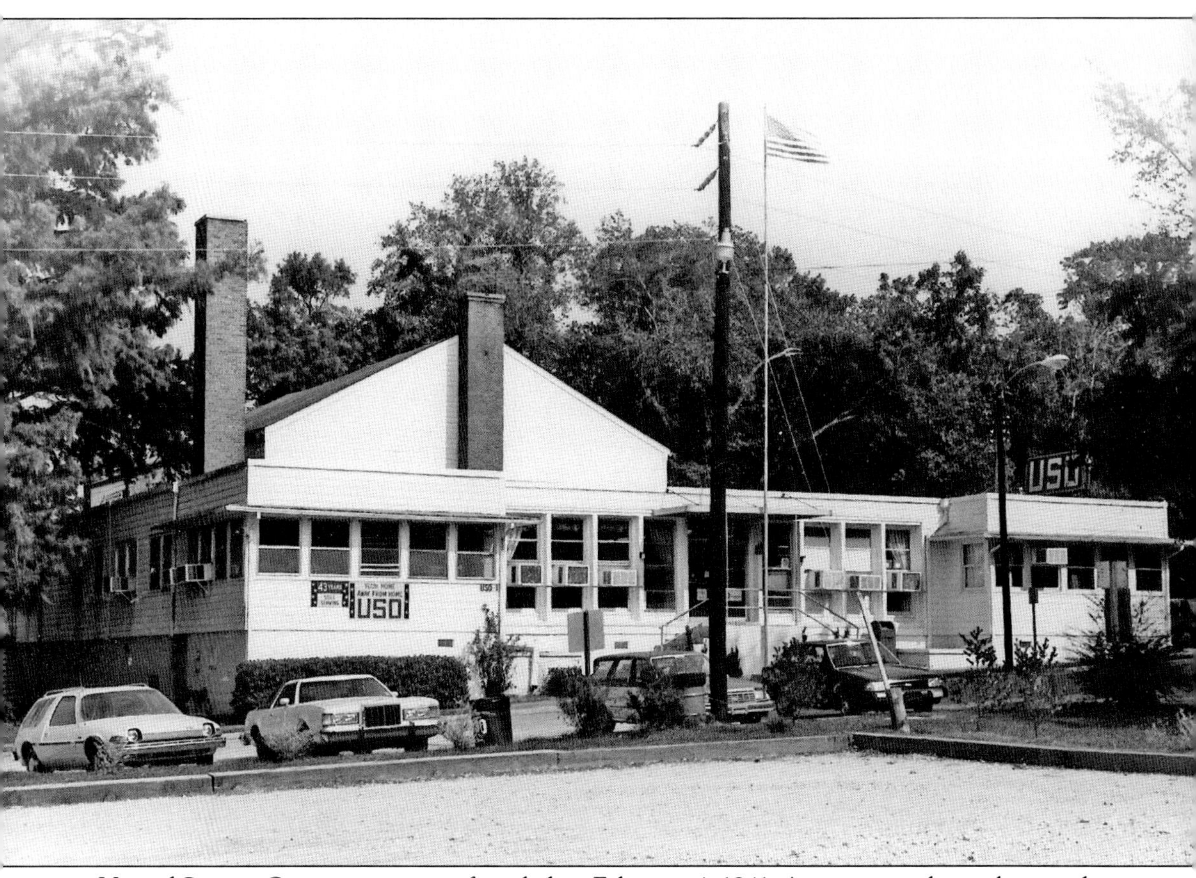

United Service Organizations was founded on February 4, 1941. As troop escalation began, there was a need for a USO in Jacksonville; it was originally opened in the old Pine Lodge building in December 1941 and moved to the Tallman Street USO in the spring of 1942. USOs for African American troops were located on Poplar and Newberry Streets before desegregation. Jacksonville's USO, a haven for homesick troops hungry for a friendly face, is the oldest continuously operating USO in the world. (Courtesy of Onslow County Museum.)

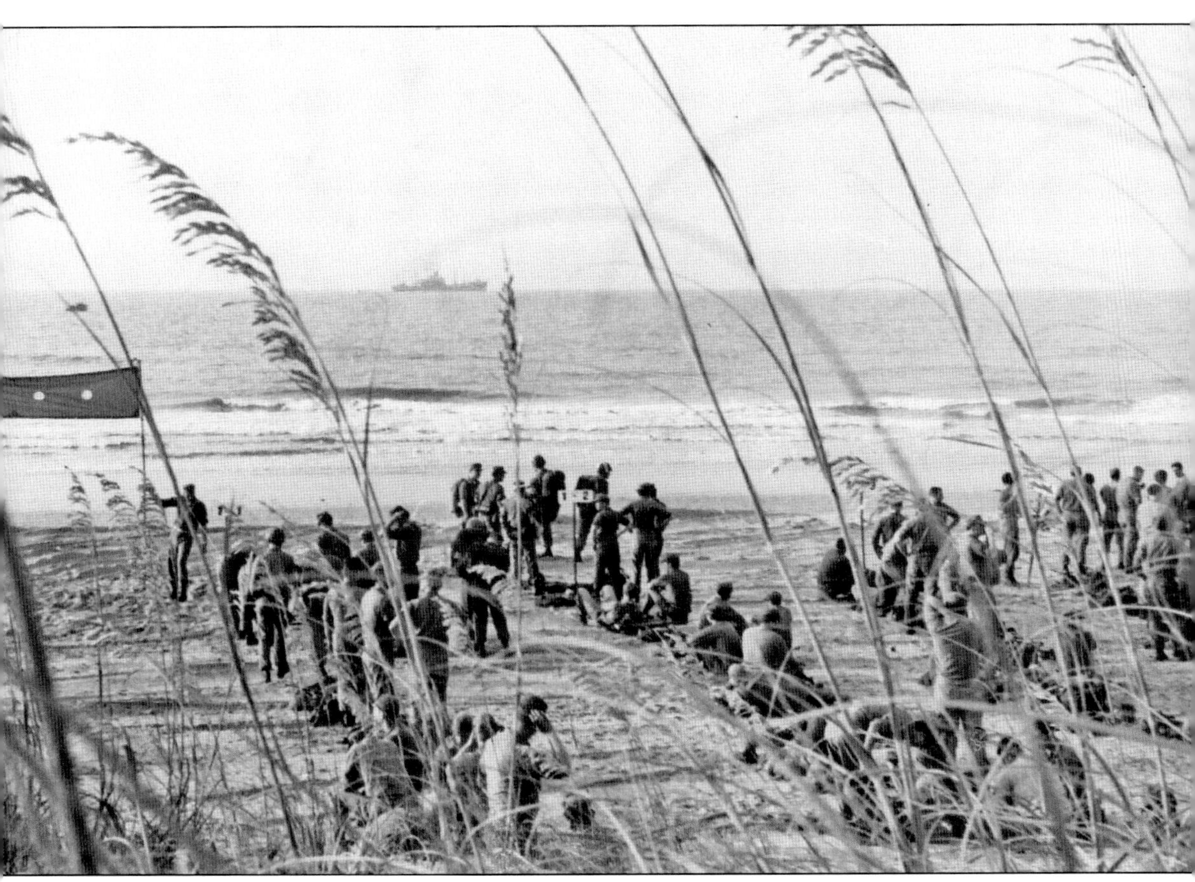

Marines hit the beach via landing craft at Camp Lejeune during a four-day exercise in July 1971. Troops of the First Battalion, 25th Marine Reserves were at Camp Lejeune for their annual two-week training. Camp Lejeune's location in Onslow County still makes it the best place in the world for the amphibious training of US Marines. (Author's collection.)

Consistent with our mission to preserve history on a local level, this book was printed in South Carolina on American-made paper and manufactured entirely in the United States. Products carrying the accredited Forest Stewardship Council (FSC) label are printed on 100 percent FSC-certified paper.

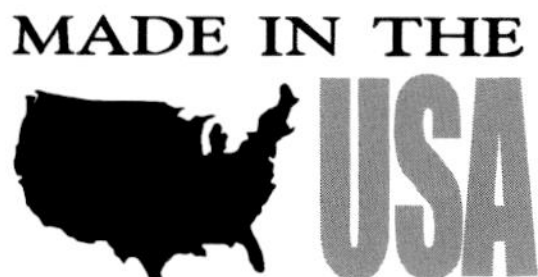